VALVANO:

THEY GAVE ME A LIFETIME CONTRACT, AND THEN THEY DECLARED ME DEAD

JIM VALVANO
and Curry Kirkpatrick

POCKET BOOKS

New York   London   Toronto   Sydney   Tokyo   Singapore

POCKET BOOKS, a division of Simon & Schuster
1230 Avenue of the Americas, New York, NY 10020

ISBN: 0-671-73253-6

First Pocket Books hardcover printing March 1991

10 9 8 7 6 5 4 3 2 1

POCKET and colophon are registered trademarks of
Simon & Schuster.

Printed in the U.S.A.

I dedicate this book to my family and friends, who "rekindled my inner spirit"—and especially to Pam, my wife of 23 years and friend for life.

Acknowledgments

My sincere thanks to Jack Romanos and Irwyn Applebaum, who made this project possible. Special heartfelt thanks to Leslie Wells, who not only is an excellent editor but one who figuratively and literally went the extra mile. To her assistant, Ellen Cowhey, who was always there when we needed her. To Art Kaminsky, my friend, who has always believed in me, in good times and in bad—thank you. To Curry Kirkpatrick, who loves to laugh and loves the game. Thanks also to Janet Pawson, who kept things on the right track, and to Stephanie Krasnow and Robert McDowell, for checking facts which time and memory sometimes cloud. And to all the players, referees, coaches and fans who have made my 23 years in basketball a joy.

A question I've been asked is why I chose to be published by Pocket Books, the publisher who decided not to publish *Personal Fouls.* The answer is quite simple. During my struggle last year, my agent and friend, Art Kaminsky, suggested that I think seriously about telling my side of what had happened. Ultimately, I decided that I would like to write a book. I felt that the integrity Pocket Books had shown in refusing to publish a flawed manuscript indicated that this is the type of organization that I would want to work with. I have not been disappointed.

Contents

1   *I Get It, the Soviets Are in Nebraska and I'm Not Fired*   1

2   *All in the Family*   6

3   *"Starting at Guard . . ."*   15

4   *Of Overachievers, Woollyboogers, and Categories*   25

5   *Difficult Meat*   37

6   *Rats to Riches*   50

7   *Daring to Dream*   60

8   *Opportunity Knocks*   80

9   *Pig-Pickin's Is What It's All About*   90

10   *Seven and Seven, Go to Heaven . . . But Don't Go to the Corner*   103

11   *Survive and Advance*   113

12   *The Gift My Father Gave Me*   136

13   *Planes, Trains, Hi's, Lo's, Spuds, Shacks, and Treys*   150

14   *Still Harm, Still "Fouls"*   173

15   *Forget the Old Italian Proverb; It's Over Before It's Over*   217

16   *Problems and Prescriptions*   249

    Epilogue   257

Chapter One

I GET IT, THE SOVIETS ARE IN NEBRASKA AND I'M NOT FIRED

IRONY. ABSURDITY. THE IRRATIONALITY OF LIFE. I'VE CARRIED CERTAIN notions—call it an attitude—about our daily existence since at least the third grade. Catching the humor, appreciating the funny side, smiling, laughing, staying upbeat, thinking positive, cracking a joke. These have been practically like commandments in my life. Or maybe crutches.

Of course I needed every bit of this attitude last April when I was fired from my job as head basketball coach at North Carolina State University. You may have heard about it. It was in all the obituary sections, although I felt it merited at least a separate cartoon supplement. If you were me you might have sensed the irony. You might have remembered that in April of 1983 the Wolfpack of N.C. State which I happened to be coaching at the time had won the national championship in one of the more memorable games in history. After our team upset Houston 54–52, on that spectacular final second jam by Lorenzo Charles, a play which I designed off the top of my head in the preceding huddle—okay, okay, so Lo's basket was a miraculously lucky rebound of Derek Whittenburg's air/prayer ball; picky, picky—I helped my team cut down the nets in Albuquerque, New Mexico. To consecrate the greatest moment of my life I subsequently vowed to name my next child Al B. Kerky.

This was barely seven years earlier. Oh yeah, and just about seven months earlier I had been given the highest honor the North Carolina State Alumni Association can bestow on a non–N.C. State graduate, the Alumni Distinguished Service Award. So there I was: a guy who had coached the University's basketball team to a national championship; who was a lifetime member of the N.C. State booster club; who'd given an academic scholarship to the school not to mention three daughters;

Nicole, a junior, Jamie, an entering freshwoman and Lee Ann, ten, a kind of cheerleaders' mascot for the Pack. I was also a distinguished service nominee and a coach with a lifetime contract and on April 6, 1990, I was pronounced dead in Raleigh.

Oh, nobody read the last rites. But then nobody said I was fired, either. Oh no. The euphemisms for that painful little scalping could fill up another whole chapter (and we'll touch on them later). All I know is that at ten P.M. on that dreaded day my North Carolina lawyer, named Woody Webb, called me up at home and said quite plainly that I didn't have to go to work the next morning.

"I don't have to go in tomorrow?" I said.

"Right, but that doesn't necessarily mean you're fired," Woody said.

"I know. I've got a lifetime contract. I can't get fired, right?"

"Exactly. What they're asking is that you come to an agreement to part company," Woody said.

"Oh. But I'm not fired?" I said.

"Exactly. What they're saying is they would like you to step down," Woody said.

"Oh. But I'm not fired?"

"Not at all. Just don't go in tomorrow. Or ever," Woody said.

"I get it. I'm not fired. I'm only totally dead as a doornail, right?"

"You *do* get it," Woody said.

You can imagine my state of mind a few days later when I finally did go back to my office to pack up all my belongings. The previous ten years had been a roller coaster, eight and a half of heaven, the last year and a half of the other place. Now I was being asked to step down from a lifetime job. And I had to clean out my office, besides. Really, now. You only see this on television: cleaning out the office. Where do you get the boxes? Where are you going to put everything? How do you have enough time? After ten seasons, N.C. State had given me all of a week to be dead and gone.

Anyway, the following is a True Story:

I was in my office that day, minding my own moving, when I looked up to find a strange man I had never seen before standing on the other side of my desk. He was wearing a Chicago Cubs baseball hat, khaki work pants, and basketball shoes of undetermined origin. I had a hunch he had not been paid to wear these shoes. Actually, he was standing across the room by the door, which was the only way into my office and for that matter the only way out. It was very early in the morning. I had been unable to sleep at home, so I'd come in to begin the unpleasant task of attacking the boxes. My secretary wasn't in yet, it was so early. Nobody was in but me . . . and Mr. Cub.

"What can I do for you?" I said.

"Are you Jim Valvano?" he said.

"No, I'm Mike Krzyzewski," I said.

"No, you're not. You're Valvano. I see you on television," he said.

"OK, I am. What do you want?"

"I want some money," he said.

(What was this? Here I'd just lost my job and was spiritually *dead.* Now I was going to be murdered in my own office and be honest-to-goodness, truly dead.)

"I don't have any money," I said. "I just got fired. I'm broke. Nada, nossink, nothing at all."

I could see the guy wasn't playing with a full deck. He moved a little bit and I thought I might be able to get out the door, but he didn't move far enough.

"I thought you would give me some money," he said.

"I don't have any money. I mean it," I said. "Anyway, what do you need money for?"

He said: "I'm on the lam."

Recalling that I'd just lost my lifetime job, I had no opportunities knocking down my door, I had three growing, hungry daughters and an all-world shopper of a wife waiting either at home and/or at the nearest Bloomingdale's respectively AND that now this strange, berserk guy was obviously about to blow my brains out, all I could think of was:

On the lam?

It was too absurd. Yeah, yeah. I'm on the lam too, buster.

"What are you running from?" I asked.

"I'm running from the Russians," he said.

Now I knew I was either very safe or not at all safe. I said: "From the Russians?"

"Yes," he said. "I'm the guy who stopped the Soviet Union's invasion of the United States."

"You did? What a wonderful thing to do! Where exactly was that taking place?" I asked.

"Nebraska," he said. "The Soviet Union was going to invade Nebraska."

"Obviously you are doing an outstanding job," I said, "because I have not heard one report about one Soviet person . . . not one single, solitary Russian in Nebraska."

He assured me that he had called in the alert. So I offered to phone the Governor of Nebraska to get him to send him some money as a reward. He said that would be a good idea. I said: "Why don't you go hide, do what you're going to do and come back later. I'll see if I can get it for you."

Then he got up and thanked me. But he said he wanted me to know one

3

other thing. That there was a "major corporation in America which was advocating homosexuality." Uh-oh. I had a sinking feeling that he was about to share more of this knowledge with me than I wanted to hear. He said the corporate culprit was—I should have known all along!—AT&T.

"They're forcing their employees to turn homosexual," he said. "Isn't there anything you can do about it?"

"I've got an AT&T calling card," I said. "I'll give somebody a buzz and put a stop to this thing."

My jokes weren't going a long way with this guy; he was dead serious. I probably should have been more apprehensive. I mean, there's no telling what this lunatic might have done. But the potential for humor, to do my shtick, was so great that I had to go for it. Oh yeah, and our mystery guest's final bombshell was this: The guy said he was broke because the NAACP had put a stop to his . . . "major league *baseball* career."

Right.

"Well, that's just one more thing America plainly cannot tolerate," I said.

I don't know what finally persuaded the Visitor From Inner Space to change his mind about leaving the premises. But he did. After which I immediately called the campus police.

Dum-da-dum-dum.

Just the facts, mister. To add even more difficulty to my day, now I had to explain this obviously cockamamie story to uniformed officers of the law. Like everybody else in Raleigh, they had read or seen all the media reports about me being on the verge of losing my job. They understood I was under a fairly heavy strain. So here I was at seven A.M. in my office breathlessly ranting away:

"There's a guy you should look out for. He can't be too far away. He's got a baseball cap and beard. He said he stopped the Soviet Union invasion of Nebraska. He said AT&T is forcing all its employees to become homosexuals. He said the NAACP left him penniless by sabotaging his major league baseball career. "You've still got time to catch him. Go . . . get . . . this . . . maniac."

One of the cops was taking notes the whole time I was pleading. The cop kept writing. And writing. I'm sure I saw this sentence: "V's finally flipped out." Then the cop said, "Coach, you sure you're all right?" I don't know where that poor officer is today, but if it weren't for his understanding and, it just so happened, a cleaning lady who had happened to have seen my whacked-out guest and confirmed my story, there's no telling what color my personalized straitjacket might be today.

Not counting this momentary walk on the wild side (which in hindsight could have produced dire consequences), I was about as low as I've ever been in my life last April. Not only had I recently been fired; not

4

only was I cleaning out my office of memorabilia from the last decade, with enough emotions draining through the room to flood Raleigh's Research Triangle. . . . Now some crazed psychotic had entered the building demanding money and possibly planning to shoot me. Just the same, after a while all I could do was laugh.

Chuckling through the pain. A guy needs this attitude to survive, and I'm glad I've never lost my sense of humor. If I did that, I'd know it was over. What I went through at N.C. State! I felt like I was on the late news, like when a tragic fire rages through a house and somebody bursts out just in time to get a microphone stuck in his face. "How does it feel," the interviewer asks, "to see your life turned to ashes?"

I went through all that. It's too painful for words. There are enough things to laugh about; why be overly concerned with the downside? My reference point has always been Brother John Driscoll, my one-time boss and president of Iona College in New Rochelle, New York. Anytime the school or the basketball team or the coach, namely me, got in a tough situation, he would look at me and say, "Nobody died."

Nobody and nothing died in my office on that final pack-up day either, except maybe a few attempted funny lines which didn't go over with my visitor.

Que sera, sera. Laughter has played the prominent role in my life— over the basketball, over the pasta and wine, over everything.

The moral of the story is not to leave the door to your office unlocked . . . especially after you've been fired.

Chapter Two

ALL IN THE FAMILY

EVERYBODY KNOWS ABOUT THE *IMPACT* PLAYER. A SILLY CLICHÉ, RIGHT? Wrong. I like the word *impact*. It has style, pizzazz, attitude. It has, uh, *impact*. I honestly believe there are *impact* stages in life. Impact grades, impact ages. My impact grade, for instance, was the third grade. My impact age was nine. Of course, I was Bart Simpson long before the television Bart was a gleam in his father Homer's stupefied eye.

Laughter took a dominant role in my formative years, from the first time I played the room in Sister Mary Helen's third grade class back in St. Leo's School, which was in Corona, Queens. An *impact* neighborhood in an *impact* borough, if there ever was one.

Tender tyke that I was, I used to go from class to class doing impressions and jokes. This wasn't so easy given the no-nonsense school uniform at St. Leo's: blue pants, white shirt, blue tie with "SLS" embroidered in the middle and, oh yes, ugly brown brogans. Befitting the glorious Catholic school traditions, not only were you going to be disciplined, you had to be dressed poorly too. Did that stop me from the gig? It did not. "Hello, America. Good night, Mrs. Calabash, where*ever* you are." I did Jimmy Durante even before I realized I had a big nose.

Any time there was a show at school or my family needed a party shtick, little V would break out the Durante. Later I moved on to more sophisticated fare. Television comedy was my life. I played lots of sports, but most of my non-jock waking hours were spent couch-potatoing in front of the tube watching comedians: Dean Martin and Jerry Lewis, Abbott and Costello, Rowan and Martin. Steve Allen, Sid Caesar, Ernie Kovacs, Jackie Gleason and "The Honeymooners." My mom and dad could hardly tear me away from the TV set, since they were watching it too. We ate a whole lot of TV dinners. Every Monday night we had people come over to watch "Lucy." We had a woman we used to call "Monday Night." That's the only name I knew her by, because that's the only time I saw her. I developed an eye and an ear, a feel for the jugular. Comic sensibility predisposes you to be silly, *smart*-silly, to look and listen for funny things.

Not that I didn't have a strange sort of C-type personality to start with (C for "cut-up"). Even my birth resulted in more than the normal excess happiness, if only because my mom had polio at the time and there was some question as to whether I'd make it.

My father said the first time I opened my eyes, I opened my mouth at the same time. My mother always said I was vaccinated with a phonograph needle. When you're the middle brother, though, you've got to have some kind of scam. Nick Valvano is three years older than me, Bobby eleven years younger. Both sets of grandparents, both sides, came from the old country, Naples, Italy. My dad's father was a builder, my other grandfather worked in the paper business. Rocco, my dad, had two brothers, Bruno and Tommy, as well as three sisters, Philomena, Marian and Rosie (not the Queen of Corona). My mother had four sisters and one brother. I joke about growing up around Italians, but before we moved to Long Island I seriously had no idea there was anything on earth BUT Italians.

The first blonde I ever met . . . the first fair-skinned thing I ever saw . . . was the lovely and talented Pamela Levine. "Hhmmm, this is kind of different," I said to myself, before I married her shortly thereafter.

But I'm getting ahead of the story.

Actually, I was born in Manhattan but we immediately moved to a triplex apartment house under the El on Roosevelt Avenue in Queens. At that time, my mother's father lived on the ground floor, we were upstairs, and my Uncle Angelo lived on top. Everybody said the Valvano family talked too fast, but in that house the subway came by every three minutes and it didn't wait for a lull in the conversation. The view from the top floor: You look out and the subway train is right there. You almost could take tolls. Whenever it rolled up, you had to talk loud. Or with your hands. And when it took off again, speed was of the essence: You had to talk fast because that sucker was coming round again.

I can't stress enough how important my family, especially my mom and dad, were as the central figures in my life. My dad was the first of the family to go to college: Rutgers, and then Savage College. Following school he played professional basketball in Utica, New York, in the old American League, a predecessor of the old Eastern League. One night driving to an away game, my father had a terrible accident in which several of his teammates were killed. He escaped with a wired-up jaw, but the accident ended his pro career.

My father was a workaholic. When he had finished playing pro, he taught and coached basketball at St. Nicholas of Tolentine High School in the Bronx during the day, and worked at the Lily Tulip Cups plant at night. It was one of those places where the employees take the job home with them, or at least the goods. I can still hear my mother ordering my dad: "No more cups. No more. We don't have enough mouths around here to drink out of all these cups."

I didn't see my dad much. He was always working. Yet every single Saturday he'd take us to the big amusement park called Playland, where we'd play skeet ball and shoot baskets and ride the roller coaster. Then on the way home we'd hit the White Castle for burgers. I think I must have put away about 842 of them every trip. My dad didn't drink or smoke, and he had a very simple concept of life: that a boy with a glove in his pocket and a ball in his hand was headed in the right direction. My life was filled with games and sports and "ball" of all kinds. When I think about it now, it's unbelievable how at seven years old, we used to take the subway by ourselves all the way out to Yankee Stadium.

Nowadays, we're afraid to let our ten-year-old, Lee Ann, cross the street by herself. Jamie's eighteen. You think we let her stay in the house alone? Remember the movie *Risky Business*?

There was so much more freedom back when I was growing up. We didn't have one organized game. We used to get up in the morning and go to an abandoned storefront we called "the cubbyhole." Do you know what a "play street" is? It was a street the city closed down for kids to play in. Simple enough, but we didn't have one. So we painted a 100-yard field on the street to play football. And Andrew Squasonie would yell and scream and argue with the entire neighborhood when he stopped all the cars from coming up the block.

Next door to me in the neighborhood were the Fernacolis, the Pizzamentis, the Capuannas, the DeSteffanos. We're talking The Italian Experience here.

We had *Maria Biocci,* "Crazy Mary"—biocci is Italian for "block off, stop"—an old woman who, whenever we played football near her place, used to come out and try to shove the ball down the sewer. If the ball went in her little garden, it was curtains.

We even had *swimming.* That's Italian for swimming. Somebody would open up the hydrant, we'd run to put on our suit and we'd get our ankles wet.

But back to Yankee Stadium. We used to sit in the right field bleachers down in the corner so we could see into the bullpen. I'll never forget leaning over one day and hearing the stunning "pop" of the ball into the catcher's mitt. "Holy cow! Hey, down there, does that hurt?" I called out. "Go f--- yourself. Get off the f------ railing," one of America's diamond heroes called back.

Ah, to be a major leaguer.

Actually, I had already heard all the bad words. Usually they were aimed at my father when he refereed semipro basketball games at Sunnyside Gardens in Queens. I remember two things about those games. After the doubleheaders were over, I got to shoot little paper cups into the baskets. And during the games I learned every naughty, dirty, crude, vile and obscene phrase imaginable. They were all directed at my dad for his judgments. At times my brother and I had to get on the man in blue, ourselves.

Nick Valvano is now a vice president and general manager for a computer firm in New York City. But back then he played for Holy Cross High School in Queens and when I went to his games it was the first time I ever saw a gym with nets and glass backboards. He was quite an idol for me, just as I became an idol for my younger brother, Bobby, who is now the head coach at Catholic University in Washington, D.C.

To fully understand how close-knit a family I grew up in—we hugged, kissed, touched and said "I love you" so often we should have been X-rated—it is necessary to explain what Sunday at the Valvano household was all about. My mother always got up early to make the gravy for the two o'clock dinner. Non-Italians call this tomato sauce; we call it gravy. But the first order of business for the rest of the family was to go to Mass where Nick was an altar boy. My family would point out that I could have been up there as an altar boy too if I had kept my mouth shut. (I got kicked out after I suggested a bit too loudly that Father DeMarco looked absolutely stunning in his new purple dress.) Then my mother would tell me not to make any noise this visit to church either or she'd alter my face.

Later at home we would sit down to our Sunday dinner and the rest of the family would come pouring in. Uncles. Aunts. Cousins. Relatives I'd never heard of. Everybody kissed everybody, not only when they came in, but also when they went out. Kiss everybody, half of whom you don't even know. One time my mother said: "I think you just kissed the plumber." I kissed so much, by the end of the day I had chapped lips.

After the kissing we all went over to my grandfather's house, who had moved out of our house by this time. I was named after him: James. You want to know his last name? I knew that you would. Ready for this? V-i-t-a-l-e. Except he pronounced it the right way. Vi-tal-ee. The other guy, Dick, I don't know where he gets off dropping the last syllable.

It was great being in an all-American neighborhood, so close to the entire family. But then came The Move To The Suburbs.

This was very traumatic for me. We moved from Queens because my dad took a much better-paying job as a physical education teacher and basketball coach at Seaford Junior High School in Seaford, Long Island (it later became a full high school). He also started a summer basketball league at Rockville Center, and he officiated sports the year round; football, basketball, baseball, the works.

The good part was that now I could ride with my dad to school and see him a lot more often. I had breakfast with him every morning. I saw him in the halls at school. I went to his office to talk.

The bad part was being uprooted from an all-Italian neighborhood. I had known only Catholic schools and uniforms. I had played ball only in the streets and schoolyards. I was twelve. All of a sudden we were leaving all my friends to go to . . . the South Shore of Long Island? It might as well have been Nova Scotia.

I'll never forget the first day of school. One kid came right up to me. I asked him what his name was and he said "Rusty." *Rusty?* I thought that was a disease from staying out in the rain. I never heard of anybody named Rusty. There were all kinds of names like that. I went to school that first day with a jacket and tie on just like back at St. Leo's. When I got there all the kids were casually dressed. When the teacher came in I wanted to say, "Good morning, Sister Mary Alice." Then we *changed classes.* I never changed classes in my life. Well, this bell rang and people went scurrying all over from room to room. I had no idea what was happening.

In Seaford all the kids drove to school. Everybody had a car. Where I came from, the *teachers* didn't have cars. One day I told somebody my mother was making "manicotti." He said, "What?" I didn't realize most people didn't eat the way my family ate.

Oh yeah. The first day at school was also the very first time I saw the extremely unbelievable Pamela Levine. I am not making this up: She was the first fair-skinned person I had ever seen in my life. I had no idea what this creature was, but I knew I liked it. Then a few weeks later she wasn't in school one day because of a Jewish holiday. I had never met a Jew, much less knew about Jewish holidays. "Jews have *holidays?"* I remember asking somebody.

Seaford High was not that large a school, but this was my first experience with sports that were actually organized. Teams and uniforms and schedules. Practices and games. Scoreboards and clocks. Going out for the first team in my life in the eighth grade was so exciting. I made it. Rusty—the disease—made it. We were teammates. The lights, the spectators, the gym. I got so psyched up, playing against another team with another uniform on. And it was the first time I had a coach, Mr. Herb Winslow. This may sound absurd, but I knew right then and there that this was what I wanted to do with my life. I was going to be a coach. No doubt in my mind.

When my dad died a few years ago and I went back to Seaford for the dedication of the gymnasium in his name, Mr. Winslow said he could still remember me being excited every single minute I was in a Seaford uniform.

As a freshman I played junior high football and basketball, and I started at second base on the varsity baseball team. As quarterback for the jayvees, we went 0–8 and I got the crap kicked out of me. In basketball, I got moved up from the junior high team to the jayvees and had a pretty good year. But baseball was my best sport. I batted .400 as a freshman and made all-league. Also, it was the only season I got to play with Nick, who was a senior and the third baseman.

One of my most important experiences in high school was playing for football coach Harry Curtis my senior year. Let's quickly review my football career: freshman year, 0–8; sophomore year, bench-warmer; junior year, I broke my ankle and didn't play. I didn't even intend to play football my senior year; instead, I wanted to concentrate on basketball and baseball. Coach Curtis talked me into playing; in fact, he saw something in me that I didn't see in myself. He worked with me all summer, and told me that I was going to be his starting quarterback, since last year's starter was gone. I didn't believe I was good enough, and yet, this man's work with me and his belief in me helped me not only to play that year, but to become an All-Long Island quarterback on the second team. To put this in perspective, this was the highest honor I'd attained in athletics, and it was in a sport in which I'd never had any previous success. It was another lesson to me about what can happen when someone believes in you. This lesson was to influence me for the rest of my life; it taught me that people can do anything they set their minds to. Later on, in coaching, I decided I wanted to find that particular something in each player and to bring out in them their best abilities.

Seaford always had good baseball teams. We made the South Shore Athletic League playoffs every year. As I progressed through high school, I became more and more a sports junkie. At St. Leo's, the measure of success had been academics. Every grade I got was 95 and up. When I got to Seaford and a whole new world of sports opened up, I became less of a student. Oh, I got grades—I had college board scores of 1135 and I was admitted to all the colleges where I applied, including Pennsylvania of the Ivy League—but sports was my life.

In my sophomore year I played basketball for Rocco Valvano on the varsity squad. Though I didn't start for awhile, I did come off the bench and made three jumpers from the corner against Malvern on a Saturday afternoon TV game. I remember because the legendary Marty Glickman did the game on WPIX, Channel 11 in New York. We didn't win, but I was still happy. I made six from the corner on the tube!

In reality, I had an absolutely Ozzie-and-Harriet (Long Island version) family; the perfect boy-next-door existence in high school. To measure that, I think the low point of my life may have come when my dad took me out of the game against St. Agnes High and benched me because I wouldn't shoot. People were guarding me, grabbing me, running at me; they were too big, too fast, too quick. I was scared out of my jock. So I figured the best thing was not to shoot the damn ball. Of course, then the other team left me open. Next day the headline in *Newsday* said: COACH'S SON WOULDN'T SHOOT. I'm serious. If I had shot, it would have said: COACH'S SON MISSES BY A LOT. I should have known even back then you can get in trouble for almost anything.

As time went on, I became a fairly big deal in high school. I was president of the varsity club and president of the student council. At home I was president of the "Why can't I drive the car?" club. Did I say my life was idyllic? Wrong. Because my father was so strict about the car, when Pam and I dated, *she* had to drive.

Actually, I was lucky I got anywhere near Pam considering my relationship with her parents, Arnie and Wilma Levine. Arnie Levine worked out of Manhattan. At times I thought he must have sold pajamas, because I always got pajamas from him on my birthday. I figured if he didn't sell pajamas, he certainly had a deal going in the peejay industry. (Actually, he was a salesman for a large textile company.) The Levines were a nice middle-class family—I always joked that I married the only "poor" Jewish girl on Long Island—and before I came along, Pam had a boyfriend whom everybody knew would turn into a rich doctor, which he did.

Pam and I were friends all along, but our first actual date was for the junior prom. (It was my first date with anybody.) About that time we started to realize: Hey, I'm Catholic, you're Jewish. This ain't going to work. But let's p--- off everybody anyway.

For instance, after I asked Pam out, her parents questioned me about what I was going to do with my life. As if what I was going to do with my life had anything to do with the junior prom.

"Well, folks, I plan to run some seriously illegal armaments to Iraq, but first—call me crazy—I'd like Pam and I to do a little twisting to Chubby Checker."

At any rate, when I told them I planned to be a basketball coach, their reaction was: "What kind of life would that be? What sort of business is that?" These conversations used to drive me nuts. Soon, the only time Pam's parents invited me into their home was when she wasn't there. Then they would sit me down and explain why the idea of the two of us together would never work. I told Pam her parents must have thought I was Spanish, because everytime I came to the house, they'd take one look at me and yell, "It's *him.*"

"No, no," I'd say. "That's *Jim.* Hard J, *Jim.* Not *him.*"

As if the relationship wasn't doomed enough, for our first date my father insisted that I *still* could not drive. Talk about embarrassing. . . . First Rocco and Jim Valvano picked up Pamela Levine and drove to a restaurant. Then Rocco picked us up and drove us to the prom. Then he picked us up and drove home. The restaurant was Carl Hoppl's in Baldwin, Long Island. I'll never forget it.

Remember now, here was my dream girl, Debbie Reynolds' twin clone. She had a boyfriend already (he was away at college) whom her parents expected she'd marry. And yet she deigned to go to the prom with this whacked-out, nervous, inexperienced Italian kid whose dad had to drive them everywhere.

At Carl Hoppl's, Pam ordered lobster tail. I didn't even know lobsters had tails, much less that you could eat the things. Then I looked at the price and panicked. I didn't have anywhere close to the money to pay for the meal. I was nearly hysterical. They asked me what I wanted and I think I ordered a tuna melt. I said, "I'll be right back," and I immediately went to the telephone to call my father. "Pop, she ordered a lobster tail. Do you know how much those things cost?" He said he'd be right over with some cash.

I remember Carl Hoppl had a band playing. Spanish band. Flamenco. Castanets. So I got up and did a little dance. I thought Pam would think it was great. "Sit down," she said.

"Hey, I'm starting to get in the spirit of things," I said. "Besides, I have to work off that tuna melt."

A few minutes later I excused myself and met my dad at the front door. He was furious, but he forked over enough money to pay for dinner. Pam never knew he made an interim trip to Carl Hoppl's. But of course he had to come back later in the evening to pick us up, take us to the prom, then drop us off at her house again.

At the end of one of the longest nights of my life, we sat at the Levines' and talked. I didn't know how I was supposed to finish the evening. Kiss her? Hug her? Do some more flamenco? Luckily, her grandfather awakened in the middle of the night and took the two French poodles out for a walk. I took my cue, jumped up and kissed the grandfather, the French poodles, and Pam good night, but not before asking for a second date (Pam, not the poodles). For some reason, she said yes.

This time we went to a movie in Merrick, Long Island. This time we took the bus. I wasn't worldly enough to understand that when you escort a woman to a movie theater, you must remember that they never want anything to eat for themselves, they just want to eat *your* food. I had enough money this time. "Would you like some popcorn and a drink?" I asked.

"No, thank you," she said.

But as soon as I brought back popcorn for me, she started borrowing some great chunks from my personal collection.

"Look, if you want a box, I'll get you a box," I said. "But this particular popcorn is mine. Food is important in my life. Don't take my food."

After I had purchased another popcorn and some soda, I was on my way back to the seats when, wouldn't you know it, I tripped in the aisle and spilled both the corn and the drink all over my date. You can imagine what her reaction was. I don't remember what movie we were watching, but the atmosphere was definitely *Gunfight at the O.K. Corral.*

It's a miracle things turned out the way they did after those two nights. Pam and I always had been friends, but we really didn't start dating until late that junior year, and even then it wasn't a breathless-second thing like most "steadies."

For one thing, I never was able to hang out like most kids. I always had my sports and "ball." I always had to be home early. Never out past nine P.M. Especially in basketball season when I played for my dad. While all the other kids would go out to eat and to dances, I would have to come home and go over the games with my dad.

Finally, after Pam and I became an "item," he did let me go to her house sometimes and she would cook me pizza, but it was that frozen stuff you put in the oven. Terrible. Everyone says Italian and Jewish families are similar, but not in the kitchen they aren't. Jewish families are nice, but I don't care what they say: They don't have good food. A Jewish deli is about it. The best thing Pam ever made were reservations.

Everyone thought after I went off to college, that would be it for us; she would grow tired of me. How many times can a Truly Beloved dance the flamenco and remain a Truly Beloved? You just don't make a comeback from these things.

Actually, I did—and Pam and I have been married for twenty-three years. During that time I came to feel as much a part of the Levine family as she has of the Valvano family. And Pam's mom, a very talented woman in her own right, has come to love basketball—and I think, me, too.

Chapter Three

"STARTING AT GUARD . . ."

THIS MAY NOT COME AS A SURPRISE, BUT I'M ONE OF THE WORLD'S BIGGEST hams. Hoops was always the neatest sport for me in high school because when you played basketball, it was an event. Lots of people watched. Basketball always seemed less a game than a Happening. I loved the lights and the noise. I loved the *Arena*.

Baseball may have been my game, growing up. But nobody cared, nobody came to the games. Back then there was no baseball draft and, if you attracted the interest of the pro scouts, you could sign for a pittance and begin a career in Class D somewhere. Representatives of the Giants and the A's contacted my father about a pro career, but he never entertained the thought. I was going to college and that was it.

Also, I never had any pretense of making it as a professional athlete. I was going to be a basketball coach and that was it; a high-school basketball coach.

At Seaford in my senior year I was captain of all the major sports. I wanted to continue playing them all in college, so I considered going to a smaller school—those schools which at the time were designated as "college division." Albright in Reading, Pennsylvania was one. Colby in Maine was another. The University of Pennsylvania was interested in me, but only as a football player. Then my father suggested I look at Rutgers, where both he and my Uncle Bruno had gone to college. I wasn't going to get a scholarship anywhere, and Rutgers, being a state school, was cheaper than the rest.

When I went for my visit in New Brunswick, New Jersey, here's how big a deal I was: Nobody talked to me. Nobody showed me around the campus. Bill Foster was the basketball coach then, and his assistant was Bruce Webster, a guy from Long Island who had known my father. We dropped in on him the day of my visit and that was enough. I had good board scores, I had been a three-sport captain and president of the student council, and I was the son of an alumnus. But a scholarship? Forget it.

Rutgers was another place where hard work and enthusiasm and desire paid off and furthered my position in life. I was an unrecruited player. I was a have-not. Always had to overcome something. Always played from behind. (I wasn't even Pamela Levine's first choice.) This experience had a tremendous impact on my determination to make my dreams come true. Going out for the freshman team at Rutgers I was one of about ninety white guys, all about six feet tall, 175 pounds, who couldn't run or jump and were just trying to land a spot on the bench. I figured out early that there was only one way I was going to make the team. So I started diving on the floor. Every chance I got, I'd dive for a loose ball. Every time the coaches were looking my way, I'd dive. Ball got loose, dive. Whistle blew, dive. You thought Greg Louganis practiced long hours on the half gainer? I took charges, blocked out and kept diving. After diving for about a week and a half, the coaches kept me. To emerge from that group four years later, and score 24 points against Walt Frazier and Southern Illinois in the semifinals of the NIT at Madison Square Garden, and make the all-tournament team—that was the beginning of my impetus for success, that would last for the rest of my life.

Rutgers usually had a couple of big-time scholarship recruits each season. In 1963–64 there was a guy named Bob Lloyd from Upper Darby, Pennsylvania; 6'2", blond, blue-eyed, handsome, a high school All-American who not only never broke a sweat, but his outfits never broke color coordination. The first thing to know about Bob Lloyd was that he always dressed in penny loafers which he kept in perfect shape by molding them every time onto *shoe trees.*

Whoa! I never saw this before. Shoe trees! This absolutely blew my mind. Lloyd also used to keep his pants precise and wrinkle-free by hanging them in the closet with *hanger clips.*

Shoe trees. Hanger clips. Always shaved. Got up in the morning and made his bed every day. Sometimes went to class in a blazer. Neatest guy I ever met, Bob Lloyd. He was just too, too perfect. But I figured out the only way to get him back. Whenever we were eating out at a respectable restaurant and he'd wave hello to some friends of his—"That's Mr. and Mrs. So and So," he'd say—I'd be sure and order ice cream for dessert. Then I'd take an entire scoop, shove it in my mouth and spit it back into the dish. Do that quite a few times, and sure enough Bob would say, "Why do you have to do those things?" Bob Lloyd would have made a wonderful wife. I ought to know; we ended up as roommates as well as backcourt partners our last two years at Rutgers. We've also remained lifelong friends.

I was a bench-warmer for the freshman team for the entire first semester of freshman year. I finally got to start the first game of the second semester against Trenton Junior College. You can imagine how I felt, starting my first college game alongside the All-American blond bomber, Bob Lloyd—the guy we nicknamed "El Rubio" (The Blond) and "El Rei" (The King). It was a big night for me: I scored 29 points. My career had begun. In the same game, Lloyd had 30-something, and for him, this was average. The Rutgers varsity that year won five games, but our freshman team won most of the prelims with Lloyd averaging in the high 30's; I think he hit 50 a couple of times.

This didn't compensate nearly enough for the ineptitude at the varsity level. The Scarlet Knights were, let's face it, pathetic. On one occasion, the Rutgers varsity played Lafayette in Easton, Pennsylvania, where they had an old clock which turned orange for the last minute of each half. It didn't matter; in any color it was impossible to tell how much time was left. On a defensive rebound, our guy, Phil Robinson, our best player, grabbed the ball late in the game and thought he saw orange on the clock. He took one dribble and threw the ball the length of the court. The baskets hung from a second-floor track at Lafayette, and after Robinson's shot came clanging up at about the 220-yard mark on the first turn, some fans grabbed the ball and wouldn't throw it back down. Meanwhile Robinson, thinking time had run out, merely walked off the other end of the court and continued downstairs to the locker room. I was sitting behind the bench at the time. Foster didn't miss a beat. "Somebody get Phil and bring him back up here," the coach announced. There were still *four and a half minutes* left to play.

I'll never forget sitting in a film session with the varsity that season. Rutgers was roaring down on a 3-on-1 fast break against Delaware when our guy, Sal LaSala, on the right wing got set to catch a perfect lead pass and take it in for the easy bucket. On the screen, here came Sal and here came the ball at the apex of the play and . . . Sal LaSala ducked! I mean, the guy flat-out buried his head into his shirt, as if the basketball was a grenade about to blow his eyeballs into the next county. Now Foster had watched this film what, maybe 864 times already? But I could tell he was still ready to crack. He couldn't believe Sal ducked!

"Sal, uh, why would you duck there?" Foster said.

"I didn't see the ball," LaSala said.

"Sal, you're the only player anywhere near this play. Why would you duck?"

"I thought the ball was going to hit me in the head," LaSala said.

17

VALVANO

"Well, why wouldn't you *catch* the ball?"

"I didn't see it."

Which is why, the following season, Jim Valvano became an immediate starter on the Rutgers varsity, helping his fellow sophomore, Bob Lloyd, lead the team to a spectacular 12–12 record. Well, at least that was seven more wins than the year before.

At our first varsity meeting, Foster swore it was a new era. No more Lafayettes or LaSalas. "I know academics have to come first, but you guys get with your advisors to schedule classes so they don't conflict with the practice times. Especially you engineering majors—you're missing too many practices because of labs."

"Coach," said Eddie Thiele. "I'll make every practice this season."

"Great. That's what I'm talking about. That's the kind of cooperation we need," said Foster.

"But coach," said Eddie. "I'm going to have to miss about 12 games."

And he did miss a lot. We'd be in the locker room getting dressed for practice, and Eddie would come in and ask how we did last night! This was such a different era.

I'll never forget the time we played Princeton and Bill Bradley. The Tigers, right down the road in New Jersey, were our big rival, and Bradley, a senior then, was the nearest thing to God in short pants. Prior to the contest, I went to the men's room for my traditional pregame appearance, when who should come in but Bradley, the Great One himself. Bad news flash: He was in the same row of urinals as me. Bad news flash two: He spoke.

Does everybody know how there are some games in which they are convinced in their heart of hearts that they have positively no chance? Right then I knew about that game. In the men's room at Rutgers not only couldn't I say anything back to the future Senator from New Jersey. That was embarrassing enough. I *couldn't even go!*

I wasn't alone in my awe. Dennis Earl was the Rutgers defensive specialist who would guard Bradley. At the introductions, when Bradley's name was called, Earl started clapping. Needless to say, we got buried.

That same year we played Connecticut and a kid named Wes Bialosuknia. Since Lloyd always guarded the guy who had the hamstring pull, who was coming off knee surgery, who had an appendectomy, I drew the tough assignments. We were in the locker room before the game, and Foster was going over the matchups. "Robinson: you've got Toby Kimball. Earl: you've got Bill Holowaty. Lloyd: you've got the guy coming off the triple bypass." Then he gets to me. "Valvano: you've got Bialosuknia. Listen, this guy was a high-school All-American, and the leading scorer in the country as a freshman. They set picks for him all over the court. He's a great jump shooter from downtown, but he drives like a house afire. And he's good-looking too. Can you handle it?"

Handle it? I didn't know whether to guard the guy, or ask him for a date!

Actually, that whole evening up at Storrs, Connecticut was an embarrassment. During the warmups, a U. Conn. cheerleader named Barbara Gross called over to me. I went to high school with Barbara, but I couldn't look at her because I was taking my lay-ups. Finally she came over and stood right next to me. I had to say hello, but just as I whirled back to the hoop a guy's pass hit me square in the shnozz (which wasn't the smallest of targets, granted). But my eyes were watering like fountains. Of course, Foster happened to be looking right at me.

Back then, the folks at Connecticut used to turn out the lights to introduce the home team. The Huskies came running out in a line and everybody dunked the ball. The place went nuts, absolutely crazy. I had just been hit in the face. Now the lights went out, and I didn't know if they were really out or if I'd fainted. I wasn't feeling so hot.

The game started, and on the first play U. Conn. dunked. Now we took the ball out of bounds, me into Lloyd. He passed back, they pressed and I coughed it up. We took it in again. Halfcourt trap. They pounded the floor. Some guy with the wingspan of a 747 played the middle. This guy could touch both sidelines from the middle of the court. I coughed it up again.

Every time I threw it in, Lloyd passed it back. The referee stood next to me, counting, "3 . . . 4 . . . 5 . . ." And where was my roomie, Lloyd? He was at the other end in the corner with his hand up, calling for the ball. And here I had about 3.5 seconds to figure out how to get the ball in past this spider monster. I jumped across the line: strip, boom, dunk. I jumped, got double-teamed and here we went again: boom, dunk.

That was on offense. On defense, it was another matter—I was worse. At the half, Bialosuknia had about 28 points. On the way back to the locker room Foster was enraged. "Hey Valvano, don't you know who the hell you're guarding?" he screamed.

"Yeah, the good-looking guy," I said. "He's beating the hell out of me."

Things were better my junior and senior seasons at Rutgers. The Knights won 17 and then 19 regular season games, earning a bid to the National Invitation Tournament. When I was a senior, Foster used to let me take the microphone on bus trips to loosen up the squad. I'd usually rag on the sophomores and juniors on the team, who always dressed as if they had purchased their clothes by mail order.

The climax of my college career was that NIT in Madison Square Garden. We beat Utah State in the opening round; Lloyd scored 42 points. We beat New Mexico in the second game; Lloyd had 23. In between, we appeared on the "Merv Griffin Show" and ate at the 21 Club.

The neatest thing in New York was meeting Muhammad Ali. One day I got a call at the team hotel. "I watched you guys play. You were great. Come on downstairs." It was Angelo Dundee. I went to the hotel coffee shop and had a coke with Dundee. Ali was training for his title fight with Zora Folley at the Garden that week, and we invited him to our practice. I played him one on one. He traveled and I called it. He said he didn't travel. I said OK, we may as well skip that one.

The next day we played Southern Illinois in the semifinals. At the half I had 20 points—draining eight straight jumpers at one point—and we were ahead by nine points. Then the Salukis went to a triangle and two on Lloyd and me. Bob had 20 for the game. I got two more baskets and we lost, 79–70.

In the consolation game the only things I remember are that we beat Marshall, that Soupy Sales (a Marshall grad) was there and that we played at ten in the morning.

All this was great experience, and we had a lot of laughs. But college wasn't total unadulterated joy, either. At Rutgers, I faced prejudice for the first time. Back in New York on the fringes of my Italian neighborhood I grew up with all kinds of minorities: black and Jew, Polish and Irish. Each had their own "turf," but it never seemed we couldn't get along.

When the Rutgers team played at Jonesboro, Arkansas in my junior year, however, I experienced some real ugliness. I was getting a hot dog when a group of people near the concession stand started calling me names: "Dago." "Wop." "Hey, you boys ever see a Guinea? There he is now." Perceptive, intelligent stuff like that. I brushed it off and walked away, but this incident had a tremendous effect on me. If this was the way I felt after merely being called some names, I couldn't begin to imagine the indignities suffered by black people when they weren't allowed into restaurants or when they had to use separate toilets.

Nowadays there is hardly a coach anywhere who doesn't vigorously recruit black players, but I take great pride in having brought some of the first blacks to Johns Hopkins and to Bucknell, the two schools where I got my first head coaching jobs. Personal hurt and anger while eating a hot dog in Jonesboro, Ark. had a lot to do with my thinking in this area.

More than anything, though, Rutgers was about Dreams Coming True. I was a walk-on at Rutgers, just another no-name, non-scholarship bench guy when I first arrived. I wound up having a terrific career, being elected captain, making All-NIT, setting some records, making a little history at Rutgers. My basketball life in college showed me that a person of limited means could accomplish wonderful things if he believed, if he had people who believed in him, if he kept on dreaming.

By the end of four years at Rutgers, I was playing in the same tournament with the Dukes and the Marquettes, with the Bob Vergas and the George Thompsons. By the time I was a senior, I guess I truly believed that Bob Lloyd and I were as good a backcourt as any in America.

Naturally, playing in Madison Square Garden was the crème de la crème, but it took the Garden folks practically our entire college career to realize Rutgers would be such a great draw in the Big Apple. I mean, it was a major event when we played there. Students lined up for hours to get tickets. When we finally made the NIT, they closed the school for us. Classes were called off. That's how big it was. The NCAA's were nothing at Rutgers compared to the NIT. It was absolutely unbelievable.

But even before that, we played two games my senior year in the Garden that I can still remember almost play for play. The first was against Missouri. My first Garden packed house; nearly 12,000 screaming Rutgers fanatics in the stands. Back home in New Brunswick, we never got to be introduced or to run out onto the court. We were usually taking our lay-ups when they announced our names. Then we walked out later for the tip-off. But that night against Missouri I sat there on the bench waiting and listening for only one thing: the famous Garden PA guy, John Condon, who would say, ". . . And at guard for Rutgers University, from Seaford, New York, Jimmm Valvanoooo."

Later on during my years as a summer camp lecturer, I based an entire routine on how different guys run out onto the floor when their names are called in the introduction. I just got a kick out of the way everybody is so different. I would tell the kids not to be embarrassed; this was their moment. This was a part of the game they should really enjoy. I told them they should even practice running out there. Get a style. Cop an attitude. Let's see a little originality. Bill Russell ran out one way, Earl Monroe a totally different way. Myself, running out, I used to practice *the low five* (I was way ahead of my time). But high fives, low ones, sideways, stroll, sashay, whatever, I insisted all the camp kids do it with style. This was my camp spiel, and it all harkened back to that night when I was introduced against Missouri. Sure enough, I came running out and gave my teammates a little behind-the-back palm.

It took almost twenty-two years of my life to finally get a big night at Madison Square Garden; it took me over forty minutes more to score my first basket. As ridiculous as this may sound, not only didn't I score within regulation time during the game, after all that I was still the one who was supposed to take the potential game-winner!

This was in the no-clock, stallball, dribble-out-the-time era. With the game tied, our ball, we set up for a final shot. Whenever we needed a basket at the end of a game, naturally, our only option was to go to Lloyd, who would dribble his brains out until he got open for the game-winner. Pass? Perish the thought. Bob Lloyd never passed in his life—we used to joke that the only pass he ever made was at teammate Rick Harley's girlfriend.

But then, that night, the craziest thing happened. All of a sudden, Lloyd threw the ball to me. Lloyd hadn't passed to Valvano in four years. But now I got the rock and the clock was ticking down so I shot it. What? I missed? I hadn't scored all night, hadn't made one single, measly basket. And now I was supposed to be the hero? Still, Lloyd passed to me because, he said later, "You were open."

"Hey, Rooms," I said later, "I've been open for a career and you never saw me. By the way, you know why I was open? Because nobody guards a guy if he hasn't made a basket all night. Oh, and you were covered? Darn! That's right, you've never been covered before."

Anyway, after not scoring in regulation, I made 12 points in the overtime and we beat Missouri going away.

The second game we played in the Garden that year was against NYU and Mal Graham, the leading scorer in the nation. I got Mal Graham on three—count 'em, three—offensive charges. And that was the end of him. Listen, I could play some D. I picked up full court, got after guys, yelled at them and hit them and entertained them a little bit, too. So Graham ran over me three times that night and Lloyd set the record for consecutive free throws in the Garden: 19 in a row.

That's nothing, really. At one time that year Bob made 60 straight foul shots, which was the NCAA record. No surprise to me, of course. I must have held the NCAA career record for passing the ball back to a foul shooter. When we were freshmen we hooked up one day after practice and—I didn't know who this was, remember, how good he was or that he was a practice maniac!—we agreed to shoot some free throws. Lloyd turned out to be one of those guys who ended every practice by taking a hundred jump shots. Then he ended the jump shots by taking a hundred free throws. "Let's go to the line. Shoot till you miss. You go first," Lloyd said. I got up there and hit a few, then missed. Now it was his turn. Half an hour later he was still swishing 'em in and I was still standing there bouncing 'em back to him.

Not only was Lloyd a great foul shooter, he tended to get fouled a lot. Our senior year he must have taken 277 free throws, and made 255. I tell you, my roommate was a great, great college player.

As I look back, the way Foster the coach, Lloyd the star, and I communicated and interacted went a long way in determining my own coaching philosophy. From Foster I got a marvelous sense of organization. The man has since gone on to direct the basketball operations at four different universities: Utah, Duke, South Carolina and, currently, Northwestern. He's overcome a heart attack. He's made the Final Four (Duke, '78). He reeks of class. Moreover, I'd say Bill Foster was one of the very first of the exceptional businessman/entrepreneur coaches. He made sure he touched all the bases: meticulous in preparation for both practices and games, innovative in recruiting techniques, aggressive in promotion. Foster practically invented such modern-day coaching staples as the recruiting letter and the summer camp.

Because I played for my father in high school, there was no guarantee that I would fit into any structure that wasn't similarly nurturing. Plus, I was quite the ball buster. I had a *player's* temperament. But, above all, I played for the *coach.*

At Rutgers I didn't give a single day's problem regarding work, effort, handling defeat or accepting a role. Bob Lloyd got the ball all the time because he was the best player. I could handle that. I knew all about the coaching life and star system. I lived in a household embodying both. I knew what a coach feels and thinks and how important practice is to a coach.

While most players dog practice, coaches *live* for practice. Players think coaches play favorites. But once a game starts, a coach doesn't like anyone on his team more than anyone else. All a coach wants to do is win the game. He could care less if one guy scores 100 and no one else scores at all. Remember Al Davis' motto: Just Win, Baby. Hey, nothing else matters. In a perfect coach's world, of course, everybody on the team scores 12 and everybody stays happy. But the ratios don't matter if a team is winning.

Other than my initial fooling around, however, I think Foster would say that I was always ready to play, always ready to practice. Oh, sometimes he would get upset and scream and yell at me, but he had to put up with some pretty bizarre stuff. Once when a huge crowd at Rutgers greeted the team bus on our return from an important road victory, I got off the bus to a whistling, screaming ovation—one so loud and invigorating that I snuck around behind the bus, opened the rear door, and got back in so that I could emerge a second time to another, equally warm and thunderous reception.

It usually took me two exits to match the applause Lloyd got in one. Upon our graduation, Bob was voted a consensus All-American, along with—these names may sound familiar—Providence's Jimmy Walker, Wes Unseld of Louisville, Elvin Hayes of Houston, and Lew Alcindor of UCLA. A hot property, Bob was drafted by the Minnesota Muskies of the ABA. This was before the NBA draft had taken place. But then it got out that he preferred the newer league. As a result, the Pistons drafted him in the sixth round behind their first choice, Walker, and he got cut. Lloyd ended up playing with the New Jersey Americans (which became the New York Nets) of the ABA for two years before retiring to take a job with General Electric. He later worked for Spalding and the Italian athletic clothing line, Fila. He brought the Mizuno batting glove from Japan to America, or rather he brought the guy who invented the glove. Then he became president of a company called Data East. Now he's semiretired, lives half a year in Los Altos Hills, Calif., the other half in Hawaii. And he plays golf every other hour.

As for Lloyd's ex-roommate:

I had four options out of Rutgers. 1. Pursue the newly formed ABA. I knew I was as good as most of the guys going into the league, but I also knew I wasn't capable of making a career out of pro ball. 2. Play with the Akron Goodyears at the AAU level. 3. Coach the New Brunswick High School team. 4. Stay at Rutgers and work as an assistant coach under Foster. The latter being the lowest-paid and possibly least prestigious of all the opportunities, that was exactly what I ended up doing.

Of course now I'm retired from coaching, and play golf once in a while myself. And I didn't even have to move to Hawaii.

Chapter Four

OF OVERACHIEVERS, WOOLLYBOOGERS, AND CATEGORIES

S OMEONE ONCE SAID THAT GREATNESS IS FINDING A VOID AND FILLING IT. Or that survival depended on filling the void. Or was it that survival in coaching depended on filling the void with greatness? Something like that. At any rate, at the same time Rutgers was a rite of personal passage for me as a human-type being, my experiences there as a player—and no less as an ultra great void-filler—established a foundation on which I based an entire coaching philosophy.

Initially, there was nothing unique about me or my abilities that distinguished me from the crowd. I wasn't quicker than a lot of guys. I certainly wasn't going to be a better shooter or scorer than Bob Lloyd. "What does this team need? Where is the lack? What can I do to fit in?" These were the key questions. Even back then, I think I figured out the answers from a coach's point of view. I could play defense, take the charge, dive for loose balls. Put me on a guy and I picked him up full court, breathed all over him, pulled the hairs on his legs. I was an irritant, a maniac. I did all the blue-collar stuff. This is embarrassing and I don't let this out too often, but I didn't get the nickname "Sparky" from singing in the Rutgers chorus.

As a college coach I later was to use a 1–3 and a chaser defense: a direct steal from my MO on the lines of fortification at Rutgers. Every coach's best teams always have a couple of sacrificial role-players who are willing to give up their bodies for the chemistry of winning. V the coach had a guy like V the player every place I went: John McFadden, my first year as the Rutgers freshman coach; George Apple at Johns Hopkins; a kid

25

named Paul Biko at Bucknell (Biko got into a car accident and nearly killed himself; he had no socket in his left arm but came back to be one of my best players); Tony Iati and Dave Brown at Iona. I loved finding these guys out recruiting. I had to have them.

At North Carolina State I inherited Sidney Lowe and Dereck Whittenburg, both of whom a lot of people think were highly recruited out of DeMatha High School in Hyattsville, Maryland. The truth is, this NCAA championship backcourt wasn't as sought after as everybody believes: They never even visited Raleigh before they signed. Both Sidney and Dereck were blue-collar role-players—as was the center on that same team, Cozell McQueen. Everybody knows Cozell's famous quote. The kid was from Bennettsville, South Carolina and when he signed with State, I thought it was because he wanted so much to play for this charming, dynamic new coach. Oh no. Cozell chose N.C. State because, he said, "I always wanted to get out of the South." But what I'll remember most about Co was what he said in the locker room before our NCAA championship game against Houston and Akeem Olajuwon in 1983.

"He ain't nothin'," is what Co said.

"Pardon me?" is what I said.

"He ain't nothin'," McQueen said before going out and getting 12 rebounds against Akeem.

You gotta believe.

At State, we did that. We had Terry Gannon, who wasn't big enough or quick enough, and Vinny Del Negro, who, after I told him as a recruiter he might never play at State, said, "Yes I will." And my last quarterback, Chris Corchiani. Whew! It used to be said of the nasty old pitcher, Early Wynn, that he would knock down his grandmother to get the win. I'm sure Corchiani's grandma never even thought about getting into a halfcourt game against Chris.

The term "overachievers" doesn't begin to explain these guys. Gannon may have been my all-timer. A skinny six-footer who hardly ever got in a starting lineup, he suited up every night with the attitude that he was going to kick rear and take a name. And the name might as well have been "World."

One night in 1983, in Raleigh, in a game against North Carolina, a team which State had never beaten up to that time with me as coach, Gannon inevitably got too big for his britches. We were blowing a big lead. Michael Jordan was starting to explode. I was in my usual panic. "Can't anybody stop him?" I screamed from the sidelines.

"Put me in," came a voice from down the bench.

I didn't have to look to know who it was.

"Hey, Terry," I said. "That's Michael Jordan, not Hamilton Jordan."

But I put him in anyway. While Jordan finished with 19 points, Gannon scored 15. We won 70–63.

In the finals of the ACC tournament that year, we were ahead of Virginia by one point with a few seconds left. Where was the ball going? The ball was going to Ralph Sampson. Everybody in America and all the ships at sea knew it was going to Ralph. But the guy who did something about it, who stepped in to strip Sampson of the ball—not only stripped him but somehow grabbed the ball and passed it to Whittenburg for the clinching free throws—was Gannon. Now are we going to compare this spindly-legged little Wolfie to Jordan and Sampson, two of the best college players in history? Of course not. But Gannon was like that. He loved taking the three-pointers. He loved being at the line in the clutch moment. He was a dreamer. He believed in himself.

You think a guy like that didn't remind me of a big-nosed college guy twenty years earlier who entered Rutgers as a walk-on and wound up as the sixth leading scorer in the school's history? My father pounded the capital B, Belief, into me; as I grew into coaching it seemed obvious that the most important thing a coach could do for his players was to engender that same Belief.

Throughout the down times at Rutgers I don't remember ever wavering in the desire to make coaching my life. Of course, there were other jobs I might have taken which required a high degree of motivational ability.

For a summer I sold Encyclopedia Brittanicas door to door. Buying leads. Following up. Home visits. Pitching the sale. Closing the deal. In retrospect it was great training for the recruiting wars.

And there was my stint one summer as a swimming pool attendant at the apartment complex where I lived in New Brunswick. I always said: "Kids, if you're going to drown, do it very close to the edge so I can reach in."

Lifeguarding was a terrific way to keep cool in the Jersey summers. But one day the heat became so bad that I actually had to get in the water. I didn't want anybody to see how weak a swimmer I was, though, so I pulled off one of those dives where you do a swan move out from the side far enough to enter the water, glide under it and come up on the other side without swimming a stroke. The only problem was at the moment I glided up for my elegant exit from the deep end, I misjudged the distance and slammed my face into the wall, breaking my nose in several hundred places. This is probably why it looks like a Pontiac hood ornament to this very moment.

"Wing Nose," to be precise, is what my Sergeant, Drill Instructor LeCrois, called me during my basic training duties at Lackland Air Force Base in San Antonio, Texas. Being a collegian in the mid-sixties, on the cusp of the Vietnam War, meant that a fellow was eligible for the military draft upon graduation—unless he opted for the Reserves. Early at Rutgers, Bob Lloyd, always thinking ahead, had signed both of us up for the Delaware Air National Guard. And so four years later, there I was.

A Reservist. An Italian. A college graduate. A New Yorker. What's that, four strikes against? You could probably guess that I didn't exactly get with the program at Lackland, a place which featured a quaint routine where every time I sat down, they told me to "Stand Up," and every time I stood up, they told me to "Sit Down." I figured the decision-making machinery must have broken down somewhere, but who was I to think? I was just another weekend fly guy who for the stupendously important moment known as "inspection," couldn't face the nozzle on his deodorant to 0300 hours.

I did learn to hunt down and destroy a "woollybooger," however. If you don't know about "woollyboogers" you are quite possibly a "dumb ass" (Military Term), just as I was for the better part of a day— specifically, the day that Sgt. LaCrois announced we were going to hunt for the "woollyboogers," which turned out to be, quite naturally, the little fuzzballs that pocked up our federal-issue blankets.

"Here Woollybooger, Here Woollybooger," I called out, peering under the beds on all fours.

"You're calling too fast, Wing Nose," Sgt. LaCrois said. "You're going to scare them."

"Yes sir," I said.

"When you find one, you jump to attention, say 'I found a woollybooger' and then come to my office and knock," LaCrois said.

"Yes sir," I said.

If you can envision a whole barracksful of college graduates on their hands and knees calling for woollyboogers, you have a solid picture of how the U.S. Air Force prepared its reservists for war.

And if we found a woollybooger? Well, I did.

Knock, knock.

"What are you knocking for, Wing Nose? What's the damn matter with you? You a crazy fool?" Sgt. LaCrois said.

"Yes sir. I found a woollybooger, SIR," I said.

"Is it male or female?" Sgt. LaCrois said.

"Yes sir. I don't know, SIR," I said.

"You don't *know?* What's the matter with you? You one of those kind who don't know the difference between a male and female, Wing Nose?" Sgt. LaCrois said.

"Yes sir. I haven't looked, *sir,"* I said.

"Well go ahead and look," Sgt. LaCrois said.

"Yes sir." Pause. "It's a female, *sir,"* I said.

"How do you know?" Sgt. LaCrois said.

"Sir. Well, I just can tell, *sir,"* I said.

"You come in here and tell me it's a female and you know that because you just can *tell,* Wing Nose? What in the hell is that? How do you know? *How?"* Sgt. LaCrois said.

"Sir. Because this woollybooger, she has all the apparatus, *sir,"* I said.

"What? What did you say? Oh my God! What kind of mind are we dealing with here, Wing Nose? I'll bet you'd like to *kiss* her, too, right? (Only he didn't say kiss.) I'll bet you'd like to hug her, right? (Only he didn't say hug.)" Sgt. LaCrois said. "You make me *sick.* Get out of here, *Wing Nose."*

My initial terror soon having abated, sure enough my big mouth was guaranteed to place me in constant turmoil amid the stiff military regimen. There was the food, the attitude, the marching. After spending what seemed like several light-years learning how to march—"Left, right . . . You're bouncing . . . You're bouncing . . . Your left, your left . . . Stand tall . . . Be proud . . ."—one evening we marched all over the base until ultimately we arrived at the baseball field where Sgt. LaCrois' son was playing for the base Little League team.

"Baseball is a great game. That's my son out there. Pretty good player, right? Men?" Sgt. LaCrois said.

"Yes sir," I shouted. "But can he march, *sir?"*

Not surprisingly, that remark was worth about nine days and nights on guard duty and latrine cleanup.

Nothing in basic training, however, could have possibly prepared me for the following summer when, working in the Rutgers coaching office, my reserve unit was suddenly called up to defend the Delaware Power and Light Company from the rioting that was breaking out in the streets of America's cities over Vietnam and the Civil Rights struggle. One hour I was figuring out how to break the zone press. The next, I found myself in uniform in the streets carrying an M-1 rifle.

It was one of those deals where you got your orders, your weapon and some dire warnings, and all you could think of was how pathetic your legacy would be.

How did your husband die, Mrs. Valvano?

Oh God, fighting in the war.

The Big One?

Yes, In Wilmington. Someone was going after a Zenith big screen.

Needless to say, when my six-year reserve obligation was ending (I had been promoted all the way up to Staff Sergeant, by the way), I met with the commanding officer of my unit. Normally, in those days, they tried to get you to re-up, to whet your interest in staying aboard. But for me, an exception was made.

"Sgt. Valvano," said Top Brass. "The military is not for everyone. Adios."

In one important characteristic, Air Force Reserve duty was but a continuation of the ambience on my college campus, because when I went to Rutgers it was all-male. In fact, if there was ever a time Pam and I seemed as if we weren't going to make it, it was when she visited New Brunswick. She was a working girl then, dealing with sophisticated businessmen in New York. I was getting up and going to morning class in my pajama top, because that is what slobs at Rutgers did. For some reason she could never appreciate my understanding of what a perfect weekend was. And to think she got a choice as well: Go to a ballgame and throw up or go to a fraternity party and throw up. What was so difficult? I wasn't exactly overly serious about life at that time.

Cracks aside, I should pause here to reaffirm how important education has always been to my family and myself. My father went to school long enough to earn a Master's degree. My brother Nick graduated from Rider College in Lawrenceville, New Jersey with a Master's, my brother Bob from Virginia Wesleyan (as a 1400 SAT student). My oldest daughter, Nicole, was a 3.85 chemistry student at North Carolina State, annually on the dean's list. Jamie, my middle daughter, graduated last year with a 3.9 average. My youngest, Lee Ann, gets straight A's, and might be sharper than any of us.

In my career I've coached some of the smartest, brightest athletes you'd ever want to know—at Johns Hopkins, Bucknell and Iona. And I was very proud that Terry Gannon was a two-time academic All-American at N.C. State. Of the players I coached before I arrived at N.C. State, all but two were graduated. The fact that I never changed my philosophy on either education or life in the ten years I coached at Raleigh seems to have been overlooked at times. And to think I majored in English, which should have guaranteed there would be no failure to communicate.

Having always loved to read, English was automatically my favorite subject in college. Then too, I noticed early on that English majors are well versed and articulate, and that always impressed me. Just as my father and Harry Curtis believed in me athletically, which helped me to reach my goals, I also had two English teachers who believed in me academically and who fostered a love of language and literature that stayed with me for the rest of my life. They were my high-school teacher, Mr. MacIntyre, and my college Shakespeare professor and advisor, Mr. McGinn. This was another instance in my life where someone who believed in me helped me to excel.

As anyone knows who has slipped into a North Carolina State basketball press conference during the last decade, I continued to take solace, wit and wisdom from the words of others. During my final, tough eighteen months at State, for example, Rudyard Kipling's *If* was daily reading material for me. I can now recite it by heart and I used it in my speeches quite often. At the beginning of each basketball season, I used to read to my team from A. E. Housman's *To an Athlete Dying Young.* Last season, in fact, one of our best pregame chalk talks—this at Clemson, believe it or not—centered around Shakespeare, not offensive rebounding.

I had been reading *Lear* on the bus ride to Clemson. The assistant coaches and players were ragging me for this, and I told them that the reason they didn't like Shakespeare was because they didn't understand the language. For instance, in *Antony and Cleopatra,* when two of their friends are standing there talking about Cleo and the one says Caesar "ploughed her and she cropped," they've got to figure what that means in their own argot (which I hesitate to reprint here). We talked about King Lear. We talked about *Romeo and Juliet* being the basis for *West Side Story* and *Pygmalion* turning into *My Fair Lady.* It was one of the best pregames we ever had. Then we went out and blew a 15-point lead to Clemson. Got plowed and cropped, sort of.

The point is, different coaches communicate in different ways. Whenever I had trouble explaining anything in my own words—to my players, the press or whomever—I didn't hesitate to call on my background in English literature. This came in especially handy whenever the subject of my "outside interests" at N.C. State came up, which was just about every other time I took a breath in a press conference.

One of the major failings of the coaching profession is that we've let ourselves be categorized too easily. As control freaks, jock manipulators, x and o geniuses, slick recruiters, game coaches, practice planners. We're either this or that, but we can't be *those.* Because I was the athletic director and on TV and on radio and did commercials and made speeches and goshknowswhatelse, all I ever got in media Q and A was: "Why do you do all these things?" Fed up one day, searching for an explanation, I tap-danced with the media by paraphrasing some of my favorite authors:

"As T. S. Eliot wrote in *The Love Song of J. Alfred Prufrock:* 'Do I dare ascend the stair? With a bald spot in my hair?' Or as Thoreau said in *Walden:* 'Some people march to the beat of a different drum.' Or as Robert Frost wrote in 'Two Roads Diverge in the Yellow Wood': '. . . and I took the road less traveled.'"

"Let me go on," I said. "Andrés Segovia, the classical guitarist, once played a piece particularly fast at breakneck speed, and all the critics in the room asked him afterward why he had done this. 'Because I can,' he said. Maybe the answers to your questions include a combination of the explanations offered by Eliot and Thoreau and Frost. I'm not afraid to show my bald spots, to make mistakes. I want to do other things, learn about other professions. I refuse to limit myself to whatever boundaries you may think surround a coach's position. Very simply, I enjoy diversity."

I thought that solved everything, until I saw the next day's papers. One guy actually wrote—I am paraphrasing here, but the drift's the same—" Valvano explained himself by quoting some poetic gibberish and admitting he was afraid of going bald." So much for communicating with the media.

The profession was all blue skies back in 1967 when I started as one of Bill Foster's assistants at Rutgers. As I mentioned, my choices were to try to continue playing in the ABA or the AAU, to go into high school coaching, or to stay in New Brunswick. I was happy at Rutgers, happier than I'd ever been. And as I told myself for the first time—but certainly not the last—"Don't mess with happy."

I never messed with happy, for instance, at North Carolina State. Up until the traumatic time I was, ahem, asked to leave the University, I was totally content in Raleigh. There had been several opportunities to pursue with the Knicks, the Clippers, ABC Television and UCLA—but my wife loved N.C. State, my daughters loved it, I loved it. Oh, there were many attractive tangibles about the coaching position at UCLA, most especially the opportunity to spend time with John Wooden. But . . . oops . . . here came the Happiness Factor. When we went out to Los Angeles to interview, the first house we looked at cost 1.4 million dollars. That was the pool house. Not really, but you get the picture.

To show you how close we had grown to N.C. State, when we were considering UCLA, Lee Ann was so traumatized she refused to leave unless we assured her we would change the UCLA blue and gold colors to Wolfpack red. *Don't mess with happy.*

This whole outlook obviously began with my father, who stayed in the same position and coached at the same high-school level all his life. In some circles that might be attributed to a lack of ambition. But my father never accepted anyone else's concept of what and whom he should be. In an age when men drank and smoked to excess, Rocco Valvano did neither. He laid out an atmosphere for his sons in which you were permitted to fail. In life as in sports he never pushed, never exerted pressure. He thought that just to be an athlete was a good enough experience in its own right; forget how good you were. Of the games, he used to say all the time: "Did you have fun? Did you have a good time?"

I have a message in needlepoint that's been mounted in my office so long I can't remember who I copped it from. Not that I'm a big-time philosopher or anything, but the message says: "The goal of life is to be able to sit in a room all by yourself and enjoy the company." The family of Rocco and Angela Valvano, every last one of them, reached that goal a long time ago.

And so I stayed on at Rutgers. The comfort zone in New Brunswick was such that I was not only an assistant coach, I was a head coach too: the head coach of the freshman team. Freshman only became eligible for varsity play in the early '70s, so back then the competition at the frosh level was hot and heavy. Our big rivalries were with Princeton and Pennsylvania, Columbia and St. John's. Our first game was always against the Penn freshmen . . . coached by Digger Phelps. If he says he forgot that we won 99–96, I'll take the scissors to one of his three-piece double-breasteds and sprinkle the remains all over Touchdown Jesus.

The best thing about that initial coaching experience was that the frosh were *my own team.* Assistants today don't get the opportunity to run the show. They sit on the bench, man the clipboards, catch the towels, maybe occasionally call a play or two. But as someone once said: The difference between an assistant and a head coach is the difference between a suggestion and a decision.

So freshman ball became a terrific training ground. I learned how to prepare practices, to deal with players, to adjust to game situations, and to find a way to win.

I mentioned before that it was wrong to "categorize" coaches. I know everybody used to say about me that I was a better game coach than I was in practice preparation; a seat-of-the-pants guy who had no strategic plan. Well, coaching freshman ball *made* me a game coach. You had no tapes, no film. You may never have seen the opposing team play or any of its players. You may not know their names! Much of your own team may have been unrecruited. So you matched and melded your personnel. Then when you got to game-time, you played the first half and assimilated everything you could. At halftime, you made corrections. You whipped serious butt, if needed. In the second half, with all that behind you, you could try to win the game.

Coaching the freshmen at Rutgers actually laid the seeds of my strategy of winning NCAA tournament games many years later. It is a very simple concept really—just win the game you play as opposed to building toward something down the road. Survive and advance, I call it. In tournaments you haven't got a whole lot of time for strategic brilliance or concentrating on scouting reports, anyway. You've got to catch as catch can and beat the other guy on that particular day. If Joe Swell, the 65-percent shooter, is off, and Frank Frompf, the injured seventh man, is draining everything from twenty feet—hey, you're going to have to adjust. And wear out the seat of those pants.

Ultimately, back in freshman ball, you didn't have the luxury of being able to choose whether you wanted to be a system coach—i.e., the players conform to your system—or a nonsystem, where the system is developed around the players each year. (Personalized respectively in the Atlantic Coast Conference by Dean Smith at North Carolina, and by Bobby Cremins at Georgia Tech.) All you could do was take a look at your players and figure out what system they could handle that particular year. If you were lucky, they could handle one of them.

Fortunately for me, Foster didn't care whether the freshmen ran the same plays as the varsity. He always said he wanted me to grow as a coach, to develop my own ideas and run the team as I wished. If that wasn't *carte blanche,* it was the next best thing.

My first day of practice with the Rutgers freshmen was also my first day as a physical education instructor; the opening course was archery. I told the kids, "I've never arched before. Just point downwind." If that was an inauspicious beginning, you can imagine how I felt when I found out what "open" tryouts meant.

Remember, I had played the game all my life. I wanted to be a coach. I was merely dying to be a coach. Full control. This was it! My first practice with my first team, ever. So I walked out onto the court and was greeted by . . . *ninety* players! So what do I do? Run two lay-up lines of forty-five guys each? Take down all their names? Memorize faces or gym shorts? Scrimmage with eighteen teams? What I actually did was get very, very nervous and suddenly I had to announce that I was going to the bathroom.

And I left. Downstairs. With ninety guys upstairs. Unsupervised. (Three lay-up lines, thirty apiece, maybe.)

While I was off answering nature's call, who should mosey into the gym but Coach Foster himself. But that's not the worst part. The worst part was that the bathroom—we've all visited these state-owned, bureaucratic mausoleums—had no toilet paper. And all I had was my Rutgers T-shirt. Well, a guy's gotta do what he's gotta do.

When I returned to my first practice, Foster asked me where my shirt was.

"It's lost," I said.

But you can't keep a funny story down on the farm. The next day Foster wrote me a note which said: "Before long trips, and first practices, always use the men's room."

As if that wasn't a humbling enough experience, my first and second Rutgers freshmen teams combined to teach me the true meaning of the word *chemistry*—not to mention the actual meanings of a couple of other words. Like *barely* and *five hundred.* That was the record posted by a van-load of blue-chip recruits whom we had brought in in my second year. And that was after my first team went 13–2, consisting mostly of undistinguished walk-ons, one of whom would go on to coach at Duke, South Carolina, Jacksonville and the New Jersey Nets before winding up as the current head coach at Rutgers; his name is Bob Wenzel.

Prior to ESPN, scouting was a tedious drawn-out exercise consisting of all-night car trips and diners, followed by long hours of writing out players' abilities, tendencies, and brands of deodorant, as well as suggested matchups with your own guys. Naturally, the head coach expected you to exaggerate your own weaknesses and play up your opponents' strengths so as to avoid any overconfidence in your own locker room.

"It was a tough trip," I began the report of my first scouting foray to Colgate in upstate New York. "I locked my keys in my car. Had to break in with my shoe. Had to drive home with the freezing rain pouring in my little green Volkswagen."

I was reporting this not only to the coaching staff, but to a team of which I was a member only a few months earlier. Head Coach Foster also was sitting there when I shouted to one of my former teammates, Dick Stewart (who would later work for me at N.C. State), "Hey Dick! You remember what it's like up there in that Ice Palace? I didn't even get a chance to go bowling!"

Ultimately I ended this soliloquy—by which time my boss, Foster, was just about passed out in shock—by telling our team: "Listen, I played with you against these guys for three years. It's no contest. These dogs can't hunt. They couldn't beat us if we showed up in handcuffs and leg irons."

Sure enough, we ended up burying the Red Raiders, probably saving my job. Unfortunately, I wasn't quite so accurate on another scouting mission. This one was to check out a high school kid whom my brother, Nick, had touted to me. The kid played in the same league on Long Island that I had at Seaford, and despite the fact that he was a 6'3" center, Nick swore to me that he was a great prospect.

Okay, I went to see him practice. He was okay. I went to see him in a game. Same thing. I even went for a home visit, because I figured we owed the kid the courtesy. But nothing came of that either. Nick and the kid's coach, Ray Wilson at Roosevelt High School, both told me he was going to be great. I said: "This is my business. Six-three? Center? CNP! *Can Not Play!*"

Oh, the kid visited Rutgers on his own anyway and still seemed very interested, but I convinced Foster he couldn't play at our level and that we should go after another player named Alan Cotler from Flushing High.

I lost Cotler to Penn. He's now a lawyer in Philadelphia. I lost track of the other kid. He was in Philly too, but I think he became a doctor or something. Ray Wilson is his business manager. You ever hear of him? Kid's name is Julius Erving.

Chapter Five

DIFFICULT MEAT

VINCE LOMBARDI, ANOTHER COACH WHO KNEW THE DIFFERENCE BETWEEN tomato sauce and gravy, once said the best feeling in sports was "lying exhausted in victory." Then he was asked what the next best feeling was, and Lombardi said, "Lying exhausted in defeat." Let me tell you from my experience that between the best feeling and the next best, it ain't even close. But the old Packer was right about the intensity of those feelings. One of the real fears I've always had about not coaching—why I never left the profession voluntarily—was that I would miss the emotion so much. And I have. It will take a long time for the withdrawal pains to subside.

Conversely, when I switched from playing to coaching at Rutgers, it didn't take more than a few losses to figure out the difference. Let's get that one out of the way real fast. There is positively no comparison between being a player and a coach. The animals aren't even in the same kingdom. Forget it.

Playing the game is easy. Playing is putting your sneakers on and answering the intros and running and jumping and shouting and getting it on. If you play great, you feel great. If you win, you feel great. If you lose, you still feel great. Oh, you might put on the long face after a defeat, but if you've had a good game individually, it doesn't bother you that much. As a player, the way you play affects how you feel more than winning or losing. That's why on a losing-team bus I've never insisted players show remorse or don't talk. Don't give me that silent, sad act. Fans take losses harder than players. I don't care what anybody says; the player who goes for 40 big ones in a one-point loss and says he's

37

crushed—hey, take that outta here. And, even if you win big, the players who didn't get into the game aren't going to be happy, either.

As a coach it's a different mind-set. You can't coach well and lose and still feel good. You win, you lose. The preparation in coaching is a hundredfold greater than in playing. I didn't get nervous before I played. Playing was an absolute joy. Coaching was like giving birth. It's labor, it's work. Same as, say, writing. I haven't done a lot of writing, but you can't tell me writing's a lot of fun. The fun is when it's done and it's a nice piece of writing and someone compliments you on it. The actual process of writing has to be torture.

Multiply that by several turnovers and you've got coaching. Did I say it's like a birth? It can be like a death in the family, too. The thing is—unlike being a player—as a coach, that game is yours, win or lose, comedy or tragedy. It belongs to you. In that way a coach is an artist. When you make a beautiful canvas, you're proud. When you don't, all the work and energy and effort is for naught. You've failed. You feel that failure deep inside your every bone.

Look at it this way, the way it is in everyday society. A player can make maybe five million dollars a year and not have a winning season. How many winning seasons have Dale Murphy's teams had? Ernie Banks never made it to a World Series. Look at Michael Jordan! He's considered one of the greatest players ever, win or lose. Great athletes aren't considered failures if they lose a few games, but coaches don't have that luxury. Continue to lose, and you're gone. You're fired, a bum.

Lose a close game and a coach feels like blowing his already jumbled brains out. A player loses the same game and he wants to know the fastest way to get dinner. That's number one. That and where is his girlfriend, his mother, his homeboys. Where is everyone? And where can we get some burgers? If this happened once, it happened a thousand times after a loss. I'm bleeding my guts out and my players are figuring out whether to order double cheese.

For coaches, the questions proliferate. "Why am I doing this?" "What am I, crazy?" Even after victories, there's only a temporary feeling of relief. But then it starts all over again. What time is practice tomorrow? Do we have the scout tapes? Who are the refs for our next game? It's a process like nothing else on earth.

Playing and coaching have so little to do with each other that it should come as no surprise how few players enjoy coaching when they've finished their active careers. They think they'll like it because they want to stay "close to the game." Then they find out it isn't a game anymore.

It's total business at this level. On the one hand it's a discipline; on the other it's art. But it's a discipline first, and a lot of people don't like that: the hours in the tape room, the schmoozing with the media, the recruiting, the boosters, the alumni, the practices, the road trips, the X's and O's. What they see on TV is the nice suits and the guys in control; immediately they want to turn in their uniforms and move down to the business end of the pine.

In my first two years of coaching, I learned both the highs and the lows. My first year, everything went right. Like the night at Lehigh when we had four seconds left, no time-outs, and Bobby Carr of the Rutgers freshmen turned and threw the ball in from halfcourt so we could get into overtime and win the game. Everything went like that my first year, and everything went the opposite in my second year. At Army I gave my pregame pep talk, the players were psyched and we roared out onto the court—only to discover we were in the *wrong gym*. I don't want to say this wasn't a big-time game, but I had the feeling that one ref was a soccer coach at the Academy and the other ref was a lieutenant.

Needless to say, we got beat.

But at least we recovered to get to the right gym.

By the time I had coached two years of freshman ball at Rutgers, I knew the vagaries of the profession like the backs of my trembling hands. I was all the way up to $7,200 a year salary, Pam was pregnant with Nicole, and it was time to move on.

In 1969, I interviewed for the head coaching job at Johns Hopkins University in Baltimore, Maryland. The Rutgers athletic director, Albert Twitchell, was a good friend of Marshall Turner, who held the same title at Hopkins. Back then there were only university- and college-division schools; Hopkins was on the lower level size-wise, but it was tops in academics. I was panting for a head coach's job and, what was key, they seemed to want me.

Twitchell sent me off to my second interview with Turner by assuring me I was Hopkins' guy, he just didn't know how much the salary offer would be. I was afraid it wouldn't be as much as I was making at Rutgers so I strategized: i.e., I devised a weasly game plan which consisted of writing down different dollar amounts on pieces of paper and stuffing them in my pockets. I had listed amounts running from $8,000 up to $9,500, and if Turner—who smoked a pipe, by the way—offered me the job for $8,500, for example, I would tell him that before I arrived in Baltimore I had written a number down below which I couldn't really accept. Then I would dramatically pull out the slip with $9,000 on it. Hey, my family needed every extra penny.

As luck would have it, Turner, puffing away on a pipe, offered me $10,000. My eyes popped out of their sockets, ricocheted off a nearby lamp and luckily rebounded right back into my head. "Ten thousand? TEN thousand?" I fairly yelped. I had no card for ten-five.

"I imagine that means yes," Turner said.

"Uh, yes, that's great," I said.

What the AD didn't tell me until I had packed up my family and moved to Baltimore, the furthest away from home we had ever been, was that my duties also encompassed teaching gym classes and being the head baseball coach and the assistant head football coach. This really ticked me off. I had worked all my life to coach basketball. I hadn't played baseball in five years and now I was supposed to spend time with all this other stuff. And football? There went my summers. They start working that sport far too early for me.

Not only that, when I went to talk to Hopkins' football coach, Alex Sotir, about all this and asked him if he had any extra jobs, he said he coached freshman lacrosse. "How much extra you getting?" he said.

"Extra?" I wailed. "You get *extra?* That SonofaBee never told me that."

I marched straight to Turner's office and literally pushed his door open. This nice, quiet man was sitting in his nice, quiet office smoking his nice, quiet pipe.

"What is the financial remuneration for these other jobs that I was unaware of?" I demanded. I had my hands on the poor man's desk like I was ready to leap across it.

"I hadn't thought . . . I, uh . . . ," he mumbled.

"You hadn't thought? Who do you think you're dealing with, some no-brain rube? What do I get for all these other coaching jobs?" I said.

"Well, would an extra $800 be okay?" he said.

"That's more like it," I said.

Afterward, I walked into the other coaches' office complex. Everybody seemed to be laughing. They figured I had gotten ripped apart or something. They also didn't hesitate to tell me that they had been joking: None of the other guys got any extra money for their additional coaching or teaching duties.

"You don't? Well, I just got eight hundred bucks more," I said.

Now look who was ticked off.

Later, when I went in to apologize to Marshall Turner, I said I understood there'd be no raise unless he wanted to give me one anyway. Mr. Turner accepted my apology but did not take my suggestion about the raise.

One of the best learning tools of my early career was coaching a various number of sports at Johns Hopkins. I always felt football was way ahead of basketball in terms of the approach coaches took. The specialization. The breaking down of offenses and defenses. The detailed use of film. There was always a tendency to think of football as being more complicated than basketball and that you didn't need more than one guy, the head coach, to handle everything.

Difficult Meat

With expanded staffs and delegations of authority, basketball coaching has caught up. The most important thing I learned that first year of football at Hopkins, in fact, was the utilization of different coaches to break down the position of the plays. I was the coach of the wide receivers, which meant I spent a lot of time saying "down and out." But I also had to learn what my position players did on every play call—split, crack back, z-out, spin and all the rest. I didn't pretend to understand any of it:

"Coach, what do I do on the 24 Bam from the pro set, 18 Flex, R Series?"

"Down and out, son."

But I learned so much about coaching and a lot more about delegating. I saw the value of taking a coach and giving him a task to teach and letting him devise as many drills as he wanted and really focus in on his specialty. My specialty still happened to be scouting. And, boy, there were some bad teams to scout in our league. Swarthmore. Haverford. I don't think either of those could win their own intra-squad scrimmages. First thing you go over in a scouting report is the kicking game. Poor Haverford didn't have one. "We have two options against their punter, men," I told the Johns Hopkins team. "We can either rush in and block the kick and scoop it up for our own touchdown. Or for a really interesting time we can let him kick it—because three of his punts in the last game went back over his head."

Coach Sotir was patient with me. He was a former Marine fighter pilot and his teams had won three straight Middle Atlantic Conference South championships. I learned never to rile football coaches. That's why I always explain that my views on their games are entirely tongue-in-cheek and please don't hit me.

But really. Why would anybody coach football when they had a choice? When they could coach basketball, the most beautiful, elegant, challenging game in the world with the best, most graceful athletes?

Look, here's the story of football. First, there are no mind-boggling upsets. There are never any upsets in college football and no wonder. It starts like this. WoooOOOOOO-OOMPF! And Oklahoma kicks off. The other guys get the ball and they try to run it back and Oklahoma tackles them. Whoops, *fumble,* Oklahoma's ball. And the Sooners go in for the score. Early in the season, Oklahoma is always playing somebody helpless, and it's 28–0 before the national anthem. So Helpless finally gets the ball and it's like "Hut . . . hut" and Oklahoma kicks the hell out of them. They go back in the huddle and try something different. WooooOOOO-OOOOMPF! Runback . . . to the 40, the 50, the 40, the 30 . . . all the way. Sooners 35–0.

I mean, this thing keeps going on and on. There's a clock and Helpless

41

keeps having to come out of the huddle again. OK, we'll try this one. *Woompf!* No? How about this one? *Woompf!* Three downs of that and the third one is a quick pass that the Helpless quarterback fires 40 yards out of bounds. Helpless punts, one of Oklahoma's speed guys gets it. WooooOOOOMPF! 42–0. Horns go off, cannons boom and now they start again.

Hey, we all know . . . what's going to happen! The problem is that in football they make you come out of the huddle. They make you play. You get killed? *Woompf!* Sorry, you're coming back out.

See the difference? In basketball if one team is better than the other, what happens? The weaker team holds the ball. They don't play. Nobody makes them. They hold it, shorten the odds, narrow the game, give themselves a chance. It's a game you can really, you know, *coach.* If Pete Carril is coaching Princeton against Georgetown, hey, watch out. It's interesting. It's no fun to coach or play against Pete. Coaches are afraid to do that. You think Oklahoma would be afraid to play Princeton in football? The Sooners would go WooooOOOOMPF! and knock some serious brains out. Oklahoma has guys who never play who can score touchdowns. *Woompf!*

As a former head basketball coach—I coached the offense and the defense, believe it or not—I just get totally confused with football. They have an offensive "coordinator" and a defensive "coordinator." They've got a wide receiver coach, a guy who coaches the linebackers, backfield coaches, line coaches. Hey, what does the head coach do? He's up in the tower somewhere. I met a football coach a while ago who said he coached the "down linemen." I said, what, are they depressed? Does he go around patting them on the ass telling them to get their heads up?

The game tapes alone in football would drive me nuts. What maniac invented that deal where the players go forward . . . click . . . and backward . . . click? The coaches in the film room are always writing the plays down, then playing them back. Forward . . . click . . . and backward . . . click. I love that move where the quarterback takes the ball out of the fullback's belly and shoves it back under the center's crotch. Oh, that was backward? Oh, excuse me. I always get in trouble when I ask the football coaches about that one. There isn't a lot of laughs in the football film room, anyway.

Then there's the terminology. The quarterback coach is always watching the quarterback, hunting for that terminology. He's seeing if the QB is "meshing" with the fullback. I love the terminology in football. The QB never gives the ball to the fullback or hands off to him. He "meshes" with the guy. He's got to "mesh."

Or he's got to "read." The QB "reads" the defensive end. The meshing fullback "reads" the inside linebacker. The linemen "read" everything else. Everybody in football is always reading their asses off; they must need glasses, they read so damn much. And the injuries. You've heard about this one: the "hip pointer." Everybody in football gets "hip pointers." I have no idea what these are. I never had a basketball player get a hip pointer. Is it kind of like an uncontrollable urge to point your hip in a particular direction? I can see this would cause a problem. If I wanted to go right and my hip kept pointing left . . .

Also in basketball, we usually know which of our guys are going to play in the games. In football they never know. They play once a week—not too difficult to keep track, men. But they never have any idea who's playing. "Well, Bronc's questionable this week," the coach says. No idea. Doesn't *know*. But now it's the game, fourth quarter, and Bronc takes off his parka and runs out there. Hip pointer and all. Hip pointing every which way. You know what happens to Bronc? Nothing. His team loses. Afterward in the locker room the press asks the coach how Bronc was able to play if he was so questionable.

"Yeah, I was a little surprised to see him in there myself," the coach says.

Which is *unbelievable!* Only a football coach can get away with that. Can you imagine a basketball coach saying, "Hey, how did Phil get in the game? Who put him in there?"

And my favorite is after the game, after Oklahoma beats Helpless 64–6 and the press asks the losing coach what happened. I love this one. "I'm not sure, guys," he says. "I'll have to see the tape."

Have to see the tape? Hey, coach! I can tell you what happened. 64–6 happened. You got the bejeezus kicked out of you. You got your asses kicked in. You got *buried,* babe! There was a whole lot of WoooOOOMPF! out there. All over your face! I mean, get serious. This really happens. He wasn't sure? Where was he, Kuwait? He should have asked somebody. They could have told him what happened. Basketball coaches know what happened. The press asks a guy who got beat by 36 . . . hey, he knows. He can tell his team got killed.

When did you lose this one, coach?

When we got off the bus, Bozo.

The next day, though, the football game awards are given out, regardless. The Mr. Tough Guy award. The Eight Perfect Snap award. The Super Hit award. One guy graded out 98 on the tape. Ninety-eight. The team got beat 64–6 and he graded out 98?

Yeah.

Next?

Anyway, you get my drift about football. Just don't break the news to Lyle Alzado.

With all that I gave to Johns Hopkins on the gridiron, my contributions in baseball must be noted. As the freshman coach, my team was victoryless. But at least we only played six games. The big one was Navy at Navy. We were ahead 3-0. Bottom of the ninth. Bases loaded, two out. The Hopkins pitcher was Allen Schreiber. He had pitched great and I had left him in. But it was obvious he was tired. On my walk to the mound I debated whether to leave him in the game, replace him with the righthander or try to fix my cap so I wouldn't look like a dork. I always looked like a dork in a ballcap. "One more out and we got 'em. Can you handle this guy?" I asked my hurler.

"Easy meat," he said.

"Let's go," I said, giving my man, Schreiber, the obligatory pat while being extremely certain I missed his privates. Then I confidently stalked off the mound.

It was just about the point when I got back to the Hopkins bench that I turned and was able to get a clear, clean path of the . . . sound. The unmistakable sound of wood nailing the horsehide "adios." The thunderous *craaaaack!* was quite enough. I didn't even need to look. First pitch. Outta here. Grand Slam. Navy wins 4-3.

Difficult meat.

Basketball at Hopkins was difficult in another way. I used to joke that before I came to Baltimore the basketball team hadn't had a winning season since the French and Indian war—probably because half the time they played like Frenchmen, the other half like Indians. In reality, Hopkins hadn't won for nearly a quarter of a century before the Blue Jays under Jim Valvano rallied to a spectacular 10-9 record in 1969-70.

That was a very special team for me, above and beyond its being my first year as a head coach. Remember, these guys were not exactly blue-chippers. They were what I call un-recruits. All bright, sharp, great students and great guys as well. There was my Israeli Connection: George Apple, Gary Handleman, and Hal Grinberg. George is currently in computers. Gary is a manager of the Capital Centre in Landover, Maryland. Hal teaches English at the University of Buffalo. John Lally and Andy Lynch completed our starting five.

Well, this crew had a high old time nailing Haverford and Swarthmore. We also beat Gettysburg by two points on the road. We had opened the season 3-0 and I was going nuts. On the bus ride back from Gettysburg the players called me to the back where they were sitting.

"What're you guys discussing?" I said.

"You," they said. "We just want to know one thing. Why is winning so damned important to you? We've never seen anything like this. You're irrational. You've gone off the deep end. You're consumed by this winning."

Whoooa. Nice, huh? Here I am in my first head coaching job and my guys are asking me why I want to win. This was incredible! I don't really remember the rest of the bus ride except for me wondering what Red Auerbach would have done in a similar situation. Maybe light up a cigar and give 'em what for?

I resigned myself to the fact that basketball wasn't the A Number One priority with my future teachers and lawyers and arena managers. Certain incidents kept reminding me.

It turned out that Johns Hopkins had never played in a Christmas tournament. Well, I rectified that. I fought like heck to get us in one—so what if it was the Sacred Heart Invitational Tournament (SHIT) in Bridgeport, Connecticut? Speaking of which, I had to go to the Hopkins administration to ask permission to go to the toilet so you can imagine the red tape involved in getting us into the SHIT. The problem was that a school rule said that once the semester ended, the students couldn't play an athletic event, for insurance reasons. I told the administration that there was a tournament opening, the players deserved it, and this was too good a chance to pass up. Finally, they relented and permitted us to play on one condition. We couldn't wear Hopkins uniforms!

Hey, great! We could be anybody. We could be Rutgers, Oswego State, UCLA, the Celtics. What a terrific deal! The upshot of all this was that when I went back to tell my team about the Christmas tournament, they held a team meeting and voted not to go. "How could you possibly have thought we would want to spend our holidays playing basketball?" they said.

"But guys, you can go as UCLA!" I pleaded. "You can go as Yugoslavia!"

Alas, we never did go. I had overstepped my bounds. Basketball at Hopkins was not a twelve-month sport. As novel as this may sound now, the players were there to *enjoy* basketball, get the experience of being on a team, play a few games, have a nice winter break, then finish off the season. Moreover, one day a player named Chris Beach came up to me and wanted to know why we had to practice every day. I pointed out that this was one of the prescribed ways a player gets better, that practice was a form of teaching and learning that players needed to do every day.

"The problem is that not only do we practice every day so that practice becomes mundane and repetitive," Beach said, "we practice at the same time every day! Yesterday it was so beautiful outside. Can't we be more flexible, more spontaneous?"

Ah, Red, you got a spare stogie?

Seriously, I tried everything to stir up enthusiasm. Charles (Lefty) Driesell had just started coaching at Maryland that season, so I started calling myself James (Righty) Valvano. I got the PA people to play "At the

Hop" by Danny and the Juniors during our warm-ups. I thought I was making inroads. Then came a big game right before final exams. Boy, did I get psyched! Stats, tendencies, plays, matchups. I was ready to rock and roll. I was going to kill 'em with my pregame. It was to be one of the most emotional pregame talks in history. I burst into the locker room and . . .

No players.

"Uh, guys?"

Nobody home.

Absolutely nobody.

Oh, the Johns Hopkins Blue Jays did come wandering in later. But they were accompanied by their textbooks, they spent their spare time in the locker room studying, they dressed out as quickly as possible . . . and we got buried. However, I was very proud of this team. We had the first winning season in 23 years, and we made the conference tournament for the first time in a long time, although unfortunately we lost to Pennsylvania Military College. With my $300 recruiting budget I went out and recruited some more doctors and lawyers who understood practice would be mandatory and who later would play in the NCAA college-division tournament. I'm just sorry I wasn't around to coach them in it.

Career-wise, I had made a calendar for myself right out of college. I had charted what I wanted to do over a period of years and, as I remember, I was way ahead of schedule. First, I wanted to be a freshman coach or an assistant on the university level—five years. Then I had figured head coach at a small college—five years. After ten years I wanted to reach the level of head coach at a larger school on the university level.

With three seasons gone, it was time to make a decision about what to do next. Was it better to stay at Hopkins as the head guy and keep turning it around? And then try to get a head job in the Ivy League? There were some strong programs in the Ivies back then—Princeton, Penn, Columbia. Or was it better to jump to a first assistant's job in the big-time, to get the experience of working on a university-division varsity bench?

I loved everything about Hopkins—the recruiting, the coaching, the academics, the philosophical repartee with the kids, just everything. But when my old Rutgers teammate, Dick Stewart, called me about an opening at the University of Connecticut, I had to think about it. Both Stewart and Fred Barakat (now the assistant commissioner of the ACC) were leaving as assistants to U. Conn. head coach Dee Rowe, and Dee needed a replacement. I said I would come up to Storrs and listen, little knowing that I had sealed my fate anyway. Ten minutes with Dee Rowe—as anyone who knows him will agree—and you are hooked for life.

Though my two years as an assistant at Connecticut do not show up on any official coaching record, the experience I had there was as valuable to my future as any period of my life. First of all, Dee Rowe is a true prince on earth. From the first moment I had dinner at his home with him, his wife and seven children, I knew that Connecticut would be perfect. Why, that first night I even heard Mrs. Rowe arguing with him in the kitchen because she didn't know I was coming and didn't have enough pork chops. This was everything I grew up with and loved.

Then there was Dee's intensity. This was the original The-Game-Is-Life-And-Death man. He loved to talk about the basketball court as Life's Stage. What you do in basketball, you do in life. He was about the best I've ever seen at the coaching juggling act of making your players believe that those forty minutes of game-time are the most important of their lives until the game is over, when they become just as irrelevant to their existence as a person and student. This is coaching's most tremendous challenge, and Dee more than anyone else helped me understand that.

It was fascinating to study at this man's knee—and listen to his long discussions into the night with another of his protégés, Dave Gavitt, who had been Dee's assistant at Worcester Academy and eventually became the head coach at Providence College. To understand how close these two disparate personalities have been over the years—Gavitt later would invent the Big East conference, change college basketball forever, then in 1990 become executive vice president of the Boston Celtics—is to realize the weirdness of human nature. While Gavitt is Mr. Calm, Cool and Collected, his mentor, Rowe, once threatened to jump off the roof of a Washington hotel after a particularly harrowing defeat.

I know. I was there. Georgetown had beaten Connecticut by about 40. Dee had declined his usual postgame scotch mist and disappeared. He left a message on my hotel phone. The message read: "I'm on the roof and ready to jump. Don't catch me."

The Big East with U. Conn. as a charter member would not be formed for another decade, but the state had no less a love affair with the basketball team back then. The Huskies were perennial champions of the Yankee Conference, qualified for the NCAA's just about every season, and were Big Time in all respects. It was at Storrs that I learned how to budget time. I had to, because among my duties I: coached the freshman team; helped coach the varsity; and headed up the regional recruiting, which meant bustling off through the blizzards of New England and learning how to drive with my head out the window to keep awake. And, oh yeah, matching wits against the likes of Mike Fratello, an assistant at Rhode Island, and a fellow named Vitale at my alma mater, Rutgers. You think that wasn't tough?

If you think Vitale generates excitement on TV, you should have seen him in the recruiting wars. He was one of the all-time best. When Dick went to a school to recruit, not only did the players get notes, the coach, the guidance counselor, even the janitor got a note, all signed with Dick's trademark, "Enthusiastically yours . . ." If I was recruiting at the same school, *I'd* even get a note. If Dicky V. sent me one note signed "Enthusiastically yours . . . ," he sent me a hundred of them. One winter night on the recruiting trail, Dick had the appointment before me. He was traveling with his wife, Lorraine, and their baby daughter. When the baby started crying for something to eat, and Lorraine didn't have a spoon, did Vitale go to fetch one? He did not—he had a recruiting appointment to keep. He recruited *me* to get the spoon. Dick got the player; I got the spoon. Dick's daughter, Terri, survived to become a tennis player at Notre Dame. And I got yet another note signed "Enthusiastically yours . . ."

Recruiting for Connecticut became my first experience in going against the heavy hitters from the ACC and the SEC; when I learned all there was to know about selling a basketball program. It wasn't that my competitors were hostile toward a guy from Connecticut. In fact, I went down to Duke one time and the Blue Devil assistant coach, Hubie Brown, couldn't have been nicer. He talked for hours. Hubie must have detailed the history of the pick and roll at least four times.

I called the ACC and SEC guys "The Leathers" because they all wore expensive leather coats on their recruiting visits. I was Polyester Pete. During that time Connecticut was desperate to sign a 6'9" center, a homestate kid named Tom Roy who was a huge, national name. But I realized right away we were out of our element. The Leathers were just so far ahead in terms of creating excitement about their programs. Tennessee was taping Roy's games and sending them to him. Lefty Driesell at Maryland would greet Roy at College Park with a uniform, a stool and a locker, all with his name on it. Kentucky would come into Roy's hometown of South Windsor and the whole community would go into orgasm. I remember telling Dee we never had a shot at this kid.

But I didn't consider losing Roy a failure. It was a learning experience. Recruiting was absolutely no different than sales. You promote, you market, you make the pitch, you close the deal. If you don't, you don't get your man. This is when I really understood that nobody wants to hear about the labor, they just want to see the baby. And Roy was some baby. He became a big factor at Maryland from his sophomore year on. If a player's worth is determined by the enmity of the opposition, consider this: Every year Maryland came into Cameron Indoor Stadium to play the Blue Devils, the infamous Duke student section held up a banner which read: TOM ROY SUCKS. The year after Roy had played out his eligibility and gone off to professional basketball, the Terps came to play Duke again. Out came another banner. This one read: TOM ROY *STILL* SUCKS.

Chapter Six

RATS TO RICHES

WITH ALL THE MONEY GROWING OUT THERE IN BETWEEN THE WEEDS OF the NCAA and television and college basketball and sneaker industries—like most coaches, I get down on my knees and pray toward Beaverton, Oregon (home base of Nike) just about every other loose ball—it's easy to forget how financially deprived young guys in the coaching profession used to be. Take me, for instance.

After Pam and I were married following my graduation from Rutgers—I actually got that marriage license before my dad allowed me to get a driver's license—my résumé in the next five years read: three jobs, two daughters, one wallet (empty). In my two years as a graduate assistant at Rutgers I made $5,800 and $6,100. In year three at Johns Hopkins my salary was $10,000. Moving to Connecticut, the Valvano financial ledger skyrocketed to entries in the range of $11,000 to $12,000. After five seasons I may as well have been working for IBM (I've Been Moved). Except that the job description called for twenty-hour days, our apartment was a cramped two-bedroom job in Storrs, and we had a beat-up Caddy without air conditioning. Obviously I hadn't been moved enough. I needed to get a head coaching position at a higher level, and get it fast.

Enter Bob Latour, the athletic director at Bucknell University in Lewisburg, Pennsylvania, who happened to be looking for a head coach. Bucknell was a respected school. Pretty location. In the university division of the Middle Atlantic Conference with the likes of Lehigh, Lafayette and Delaware. (The other division had St. Joseph's, Temple and La Salle.) And a real, live NCAA bid automatically went to the champion of this sucker. Could we call the league a cradle of coaches?

50

Jack McKinney was at St. Joe's at the time, Paul Westhead at La Salle, Tom Davis at Lafayette. This was the place.

The problem was, Bucknell had closed applications for its coaching job, which left only one thing for me to do.

Beg.

Not really, but I did call Latour on the phone dozens of times, and I also got a couple of my mentors, Bill Foster and Dee Rowe, to call. Eventually the Bucknell people agreed to see me.

I say "people" because it was more than just Latour who would pass judgment. I discovered long before this that the smaller the program, the longer the interview, and the more people are involved. You apply at a big school and it's always just one guy you have to impress. At Bucknell, after talking for a week with the athletic director, the president, the provost, the director of admissions, the financial aid rep (a guy I really needed), the doctor, the lawyer and the Indian chief, Bucknell saw fit to hire me.

It was either my avid persistence, or else they appreciated a funny line. After interviewing all day, I finally met with the provost of the school, Wendell Smith, who kept staring at me. "That's it," Smith finally said. "Joe Namath. You look like Joe Namath."

"Ironically, the difference between me and Namath is the precise reason I need this job," I told my new employer. "When you've got Joe's money, they say you're 'ruggedly handsome.' When you make what I make, they say you've got a big nose."

Bucknell paid $13,000, which wasn't much overall, considering that Lewisburg was a community without low-cost apartments; a young family like ours almost had to live in a house. So Bucknell loaned me three grand (to be paid back within the year) to help make the down payment on a house costing about $35,000. We went to see the builders one day and they turned out to be Amish—the guys with the beards, the black hats and the buggies. Naturally, a buggy is what I figured I'd be driving if I coached very long at Bucknell.

I reveal all this background information to explain why, in the summer of '72, I hopped in my car before my first season at Bucknell and took off to work every summer basketball camp in the Pocono Mountains I could point a compass at. To explain why I had to make another $150 per week every week so that we could come up with the closing costs for a house, not to mention a washer and dryer to go inside it. And to describe precisely why I became "The Camp Man."

Because my coaching life has been inevitably divided into BC/AC (Before Championship and After Championship), there are some people who never knew I existed before North Carolina State won the NCAA title in 1983. "Oh, look at Valvano," they said. "Another speech. A roast.

A sports dinner. Think this guy has enough speaking engagements or what? Ever see anybody take advantage of the NCAA title like this?" Hey, I'd been speaking all my life. Comedy engagements in the third grade naturally segued into motivational addresses at business meetings. Yes, I'm a public speaker and I make a lot of money at it. But I prepared for it long before the national championship. It was all part of the game plan. I wanted to be ready. And the key stop was summer camps.

The fact is, there may be several people out there who still recognize me more readily as "The Camp Man"—the guy with "The Super Rat"—than they do as a championship coach at N.C. State. Ah, such is fame.

Inasmuch as there already was an established circuit of famous-name coaches and players who made annual trips to the numerous camps, it was rather difficult for a young unknown clinician to infiltrate the lineup of stars. But a Pennsylvania high-school coach named Scotty Beeten, who once played for Dee Rowe at Worcester Academy, got me started by letting me wing it in speeches to kids at his small camp, and luckily my reputation spread. One day at Bob Kennedy's camp, which is one of the largest basketball camps in the Poconos, I made my key breakthrough. The main speaker had canceled. It was raining. I had the entire camp as a captive audience. I began:

"Good afternoon, everybody. The coach of the New York Knicks, or some pro player, or whoever, couldn't make it today, and because of the rain they couldn't get anybody else in here either. That's why I'm here and I want you to know a little about me. First of all, I'm a gym Rat. No other word for it. I love the game. I was a defensive player. I dove on the floor for loose balls. I grabbed you, talked to you, annoyed the daylights out of you, got in your face, *took the charge.* That's how I made the team. It's guys like me—and there're a ton of you out there—who make the game.

"Aren't you tired of most of the speakers who come in here? Every one of them . . . they're always coming from some other place. 'I was at The Cooz' camp' or 'I just got in from the coast.' Hey, I didn't fly in from anywhere. I was right here, eating the same food as you were. Every Wednesday, beans and franks. I got enough beans and franks to blow this place to smithereens. I've been here on this mountain for six weeks now and I love it. Just smell the atmosphere. It's great because we're going to play hoops and run and work and play and learn. And I mean, really *learn.*

"Know what I'm sick of? I'm sick of these Big-time guys coming in here and all they do is Q and A, Q and A. Question and answer, that's it. The guy rolls in here half a day late. We're here sitting around waiting like it's some king. The camp director is about to have a cat, he's so nervous. The agent said the guy would be here. And everybody's on edge.

"Finally he shows. Shades on, right? Hat on, maybe? 'Hey guys, how you doin?' he says. Never knows who the camp director is, who the counselors are, probably doesn't care what planet he's on.

"Next, our Big-timer *sits* on the ball, man! That's our gold, our luck, babe! You don't sit on it and say 'got any questions?'

"But that's it. That's all you get with these guys. Oh, one of you always asks, 'Who's the toughest guy you ever had to guard?' And the Big-timer says, 'There's no one that tough for me to guard.' And you all cheer. And you say: 'Sign this, sign this.' Then after the Q and A, the Big-timer gets up and says, 'Who wants to guard me?' So one of you gets up there to guard him, and he sticks his butt in the air and you run around him like an idiot and then he goes, *'Two* of you can't guard me'; and two guys do the same thing.

"But guys, that's nothing. That's bull . . . That's not what this camp is about.

"This camp is about guys who'll do the shuffle offense on the way to breakfast and who'll guard that tree and who'll wait in the bushes and when (camp director) Bobby Kennedy walks by, they'll run out in front of him and *take the charge!* That's all I want. Take a charge on him coming out of the dining hall. Take a charge on bigger guys. Take a charge on the laundry truck. Get in there and play the game.

"Hey, do you get what I'm talking about? Don't be a Big-timer. The player who comes in here from the coast and won't speak and cheats you is a Big-timer. The coach who comes in and says he was at so-and-so's camp and won't teach anything, he's a Big-timer. Some of your fellow campers, the ones who arrived with their clippings from high school—you know you're out there—they're Big-timers. But, hey, we don't need Big-timers at this camp.

"We want Rats. Rats are what the game is about. Big-timers can't make it if there are enough rats. Rats scratch and claw and fight and *take the charge."*

I was winging this speech, blurting out everything that I had piled up inside over all the years sitting and watching at camps. My father had camps. His friends had camps. They all had paid speakers who came to the camps, some of whom were great—as was Hubie Brown—and some who didn't really care. So I told the audience that we were going to start all over, we were going to tell the speaker to be good, to teach us something, to make sure we learn, to earn his speaker's fee.

"I'm going to be introduced again and I want a standing ovation this time," I continued. "You're going to say you're glad Coach V is here, that you want to do a terrific job and that you're all *Rats*. We're going to talk the game, love the game and play the game."

Then I switched personalities and impersonated the camp director. "Some of you young men have lost your keys," I said. "That costs us $18 per key per mail call. Some of you aren't picking up your mail. Billy Joe back there—your folks just died. I thought you'd like to know. There'll be a bus on Wednesday; you can get out of town. By the way, here's today's speaker: a wonderful guy, a great coach. I love him, he's a real prince . . . Jim Valvano."

And then I went back on as myself. And I didn't spare the coaches or the camp director.

"Thank you, thank you. Anybody who steps on our court during our activities today, gets a standing ovation unless he's not worth it, in which case we boo his ass right off the court. Our speakers give us everything they've got or they get the hell out because this is going to be an hour for *Rats*.

"For Rats Only.

"And you coaches! Hey! You guys sitting on your hands. We're missing you. Because you don't care, that's why. I've been a counselor like you guys all my life. I'm The Camp Man. And I see coaches who don't care all the time. As soon as the Big-time speaker gets introduced, they leave. Or they just sit there.

"But now, no more! No way! Because I'm a Rat. I don't get paid. I don't get paid for doing this. If I'm going to do this, the coaches are going to get excited and listen. Because if coaches don't coach, players don't play. And players, you're paying $150 a week for these guys to sit on their asses? Are you kidding me? Let's make sure they coach. Make the coaches coach. Make the speakers speak. Make the players play. Make this the best camp in the United States. Anybody want to leave, leave. I only want my Rats to stay!

"And how about the camp director? What a beauty he is! The first day he tells me he wants this to be the best camp in America and how special you are. Hey, he's had this camp for twenty years. Thirteen weeks a summer, twenty years running. You think he gives a flying &%$-£* about your week?

"Did the director tell you this was a special week? And you haven't seen him since? Right? Because he's been checking keys. Because the thing that worries him most is not whether you learn the crossover dribble. He's too busy hoping you don't fall in the pool and die. Because if he gets up in the morning and there's two bodies floating in the bottom of the pool, he's in trouble.

"What I'm trying to tell you all is that it's not his camp or my camp. It's your camp. You'll decide whether this is a good one or a great one. If you demand the best from your speakers and your coaches and from yourself, it will be the best camp. And when that speaker comes tomorrow, give him a standing ovation before he says a word. Blow his mind. And I guarantee you he will do the best job possible, whether he's from the coast or sitting on a ball or what. Because he won't be a Big-timer anymore. He'll be a Rat. Just like you and me."

The standard speech about enthusiasm and hard work and hopes and dreams that I've been giving to corporate America basically started out woven from the fabric of this soliloquy at summer camp. And you'd be surprised: It went over even better at the girls' camps. I loved speaking to the young women. They were like sponges. And they gave back as good as they got. At camps run by the former Immaculata College Coach Cathy Rush, she'd always have the campers pull some trick on me. One year when I got to a certain word in my speech, by prearrangement the campers threw their sneakers at me. Another year, the instant I began my talk the entire camp walked out.

To say that the Poconos summer camps, and especially Bob Kennedy's camp, were my financial salvation would be an understatement. Emotionally, they were right up there as well, especially after a friend presented me with a stuffed Rat. He had a taxidermist stuff the Rat standing on its hind legs, naturally in the position of taking a charge. I mounted it on a skateboard, tied it on the end of a leash and took it camp-hopping. The highest honor a camper could receive became my "Super Rats Take The Charge" T-shirt. The high point of my camp speaking career came when the Rat and I were invited to Howie Garfinkel's Five-Star Basketball Camp. The best players in the country are there, and this really helped my recruiting effort.

For a long time the Rat accompanied me to games during each basketball season. I'd keep him in the locker room for good luck. Then one summer afternoon, my wife, the assassin, threw him out with the garbage. Can you believe it? The Rat had taken on a life of its own and had been getting more favorable press than I was, but that was no reason to do away with him. I don't know which hurt more in my coaching life: losing my job at North Carolina State or losing my Rat.

The point of this is to demonstrate that at every stage of my career, I was learning something to prepare myself for the big show. When I finally stepped on the stage for the first time to speak before a business group, I gave them the same kind of talk I'd presented at my first camp. When I finally got a shot at being a head coach in the university division, I was a guy who couldn't help but be a product of all those experiences at Rutgers, Connecticut and Johns Hopkins.

Even though it was a different level and I didn't have what you might call the horses—the previous Bucknell team had won five games and we had everybody back, which was the real difficulty—I felt good about myself and my new job. I was at the starting gate now. The top level. The Big Time.

My first year went relatively well; we won eleven games. One of the most memorable came early in the season. Bucknell's best player that year was a 6'6", 220-pound senior named Harvey Carter. A tough kid but very mild mannered. Never said much. We were down by a point with about twelve seconds to go when Harvey made a steal, and called time-out.

I was thinking of what brilliant last-second play I should diagram when Harvey stormed over to me on the sideline, grabbed my clipboard and said, "Get me the damn ball!" Then he picked me up and shook me and set me back down! Now, Bucknell isn't exactly the Dean Dome. I mean, everybody in the place saw this. I couldn't exactly pretend nothing happened. So I reacted in the only way possible.

"Damn! Harvey, who the hell do you think you're talking to!" I screamed. "For god sakes, I'm the damn coach around here, and I'll tell you what we're going to do. Give me the damn clipboard. And if you ever do that again your ass will be out of here so fast it will make your damn head spin!"

All of a sudden the horn went off, ending the time-out. I screamed, "Let's get another time-out." But my assistant coach said we didn't have any left.

"What're we going to do?" the Bucknell players were all shouting, near panic.

"Get the damn ball to Harvey! What else?" I screamed.

We did, Harvey scored, and we ended up winning. In the locker room after the game, reporters asked me to describe that winning play. I told them, "That's the play we work on every single day in practice." This may have been the first time I really understood how important players are and what their input can mean, especially in tight situations at the ends of games. From then on I always finished practice working on last-second plays utilizing the team's best players, letting them create scoring opportunities so that when we got in game situations, everybody knew what to do automatically, even without benefit of a time-out.

We had to win our final six games in a row to make the Middle Atlantic playoffs that season. After we had won four of them, I dressed out in a game uniform for the fifth—against Gettysburg—took pregame lay-ups, foul shots, the whole schmeer. Then I sprinted back to the dressing room to get back in civvies. As the current head coach at Tulane, Perry Clark, could tell you—he played for Gettysburg that night—I should have stayed in uniform. We missed the playoffs by two points.

In my second year, reality really hit. We had to play some of the top teams in the country, like Syracuse. At Syracuse. Of course everyone was very excited. I told everybody we're going to work hard, we're going to overcome the obstacles, we'll get it done. I told the reporters we're fine, we're ready, we're not in awe, they put their shorts on one leg at a time. Something like that.

Then: Wham! Reality. I think the 'Cuse led by about 50 at the half. This was a young Syracuse, the nucleus of the Orange's Final Four team of two years later.

Opening tip: Syracuse controlled at the top of the circle. Pass to the wing. Drive. Dunk. We passed the ball in. Boom, steal, pass. Boom, dunk. Second inbounds. Lose ball. Whoops. Boom, pass. Dunk. *Time-out!* Twenty seconds had gone by. Well, it's a long game. Wish I could say it was going to be short. I could tell already that if this was a fight, they'd have to stop it on cuts.

In the huddle I was cool. "We're fine, guys. Relax. Let's alter the alignment, go a little 1–4 and maybe run the baseline. Let's go," I said. And actually clapped.

Within another minute it was 20–0 and I had called another time-out. "Men, don't worry," I said. "When you get down early, there's more time to come back. If you can't get the ball in bounds, throw it off the guy's leg. Let's run down and outs. Go down, take a right and get the damn ball out of there."

Now Bucknell went back out, got pressed and my guy called another time-out before he could pass the ball in. "Not so fast, men," I said. "I've got nothing to tell you. Nothing has changed since the last time you were here. How much trouble could you be in? We haven't even sat down."

When you're down 50 at half, you almost wish nobody'd be watching your locker room door. It was one of those "Oh no, they know we're still in here" deals.

Syracuse was a gracious host, though. They ended up beating us 110–53 and the Orange coach, Roy Danforth, led the student body in cheers when they got a 55-point lead. Walks right by me, leads them in cheers and walks back. Is this a fun profession or what? Then afterward he came in with the stat sheet to show me that everybody on their team played.

I thought: Is this depression necessary? If somebody had suggested to me in the locker room that night that ten years from now I would win a national championship, I would have asked: "In what sport?"

Let me put this on the record: I learned how to coach at Bucknell. In

57

the three years I stayed in Lewisburg we played a lot of people over our heads. In addition to those Syracuse teams, we also played the Rutgers of Phil Sellers and Mike Dabney—another team which would end up in the Final Four as seniors. We played the South Carolinas and La Salles and Pitts. We played a Lafayette team that was to qualify for the NIT. Going up against these types of teams gave a guy a taste of what tough competition was all about.

One of the most competitive aspects of college basketball is recruiting. At Bucknell, it was particularly challenging to recruit minorities. When I first came to Bucknell there were three blacks on the team, including Harvey Carter and Algin Garrett, who was Elgin Baylor's nephew. When I left, the starting lineup sometimes consisted of five black guys from the inner city.

I stepped up the recruiting of blacks even in the face of the Ivy League's increased activity in minority recruiting. Princeton, Penn and Brown all were making a big push for blacks. Harvard had one of the better freshman teams in Eastern basketball history. Likewise, Bucknell's high academic standards meant we had to identify the minorities who would qualify and get the job done—and there simply weren't a lot of Brian Taylors and Armond Hills out there.

In view of what would later transpire at North Carolina State, I point with pride at my work in this area at Bucknell. I always worked within the academic framework of the institution. Certainly the minority athletes at Bucknell met the accepted standard for all minority students. They didn't have the board scores or the class rank that the more advantaged white students had, but the University sought not only to improve the minority numbers but to lead them successfully through college life. Bucknell worked with them so that they weren't mere statistics, and they all graduated. This was a system whose application and foundations I was to find sorely lacking at N.C. State several years later.

Did the recruiting pan out at Bucknell? What I tried to do was the same thing Pete Carril has done so successfully at Princeton over so many years: find players who will continue to improve. Bucknell awarded scholarships only on a need basis—again, just like the Ivies. Conversely, the school's need was for some more victories. Fortunately, the Bison developed a strong program in the next five years. Unfortunately, I wasn't around to help them do it.

Just as all the hopes and dreams that I engendered at Bucknell were reaching fruition, I felt I had to move on. A terrific coach named Charlie Woollum—who's still there—succeeded me. But the people of Lewisburg were upset, and my own wife wasn't exactly overjoyed at the prospect of moving once again. Bucknell had even come forward and offered me a full-time assistant, an increase in budget and a significant raise in salary. But again, it has never been financial considerations that motivated me.

It was hard to leave Bucknell. They treated me well; I liked the people there, and they believed in me. When you leave a school where you've been happy, it's not just a separation. It's more like a divorce.

Kenny Rogers sang the song: "Don't Fall in Love with a Dreamer." Ironically, my dreams were pointing me in the direction of home.

Chapter Seven

DARING TO DREAM

*H*I, I'M JIM VALVANO, IONA COLLEGE.

Holy God, man. You're what, thirty? And you already own your own school?

Aside from Iona College being a one-liner waiting to happen, was this the place for me or what? A small Catholic school run by the Christian Brothers? Located in New Rochelle, Westchester County, New York, which was the fictional home of Dick Van Dyke and Mary Tyler Moore on their classic TV sitcom? A short train ride—about fifty minutes—from Madison Square Garden? Not to mention forty-five minutes from Broadway. An urban commuter school with a lot of second-generation ethnics who were first-generation college students, the first in their family to qualify for higher education? Iona was named after the Isle of Iona, which is just off the coast of Scotland, where the Irish landed and established a monastery. Some people claimed the name stood for the Irish On North Avenue (in New Rochelle). These kids were not only Irish, but Italian and Polish. Lots of vowels. Mostly middle-class. They had to work to pay their tuitions. Maybe they wanted to go elsewhere, but they didn't have the bread to go to Notre Dame or Boston College or Villanova. They had loans. They had dreams. They needed an identity. They were me.

If that wasn't enough of a match, there was the president of Iona, Brother John Driscoll, a doer, a leader, a bright, witty, warm human being with a vision of expanding the school's horizons. Bottom line, it was within his province to present Iona with its own, special identity.

Already Driscoll had improved the academic environment at Iona. In the field of science and in the MBA program, the school had made giant strides; but by the same token, Iona needed something more to compete for the New York students in an ever-decreasing marketplace of private education. Iona's competition was Manhattan College and Fordham University and St. John's. The simple fact, which Driscoll well knew, was that building enrollment and attracting corporate money can happen faster if you have a winning basketball team.

In our first meeting, Driscoll told me how he wanted to elevate the visibility of Iona. Because it was a commuter school, after the kids had driven home for the day there was no reason for them to come back. He wanted to change that. The cheapest and easiest visibility was through basketball. He said that as a kid he used to sneak into Madison Square, but that now he wanted to walk in the front door. It was remarkable how this guy touched just about every chord possible within me. Here was a man talking about visions, and I was talking about dreams. He wanted to walk in the front door off the Garden, and I wanted to play the nine P.M. game there. Here's a guy who told everyone to aspire to be whatever we wanted to be, and I was the kid from Queens who wanted to win a national championship.

Indeed, as it turned out, together our passion for Iona later became embodied in a slogan, "Dare to Dream."

My initial contact with Driscoll came when a couple of friends of mine, Bill Madden, a lawyer who had captained the basketball team at Yale, and Tom Costello, who played linebacker for the Giants, told me what a dynamic individual he was. Both men had been in the Catholic Big Brothers with Driscoll, and when Iona had an opening they called me at Bucknell to ask if I'd be interested.

But it took a long period of emotional trauma for me to make another move. Pam loved our situation at Bucknell. She loved the idea of being settled. Bucknell is three hundred sprawling acres of nice buildings and leafy glades. Iona is one sixth that size; back then it sat next to the College Diner and had no dorms. With my speaking and the camps and the coaching salary combined I was making around $30,000 at Bucknell. The Iona board offered me $20,000—which was when I took to the blackboard and proceeded to express the facts of economic life to my soon-to-be-bosses. Namely, that one of the main reasons people move to the New York area is for the culture and the art and the sports and the fabric of life in the greatest metropolis in the world. If I came to Iona on these terms, I couldn't even take my kids to the circus. Needless to say, it took a couple of visits back and forth between Lewisburg and New Rochelle, but after Driscoll met with the board, he brought me back to Iona to show me how I could not only take my kids to the circus but buy a couple of bags of peanuts, too.

61

I can't emphasize enough how important Madison Square Garden was in my thinking about changing jobs. If most coaches' aspirations and goals have to do with reaching the point where they play for the national championship, mine included the Garden. Get to the Garden, the NCAA's will come. Remember when my Rutgers teams practiced on the Garden court for the first time? I told myself, "Someday I'm going to coach a team in here."

I wasn't going to make it to the Garden at Bucknell. And so Iona would be the realization of these dreams. I was ready. Whether it was selling encyclopedias or doing camp talks with a stuffed rat, all my experiences had prepared me for this. I had learned how to articulate, communicate, sell. We had to put the pieces together, get the players, win the games, stand college basketball on its ear.

I started tap-dancing my brains out by recruiting all over the Northeast. Iona was in the mix—that was one of the edges of being there—and right away we got Dave Brown from Essex Catholic in New Jersey, Lester George from Bishop Loughlin in Brooklyn, and a kid named Cedric Cannon from Bridgeport, Connecticut. You talk about a change in target personnel.

If you're recruiting my daughters in my home, you're going to eat Italian and like it, right? Well, when I recruited Cedric Cannon, his mother fed me chitterlings and I *loved* 'em. Never had chitterlings before, but I took to those suckers right away. Then Ced's mom put on some music and we danced. This was one happy family. Before Ced made his decision, however, I was going to have to talk to his Uncle Calvin. So after eating chitterlings and dancing the evening away, I got on the phone.

"Hi, Uncle Calvin. This is Jim Valvano," I said.

"Yeah, I know. We met a few years ago. My sister's a happy woman, isn't she?" he said.

"You got that straight, Uncle Calvin. I'm not sure where we met, but your nephew's chosen a fine school," I said.

"I want to make sure he really likes it. I've been through this before. I played some college ball," Uncle Calvin said.

"Oh really? Where did you play?" I said.

"Niagara University," Uncle Calvin said.

"Did you? (Former Niagara Coach) Frank Layden's a good friend of mine. What are you doing now?" I said.

"I'm still playing," Uncle Calvin said. "I'm Calvin Murphy."

"Ohhhh, *that* Uncle Calvin," I said.

Iona had finished 10–16 my first year, 1975–76, which was about how well Pam and I did in house-hunting. Realtors said then that you could subtract $10,000 more or less from the sale price of a house for each town further away from Manhattan. But could we afford New Rochelle,

Scarsdale, etc? Forget about it. I thought we'd wind up in Canada before we found a place.

Likewise, it took awhile in finding my place on the bench. We were close enough now to my family so that my father could come to all our games, chart the plays on a yellow pad and tell me later what went wrong. And, boy, did he! I referred to some of his favorites as "yellow pad" games. One of the very first was against Columbia.

This was at Columbia, and Tommy Penders, now the head coach at Texas, was coaching the Lions. Under the guiding hands of two of the obvious young geniuses of the profession, our teams must have set a record for turnovers. We'd bring the ball up the court and bounce it off our feet. They'd get it, make a fast break, and run it out of bounds. We'd in-bounds, they'd steal. They'd foul, we'd miss two free throws. It was horrendous. Destined to go double overtime, but threatening never to end. Finally we seemed to have control: ahead by two points with five seconds left. We had the ball and they fouled Jimmy McLaurin. One and one. Even if we missed, Columbia had to go the length of the court just to tie.

So what did McLaurin do? He missed. But the ball came right back to him so all he had to do now was hold it and we win. Did he hold it? Are you kidding? McLaurin took a jump shot. Kaaaang. Columbia rebounded and called time out. I jumped up screaming. And that's the last thing I remembered. Right then and there—Ppppffft!—I went out like a light. Up and out. I guess the blood just rushed to my head and overcame me. By the time I was revived, Columbia had in-bounded, threw up a Hail Mary which missed, and we had won.

Afterward in the locker room I was totally grogged out, thought I was going to die. I was looking for some TLC and, thank goodness, here came my father.

Uh-oh. With his yellow pad.

"Jimmy! I have about nine pages here. The fast break, you guys . . ."

I couldn't believe it. We had just won in OT, I'd passed out, my own father couldn't have known I was even *alive,* and he's giving me "the fast break."

"Hey, Pop! Didn't you see me? I was on my butt out there," I said.

"Awww, I never know when you're acting," said my dad.

I would have liked to have passed out more often in that first year. Unfortunately, I stayed awake for all the games. But recruiting went great.

I had hired a guy in a polyester suit named Tommy Abatemarco, "T" or "T-Man," a recruiting buzzsaw, as an assistant coach specifically to work Long Island and New York City. The best player on the Island, Glenn Vickers, became our obsession. If we were going to turn this thing around at Iona, we needed someone of whom people would throw down their newspapers and say: "They signed *who?*" So rather than shotgun a zillion kids, we focused on signing Glenn and figured we could just swoop up any others who would naturally want to play with him.

Vickers, a 6′3″ guard from Babylon High School, was that good. He could have gone anywhere in America. He was one of those kids who had to decide whether he wanted to go Ivy League and concentrate on his studies, or be the savior of a small program like ours, or the vital part of a big-time national championship contender.

The recruiting rules were different then. There was no limitation on the number of games a recruiter could watch, so representatives of Iona were at every game, every practice. "The ball doesn't go up until Iona's here," the Babylon coach used to joke. I firmly believe it was the attention that finally swung Glenn to us. If I saw Vickers three times and Kentucky saw him three times, we were not going to get him. It was the only way smaller schools used to get anybody. That's why I think cutting back on recruiting visits for everybody hurts schools like Iona immeasurably.

We could always tell Glenn Vickers that if we're here, we can't be somewhere else. The bigger schools were—elsewhere. And when the decision was made, it was a monster. Vickers absolutely made the Iona program. When Vickers signed, another terrific guard from North Babylon High, Kevin Hamilton, did likewise. Then we got another Long Island native, a transfer from Wake Forest called Mike Palma, and Joe McCall, a junior-college player from upstate New York.

We won fifteen games with our freshman backcourt, and that record caused a lot of heads to turn. Players beget players; for the next season we signed precisely the two big men we needed. 6′10″ Kevin Vesey from Bay Shore and 6′10″ Jeff Ruland from Sachem High School in Lake Ronkonkoma, New York.

If you think the pronunciation of Lake Ronkonkoma might be difficult, you should have been one of Iona's opposing centers that year trying to handle Ruland. Kentucky, Notre Dame, Maryland, North Carolina—all the big guys had wanted Jeff ever since his junior year when he was a skinny medium-range jump shooter. He didn't just get heavy. He got huge. Though many recruiters thought they had Ruland, we knew he was coming to Iona all along.

One day a prominent coach was sitting in my office when Ruland, still a high-school senior, still sought after by just about every school in America, opened the door and popped his head through. "Hi, V," he said. And then he was gone.

"Was that *Ruland?*" the coach said.

The thing is, nobody realized what close friends Ruland and Vickers had become. All the concepts about Iona we had been selling . . . forget it. We weren't out-recruiting anybody. It was either he's staying home or he's not. Kentucky became his other option, probably because of all the attention the Wildcats paid Ruland. Learjets would fly in from Kentucky for the Sachem games and disgorge Kentucky fans who would root for Ruland, make some contact, then head back to the Bluegrass.

We all got to know each other, too. Late in the year as Ruland's imminent decision came down to Iona or Kentucky, a big Kentucky booster was sitting in the stands at one of his games and saw me.

"Iona? You mean it's just us and you?" he said.

"Guess so," I said.

"Damn! We'll buy your silly school and move it to Lexington," he said.

"Make us an offer. We may want to come," I said.

Jeffrey Ruland was raised primarily by his mother, a tough, no-nonsense woman who ran a roadhouse type of establishment in Farmingdale. It was called Ernie's Tavern. Jeff's father was long gone before I met him, and his mom, Anita Swanson, had become the titular/spiritual head of Jeff's family. Mrs. Swanson was totally protective of Jeff; the recruiting became a very personal thing with her.

Her son, meanwhile, was a fun-loving, happy kid—when and if you got to know him. Not many people got close to Jeff, which is probably why a lot of legends grew up around him. With strangers he was always a bit suspicious. Jeff was one tough cookie all right, but he was mostly a sensitive kid. If you were his friend, he was kind, loyal, even gentle. Jeff was the best player I ever coached, hands down.

Did I mention Ruland the prankster? Jeff would call me constantly on the phone, crack a joke, then hang up. He used to hide my airline tickets, just to make me nuts. Then he'd tell me where they were just in time so I had to sprint out the door to make the plane.

But as a player, if the judgment was based on efficiency and reaching one's potential, Ruland was one of the true standards of his era in college ball. He had small hands and didn't jump that well. But he could shoot, rebound, pass and outlet the ball in combo better than most any big center in the land. He got to know the inside game so well, after awhile we didn't need to teach him anymore; Jeff could have coached himself.

How good was Ruland? In the three years he played at Iona we won 17 games, then 23, then 29. In the last two we made the NCAA tournament, a place where Iona had never been before. That's an improvement of six games each season. If both Jeff and I had stayed for that one, last year . . .

Ruland was the final piece in the puzzle at Iona. It's called R-E-S-P-E-C-T. A year before he enrolled, even with Glenn Vickers, we had to struggle like crazy just to get a game in Madison Square Garden. I had kept after our people to get us on the Garden schedule, which in those days the smaller, local schools managed to do by "guaranteeing" two or three thousand seats to the Garden management. We wanted in so badly we guaranteed five thousand and said we would buy them all right then. Luckily for me (because I didn't know how we could sell five thousand tickets; I might have had to spring for them out of my own pocket) the Garden was so impressed with my perseverance, we wore them down and they just gave us a game, free.

Naturally, it was against South Florida. As an addition to an already established doubleheader. On a Saturday. At . . . *twelve noon!* Sure enough, our team bus broke down smack in the middle of the tunnel going into Manhattan. Still, we made it to the city and ran out onto the Garden stage at 10:30 A.M. In the game itself we were awarded 43 free throws on the way to a defensive battle, a simple annihilation of South Florida, 107–100. Later I celebrated and wound up toasting victory in Chinatown into the wee hours.

I mentioned respect. Here's another example, pre-JR. The next year, in anticipation of our first game in the Ruland era, we had ordered new uniforms from a firm in Oshkosh, Wisconsin. In fact, we *had* to order the uni's; with two new guys in the 6'10" range, we had nothing on hand that fit. Unfortunately, with a week to go before the opening of the season, the uniforms had not arrived, and in a phone conversation with the company I was told they may not for several weeks.

I wouldn't stand for this, of course. We were opening big-time. We had *The New York Times,* the *New York Daily News, Sports Illustrated,* everybody interested in us by now. Ruland's debut had meant that much. Immediately I dispatched one of my assistants, Pat Kennedy, to Wisconsin to bring the uniforms back personally. Piece of cake, right? Naw. A bachelor then and somewhat less responsible than he is now as head of one of the more burgeoning basketball programs in the land at Florida State, Kennedy in forty-eight hours managed to:

1. get picked up for speeding
2. have his story misconstrued so that he had to explain it to a magistrate
3. had to pay a fine, and
4. after that was cleared up, back at his hotel, get rolled by an assailant and robbed of all his money.

Needless to say, after all that, Kennedy did come back with the uniforms, even though they were only the home set. Thank God I didn't insist he get the warm-ups too; those nice folks in Wisconsin might have wrapped him in a straitjacket and tied him to the electric chair. Osh kosh oh my gosh.

A coach is only as good as his assistants—as I used to tell Bill Foster and Dee Rowe—and Pat Kennedy was actually one of the best. Pat Kennedy replaced Abatemarco on the staff at Iona, and two years later we hired Kenny Williamson, the Egg Man. Eggy, as everybody called him, was my first black assistant coach, the first guy I thought really helped me understand the black experience—what it was like to grow up black, the black home, the ghetto, what basketball meant there, how a white coach was perceived there.

When Eggy was a kid in Harlem, he used to bring a basket of eggs to his grandmother every morning for breakfast. So he became Eggy, the Egg Man, one of the hippest, funniest, city street-smart characters I ever had the pleasure of working with. The Egg Man played ball at the University of Delaware, and after graduating from CCNY, he left to serve in Vietnam. I met him when he was an assistant at Columbia. The Egg Man is still the best I've ever seen at splitting the worlds of the street and the boardroom and getting along in both. I mean, this guy could lay a rap jive on you so far out you'd think you had stumbled into a different galaxy. Then he could turn around and discuss the latest implications of a story in *The Wall Street Journal* with some MBA's.

The Egg Man is at Florida State with Pat Kennedy now, but I credit him with a big role in perpetuating the Iona program after all of us, including the Eggman, left. First of all, he knew absolutely everybody. "This guy's all right, he's from the neighborhood," Eggy would say. Or "You don't want that guy. He's got cups for hands. You got to lay the jack out there to get him." The Egg Man was tuned into city kids. He'd take me to Harlem where he'd introduce me as "the V Man . . . the white boy's all right . . . he's with me."

As I mentioned, my specialty was recruiting Long Island and the Catholic schools. I hadn't had much luck in the inner city. And we needed a big recruiting coup for after the Ruland teams left.

Matter of fact, there were three area kids I felt we needed for the future: Gary Springer, Mike Moses and Steve Burtt. And the Egg Man got 'em all. (When I left, Springer and Burtt decided to attend Iona anyway. Moses did not.) That's with an entirely different style than I was used to, of course. I'm usually in the office early, 5:30–6:00 A.M. I'd stay there and sleep there, that's how I am. But the Egg Man would come breezing in after noon and I'd never know what exactly he was up to.

"Look, do you want me here at dawn and unable to sign my main men?" said the Egg Man. "Or can I come in here in the afternoon and know I can nail them? I thought you understood, man. I thought you were into it."

"Is that the alternative, Eggy?" I said. "What is it, exactly—you need your rest? Humor me for a while and get in a little earlier. I love to see your face, maybe have some coffee together, that kind of stuff."

But the more I got to know the Egg Man, the more I realized that there are people who do things in their own personal style, and you just have to give them the space. They're *artistes.*

Whenever we recruited a city kid, it was easy to see these were Eggy's folks. The home visits were a lot more personal and sharing. You got to know the family. You got the business out of the way: You told them what courses the kid would take and who we were going to play and that *we would be there* when the kid needed us.

More than anything, the Egg Man showed me how different recruiting in the black community had to be. "Don't tell them what it's like for a black kid at Iona," Eggy said, "because, man, you don't know. That's presumptuous for a white guy to tell anybody that." If I hadn't thought much about it before, I sure did then. Nobody knows what it's like to grow up an Italian kid from Queens, either, except Italian kids from Queens. More than anybody before or since, the Egg Man made me realize how superficial, how ridiculous it was to tell any black family anything other than the truth, which is, "Your son is a great player and if he wants to know what it's like at Iona, he's got to get his butt up to campus, check out the black community there and ask the black ballplayers what it's like."

I wasn't exactly without an edge going into a ghetto area with Eggy, either. I mean, the families saw us coming and knew right away we weren't insurance salesmen. A black guy and his white sidekick sauntering through the projects? Me and Eggy were either basketball coaches or the narc squad.

My recruiting rap actually became quite different—and something that later would be taken out of context by some critics. I called this our "reality session." "I've got my education," I used to tell the kids. "Now you have to get yours. Nobody is giving it to you for free." Let's face it. When a coach goes into a home and tells a recruit, "My number one goal is you getting your degree," that's a stretch. If that's really true, okay, then let the recruit tell that coach that what he would like to do is sit out his first two years and concentrate on getting that degree. Then let's hear what the coach says.

A coach shouldn't be allowed to make education sound like a briefcase, something that he can go fetch for his player. The fact of the matter is, I'm a basketball coach. If you need help with your jumper or your defense, I'm supposed to be able to help. If you're sick or have a bad knee, you go to a doctor. Bad teeth, go to a dentist. Bad dribble, you come to me. But education? That you must get from the college itself, from professors and classes, labs and lecturers. Eggy taught me not to promise so much help and so many tutors that a kid couldn't feel personal accomplishment. He taught me not to coddle. Maybe that's what led to my trouble fifteen years later when I was accused of not having enough control.

Speaking of which, the first time I really felt out of control coaching any team might have been that first year we had Ruland at Iona. One of the things about coaching that people don't understand is that a lot of talent doesn't always equal success. Early on that season we were doing quite well before we went up to Holy Cross and got kicked pretty good. It was our first loss and afterward in the locker room there was plenty of yelling and finger-pointing and blaming Jeff. He was the star, sure, but he just wanted to be one of the guys. However, the older players were having none of it. They were mad at him for getting all the ink. Now that there'd been a defeat, everything hit the fan. We'd lost one game and the whole thing was coming apart. I'd always had a team of rats. Now they were all big-timers. It was unbelievable.

When we got back home, everybody went whacko. Ruland said he was going to transfer. Vickers said *he* wanted to transfer. We were 5–1 and my career was over. I wasn't sure how to handle this. All I knew was that I wasn't going to call a team meeting. I hated team meetings. Ruland said he was going home to Lake Ronkonkoma, Vickers to Babylon. I blew up. "If that's all you think of me and the program and your teammates, get out of here," I said. "Go on. We'll carry on without you guys."

After they took me at my word, it was one of those times you look back and say: *"Oh no. What have I done?"* The funny thing was, Jeff's mother was the one who patched up everything. She called me the next day and read me the riot act.

"What are you, nuts?" she shouted over the phone. "You let those two guys leave like that? You should have kicked them in the butt and told them to grow up and play some basketball. I'm sending both of them back." And she did. When they returned, I benched both Ruland and Vickers for our game against the Australian Olympic team. We got blown out, but the experience showed everybody on the team how much they needed each other. I've always thought that Jeff's mother should have been the first woman to be an assistant basketball coach.

I've always felt a team has to play a big game first before it's ready to win a big game. Because of Ruland, we had beefed up the schedule and we had Auburn (at home) and Kentucky (on the road) within a few days of each other in that 1977–78 season. If the team and the year ring a bell, they should. That's the season Joe B. Hall's Wildcats were ranked number one most of the year before ultimately winning a national championship.

We crushed Auburn, and now it was the night of December 23, a Friday, a momentous occasion for me. Picture this now. Three years before, Iona had been 4–19. Now we were 7–1, playing Kentucky at Kentucky, and we knew we had a chance to win! Or at least, I thought we did, before I noticed some telltale signs in the locker room. First, my guys were talking about the size of not only Rupp Arena, but the lockers in Rupp. They wanted to see what the Wildcat Lodge looked like. That was bad enough. Then one player kept asking if the game was on TV. Hey, I wanted to say, forget about it. Let's play the game. But I knew these guys were over their heads. Then I saw Kevin Vesey engrossed in reading *The Cats' Pause* (the weekly journal covering Kentucky sports). Uh-oh.

There's always something that crashes a coach back to reality. We had risen to a different level all right, but we weren't ready to win. You don't win games when you're just happy to be there. We lost 104–65, and it was one of those nights when a coach doesn't know exactly how it's going south, he just knows it is. One thing is the players' Big Eyes. Big Eyes are always trouble. Fans think that when the players come to the bench and seem all focused and intent on listening to you, that's a good sign. Curtains is what that is. It means they're sitting on the edge of their seats with their eyes bugging out of their heads totally terrified! To be championship contenders, players must elevate themselves to the level of the game. Not many can do that.

This was a big game, a big environment, a big arena, and we didn't handle it at all properly. We panicked. I decided the most important thing I could do was not say things we would all regret. A coach must never place his players in a position from which they can't come back. I wasn't about to impose on them just for the sake of a Rockne-type speech.

Moreover, it wasn't that hard to take, getting blown out. The hard losses are the one-pointers. You question yourself: I should have, I could have. But when you lose by 40, you almost never have to say: "If the 2 play had worked at the beginning of the second half, maybe . . ." Or, "I need to look at the tape." No. You just tell everybody to get on the bus and get the hell out of there. Which is what we did.

While Kentucky went on to its NCAA title, the next season we proceeded to shore up some weaknesses. We had Palma, the transfer from Wake Forest, eligible. We recruited a little point guard from York, Pennsylvania named Tony Iati to share some of the load with Vickers. And we had Alex Middleton, an outstanding 6'6" player who attended junior college in Texas. As we approached the preseason of '78–'79 we were ranked number nine by *Sports Illustrated.* To celebrate—I am not making this up—my staff and I went outside and took a victory lap around the track. The student body thought we were nuts, but to be ranked was such a milestone. I would come to learn later at N.C. State that the top twenty ratings mean very little to an established school, a team that makes the NCAA tournament every season. The only thing that matters there is the NCAA's. But when you're trying to build a program, it's so important to achieve that kind of national recognition.

So you can see why we went absolutely nuts with that ranking. It meant so much to us. I remember having a team meeting soon after that. It was my Great Expectations address. I guess I had been saving that speech for quite some time because it would be an important moment for me at Iona. I shared with the team my hopes and dreams. I told them we would make Iona nationally known. We would help Brother Driscoll get things done he felt were important to the area. We were all very emotional, coach and players—blue-collar ethnics coming into their own.

We were 23–6 that year. It was a whole new experience, having to elevate ourselves to the point at which we could take everybody's best shot. I pulled out every emotional discussion you ever heard of. I was a quotin' fool, drawing from everybody from A. E. Housman to John F. Kennedy. I changed team rules—I told them I didn't want to be a cop anymore. As a coaching staff we gave the team tests on their knowledge of what we were doing—you'd be shocked at how many guys struggled with the tests.

At times, even the coaches struggled to communicate what they wanted. Picture this scene. Late in the game, call time-out. Twelve seconds to play, down by one, our ball, set up the last play. You've seen this on TV a lot, right? The team has gone over this play approximately 37,000 times in practice. I mean, it's our pet play. The one we use to win games. This is the time, guys. Seems easy, doesn't it? Uh-uh.

The first thing that happens is I start shouting: "Get in! Get in! Get in! Everybody get in. Here we go! Here we go! Here we go! All here? All here? All here?" Now I'm at the diagram board going crazy. "This is Tommy. This is Nate. Here's Chris. No, where's the ball? Where? Where's the goddamn ball? Okay, okay. Where we going? Okay. Phil is going to take it out over here. What? Phil's not in the game, he fouled out? Okay, okay. Here we are, we're going to run the play now. It's our play, guys. The play we run in practice. Thirty-seven thousand times we've run this baby. Everybody got it?" Now I'm drawing upside down figures and numbers in a frenzy and we're going over the play. "Yeah, you go here and you go there. Okay, okay. You cut back, fake, come across the middle. Okay, you're going to get the screen and it's an easy J. All net and we go home. Okay, okay."

If I'm lucky, maybe one guy has an idea what I'm talking about. If I'm really lucky, there's time for another time-out.

"Quick. We got another time-out? Great. Yeah, time. Get another one." This is when the TV announcers say, "Well, it's obvious Valvano wants to see the other team's alignment here." Alignment, my ass. My team doesn't know what the hell to do yet, I need more time!

What we eventually did was draw up a book with all our last-second plays and key words for each. It was very clear, and I didn't have to diagram or call out anything. I just showed them the book and said here's what we're going to run. Of course, if you've got a veteran team with a guy who takes those last-second shots, they don't even listen to you. They know what to do. They just tolerate you, go out, set the play and the kid does his thing. You just hope you have practiced enough so that they can overcome your coaching in the dying seconds when you're in an absolute frenzy and all you have to remember is the key word.

I also was finally learning about the referees who were regulars at our games. Two incidents stick out. In the '78–'79 season we were playing the University of New Orleans, coached by Butch van Breda Kolff, and we had Tom Birch reffing. Now Tom Birch is one tough hombre, a well-known guy in the East. I'm not saying a tough official; I mean he was a tough man. He took no guff from anybody. When you had Birch working the game, you sat there and literally did not open your mouth. Because if you did, as soon as you did, it was a technical foul. Boom—T! Of course the first time you had the guy, you didn't know that. And sure enough, the first time I got Birch, I just stood up and he hit me with one. So the deal is, you *know* about Tom Birch. You tell your players to just let him ref. And you love to get him when you're playing against somebody from out of town who doesn't know him.

Well, the night van Breda Kolff came in with New Orleans, you can imagine . . . I knew we were in great shape, even though they had just beaten Princeton at Princeton. The game starts. It stays close. Technical. More screaming, a bit of yelling, a few bad words. Tweet. Tweet. Two more technicals. Butch is gone, just like that. Out of the game. Now it's the assistant coach's turn. He's just an echo of Butch. He's really hot, too. He wants Birch. Tweet. Tweet. Tech, tech, tech. The assistant's gone reaaal fast. We stepped to the line with about twelve free throws. I think we made eleven. Went from a five-point lead to sixteen. And now New Orleans didn't have any coaches. Hey, I'm in good shape when there are no coaches on the other bench. But I predicted the whole thing before it happened.

The other memorable time we got Birch was when the University of Wisconsin-Milwaukee came in coached by a guy named Bob Gottlieb. I knew Gottlieb was a very vocal coach, so I told my players just to let Birch ref the game as usual, don't open your mouths, and everything would work out fine. The game went along without an incident until the very end when a crucial call went against the visitors. A terrific surprise to me, of course. I don't even think Birch made the call, but Gottlieb got up and screamed, Birch tee'ed him anyway and we went on to win.

Afterward, Gottlieb ran out on the court and got right up in Birch's face. "If you didn't have that damned striped shirt on, I'd let you know how I really feel!" he roared at Birch. So—I couldn't believe this!—Birch starts to rip off his shirt right there! I grabbed the referee and wrestled him off the court and somebody else held back Gottlieb, fortunately for him. He was challenging the wrong guy. Birch is just too tough; they would have carried Gottlieb out in a body bag. Actually, it was the first time I ever helped a referee off the court.

In the postseason, Iona finally played the biggest game of my life to that point. It was the finals of the ECAC tournament. Winner to go to the NCAA's. It was against St. John's.

Scheduling the Kentuckys and playing the Kentuckys was a way to get the big games into our system. Get used to the level. Get ready to beat a national power in the nine o'clock game at Madison Square Garden. But playing St. John's with everything on the line . . . Well, this was that big game. No, it wasn't in the Garden. It was in the Nassau Coliseum out on Long Island. But this was the moment I recruited our players for, the experience I convinced them would be theirs. This was how we would make Iona a name. I was so emotional. It was one of only two times in my life I could barely even give the pregame talk. Instead, I just cried.

I *was* able to babble something before the game to the team. I said: "Here we are. St. John's for the NCAA bid. I can't really explain the magnitude of this moment for me. Coach Lou Carnesecca coached his first high-school game against my dad a long time ago. Now I'm against him. But what did I tell you three years ago? It's all here now. I didn't do it, you did it. I can't play, you guys play."

Then I just broke down. That Iona team bolted out the door and absolutely kicked ass. I think we led at halftime 36–16, and this was against a St. John's with Wayne McKoy and Reggie Carter, a team that was going to the NCAA's. The victory really was the culmination of a lot of struggles. We had been ranked. We won the conference and went undefeated in league play—no easy feat considering the quality of coaches we were up against: Mike Krzyzewski at Army, Tom Penders at Fordham, and P. J. Carlesimo at Wagner. We'd gotten over that twenty-victory hump. It was one of the first times we got to cut the nets down. It was one of those special moments in sports where the anticipation is *not* greater than the realization. I went over to my parents' house later. For the first time, my dad told me something that would become our little joke over the next several years. "My bags are packed to go to the national championship game," said Rocco Valvano.

Ultimately, Iona turned into only a national footnote in our first

NCAA tournament because we lost right out of the gate to the Ivy League champion, Penn. It was funny because there we all were—four friendly, familiar Eastern teams; Iona, Penn, St. John's and Temple—down in Raleigh, North Carolina facing off for the chance to play North Carolina and Duke on the weekend. You might remember; the ACC will never forget. When our survivors, Penn and St. John's, beat the Tar Heels and Blue Devils, it was forever called "Black Saturday."

Our loss to Penn is freeze-framed in my mind, of course. Every game you lose on an official's call is like that. Our strength and size had negated their speed—these were the Quakers who ended up in the Final Four, by the way—and we were down by one point with only seconds to go. Mike Palma made the game-winner, but here came the referee signaling a travel. Cut our hearts out, that's all. Little did I know it would be the first of many heart-wrenching contests for me in Reynolds Coliseum on the campus of North Carolina State.

We all went back home and I watched the Penn-Carolina game on TV. Contemplating what had happened, I learned some valuable lessons on that initial NCAA trip. First, I had been too loose the whole time. At practice. Dealing with the media. Preparing for the show. I mean, this was the big time. I enjoyed getting off lines, I was having a ball. But, again, just as when we played at Kentucky the year before, I fell into the trap of being satisfied just to be there. There wasn't the edge that a coach needs to be at his best. Bottom line, I wasn't ready to win a game in the NCAA tournament.

Not to mention how awestruck I was. Willis Casey, the tournament director (who as N.C. State athletic director would later hire me to coach the Wolfpack), had a meeting with representatives of the participant schools in which he explained how important it was to wear our identification badges at all times. In future years I learned to send other department personnel to these meetings, so that I could concentrate on the task at hand. But at that first tournament I must have been waiting at the Reynolds Coliseum door before they even opened the place. Casey said if we lost our badge, we couldn't get in. I pinned the thing to my underpants.

Watching Penn beat Carolina also convinced me of this: There are no levels of program, only levels of players. Think about that for a second, because it's exactly what makes the NCAA tournament the fantastic event it has become. In other words, it's why a Cleveland State can reach the Sweet 16, why Siena upset Stanford, how Austin Peay beat Illinois in 1987.

Sure enough, St. John's (a team we beat) ended up playing Penn (a team we could have beaten) for the right to go to Salt Lake City and the

Final Four. That's when I decided my sights were set too low. The next year, our goal would be to win the whole damn national championship.

Bear in mind, we still hadn't played the nine o'clock game in the Garden. We had to do that—and to win the game against a biggie—to ever be ready to do the other. I knew from the previous year that had we lost that game to St. John's, Iona wouldn't have been invited to the NCAA's. Juicing up the schedule was not enough. We had to win those juiced-up games. The schedule just wasn't tough enough. If you play enough good people and you're good enough, you'll beat those people. But they weren't going to come to Iona. We had to play those games in New York.

Imagine my surprise when I picked up the newspaper one day and read that the president of the Garden, Sonny Werblin, who used to own the New York Jets and once invented Joe Namath (the guy who was always being mistaken for me), wanted to bring big-time college basketball doubleheaders back into the Garden. Yo, Sonny! A little dip into my own chutzpah bag and in a flash I was downtown crashing some reception that Werblin also attended. I had the article from the newspaper in my hand. Luckily, Werblin, a Rutgers graduate, recognized me from my playing days.

"I'm here to answer your ad," I said.

"What ad?" he said.

I showed him the newspaper. "I'm the coach at Iona College now and we're not in here. We have the best team in the area and if you're going to bring big-time hoops back, you need us. I'm telling you. We're good enough to win the national championship. But we need to get scheduled in the Garden, and the Garden needs us."

Eventually, after my prodding, Werblin told me to call his secretary and make an appointment to see him. He wasn't blowing me off, either. When I got to the Garden offices a few days later, it was like Wonderland. I was walking on eggshells through that place. The door didn't even look like a door; it was an Entrance. The waiting room had pictures of the Knicks and Lakers and Frank Sinatra and Ella Fitzgerald. I was a long way from under the El. Rocco Valvano should see his kid now. Werblin gave me half an hour. He had to go to a meeting with some representatives of Ringling Brothers. I was, you know, impressed. Suavely, I asked him a couple of penetrating questions.

"How do the elephants get into the Garden? Do you have to bring in the elephants yourself?"

At least Werblin seemed amused. He wanted to know what he could do for me, and with that I spilled out my briefcase. Brochures, photos, clippings. I had stories about Ruland from back in high school. "We need exposure," I said, "and not through playing Manhattan and Fordham. We need to schedule a national power. Can you see it? The Garden packed. A big, traditional name school. Iona of New Rochelle. It's got to be late in the season to have an impact. The whole town will be buzzing. And one other thing—it has to be the nine o'clock game. We can't play at seven. Got to be nine." I was adamant about that.

By the time I got back to school that day, Werblin's secretary had left a message for me. She didn't have the opponents yet, but we were given two dates. National teams. Both at nine o'clock. One turned out to be Kansas on February 7th. The other would be Louisville, February 21, 1980.

I'm telling you, we were excited about these two games. From the beginning we talked about winning the Great Alaskan Shootout, winning our games in the Garden, going unbeaten in the conference again and winning the national title. We had a pro mentality. Everything was working. We were geared.

There were no more Big Eyes. We knew how good we were. I was the best coach I had ever been; my staff was the best prepared. Pat Kennedy would do all the scouting reports. There was no guesswork about what to run, what plays would work against whom. The whole team was back. I even stopped recruiting for the year, leaving that chore up to the Egg Man.

To begin the season, we swamped Texas A&M and Long Beach State in Alaska. We didn't go up there to visit the seals. We went to kick some serious ass. Now we were to play Kentucky again and, dammit, this time we had the edge. We were better, I thought, at every position. Remember, there are no levels of programs, only levels of players? The country didn't know that yet, but we knew it. Ruland threw up before the game. He had the edge; he would dominate Sam Bowie. Vickers was a senior, and he had the edge. Kyle Macy got all the ink; Vickers was better.

We were up by ten points with eight minutes to go in the game, and damn if Kentucky didn't go to that same 1–3–1 zone defense that embarrassed us two years before. To make a tragic story short, we made some horrendous decisions, we stopped hitting and then we stopped playing. It was unbelievable. Macy hit everything he fired at. We scored 50 points in the game. That's right. Five-oh. The final was 57–50. It was like a five-year journey that ended in Hell.

There we were right at the threshold of a stunning, major upset. And a huge ranking. It takes about 10 days for the Alaskan Shootout scores to reach civilization anyway—but we would have been the toasts of college basketball for a while. Three-and-oh, Alaska champs and a victory over the Wildcats was light-years away from 2–1 and just another Kentucky victim.

I went nuts in the locker room afterward. I pounded chairs and lockers, cursed out the players, destroyed personal belongings, some of them even mine. I was uncontrollable, flip city. It wasn't even okay to play Kentucky close anymore, our goals had been elevated so much.

I went out and walked the streets of Anchorage fairly deep into the night, as I vaguely recall. What did I do wrong? Why did I slow the game down? Why didn't I let the kids play? It was the second time a 1–3–1 zone had busted up our offense. We had good shooters, ball handlers, veteran players. The other team couldn't even guard Ruland. It must be me.

I'd like to say that after games like these I took solace in my family. But the worst part was that at that point in my life I had no time for domestic pursuits, as Pam will be the first to say. My family wasn't allowed to travel with the team. I had, as they say, "tunnel vision." Actually, that means I was a total asshole. Basketball dominated my life to the point that I was never, ever home. If I wasn't watching game films or going over scouting reports, I was going to Knicks games in the city.

But on that trip out West to open the season, we were far away from Iona. In fact, we went from the tournament in Alaska straight to California to play St. Mary's and San Francisco. It was like starting all over. I was looking at the possibility of us getting beat two more times. My best team in history would be 2–3.

St. Mary's was first. They were opening a new gym, so obviously it was packed and the fans were out of their minds. We were down twenty at the half. I benched all the Iona starters and our second team began pressing. We came back. I platooned. Our first and second teams alternated, and we ended up winning 79–73. It was a great comeback.

At least I was in better spirits for our game at USF. My old college roommate, Bob Lloyd, came to the game. At dinner the night before, some guy came up to me and wouldn't believe I wasn't Joe Namath. Didn't go for my funny line or anything. He followed me to the bar. "I understand you don't want people to know you're here, Joe," he said.

"Look at this body," I said. "I can't be him."

"Your secret is safe with me, Joe babe," he said.

I needed some secrets for USF. They were a terrific team, and they won 76–66. So now we were 3–2. I read *Patton* on the airplane home. I didn't talk to anybody, just read war books. Patton. Eisenhower. Anybody who'd ever been in a war. The culmination of five years at Iona—and we were 3–2 to show for it. Hardly the 5–0 of the previous year. Hell, I was 3–2 at Bucknell, 3–2 at Johns Hopkins.

"Who was the fool AD who scheduled us to start the season with five straight road games? It was me? Oh. Never mind." We righted ourselves after that, losing only two more of our first sixteen games. Georgetown beat us. Georgetown *always* beat us. And Pittsburgh beat us at their place when Sam Clancy, who later played in the NFL, got in a fight with Ruland to start the game. Clancy was a huge fellow. Every time Clancy came down the court, he would look at me. The game got vicious and nasty, and Clancy started pointing at me. Hey, what did I do? Pittsburgh beat us by twelve, but I didn't hang around to congratulate Sam.

After that loss we vowed to win the rest of our regular-season games, including our two big ones in the Garden against big-name schools Kansas and Louisville. We beat Kansas 81–77. Coming into Louisville, we had won eleven in a row. The Garden bill had DePaul, ranked number one in America, against Wagner (coached by P. J. Carlesimo). Then came Louisville, ranked number two, against Iona. Yeah, we had finally made it; the nine o'clock game in the Big Apple.

There were 18,592 people there and it was the second time that I lost my composure, choked up and started to cry during the pregame. The kids were so ready, they could taste it.

Everything about that night is still vivid. I had worn a turtleneck sweater for good luck during all our victories, so since it was the Garden, I wore a suit with my turtleneck. Louisville was on its usual late-season roll and really starting to play great. As a footnote, I might add that one month later the Cardinals won the national championship. However, on this night, though the game was tight in the first half, we knew exactly what to do.

In college ball there are "system" teams and "talent" teams, but Louisville has both talent *and* a system. We decided in the locker room at halftime that to beat the 'Ville's 2–2–1 press we would have our big guys bring the ball in bounds, then have Vickers come get it in the middle of the court. Our two outside shooters, Palma and Hamilton, would go to the corners and when Vickers got the ball he would turn and hit them deep for the shot. A poor percentage shot with nobody underneath for the rebound yet?

Forget it. We were going to run and run and break the press and stick it in Louisville's gullet. With Ruland trailing the play, if we missed I figured he'd be there.

There were no tears in the locker room. I was totally in control. I told the team I knew they could do it.

Well, we came out in the second half, and we did do it. Palma and Hamilton shot the lights out; Middleton and Ruland dominated the boards, and Vickers not only ran the offense, he was the key guy in our 1–3 chaser defense on the Louisville All-American, Darrell Griffith. Glenn chased Griffith up into the Garden mezzanine.

It was fabulous. Our shooters would fire . . . good. Keep firing . . . good, good. The Garden was rocking. Our lead went to six, to ten, to twelve. Ruland was a bear—30 points, 21 rebounds. We went four corners. They let us. And with about a minute left to go in the game, it was obvious we were going to win in a rout. It seemed as if, in the last three minutes, every one of those 18,592 was standing and roaring for our 77–60 victory.

A standing ovation for little Iona College of New Rochelle. I had goose bumps. I got all choked up. I wanted to hug everybody—my father, my brothers, Pam, for putting up with me being "focused." I never wanted that moment to end.

Finally, Jeff Ruland got the ball on the wing, bulled in and dunked to end the game. Bedlam. Magnificent bedlam. I wound up that night in Chinatown—don't ask me how. After games in New York I always wound up in Chinatown.

What I do remember was a quiet moment with Pam somewhat later. I remember telling her that she'd better start thinking about moving one more time.

Chapter Eight

OPPORTUNITY KNOCKS

I T WAS JUST A SENSE I HAD. THE HUGE, PROMINENT, NATIONAL VICTORY. THE publicity. The streak we were on. When you're hot, you're hot. It was late in the season, other coaching jobs would be opening up, and athletic directors are always searching for new coaches who are on a roll. I figured it was just a matter of time before somebody found Iona and V.

We went on to win 20 of our last 21 games, a fabulous jump into the national consciousness and the Top Twenty, right? Play a little Aretha Franklin, maestro: "Respect." But—nooooo. I went from Aretha to Rodney Dangerfield because, rather than move up in the rankings, we moved out. Right out of the Top Twenty! How could that be? Well, to me it just showed how stupid and ridiculous the wire service polls were. So what we did was use the slight to motivate us for the NCAA tournament.

Again, the polite word is "focused." We were "focused" for the playoffs as never before. But actually what we were was *pissed off*. We played Holy Cross in the first round and won easily without even being emotional. That's when you know you're both good and ready, I have decided: when you can go out and beat a good opponent on pure, businesslike terms without getting hot and bothered about it.

To get to the round of sixteen now we had to beat Georgetown. Good old Georgetown. Thorn-in-my-(back)side GT. The game was in Providence, but damn if I didn't think we would win it. They were one of only four teams that had beaten us all year, so we had the revenge factor working. Beat the Hoyas and we were two games from the Final Four. Those two games would be in the Regional in Philadelphia, where we would have enormous fan support. I really thought this was it.

It was a terrific game, too. They took an early lead. We came back and led at the half. We stormed off at the beginning of the second half and got about an eight-point lead. But now Ruland was in foul trouble and I had to take him out. Georgetown rallied, caught us, went seven points up. But we fought back. As all great games do, it came down to the wire and a couple of big plays.

With Georgetown ahead by one point, we fouled the Hoyas' star, Craig Shelton. Anyway, there weren't any worries about drawing diagrams upside down this time. In the time-out, we knew exactly what we would do. If Shelton missed, we were going to our 3–2 set with the ball in Vickers' hands. Glenn would come down, beat his man up the pipe, take the percentage jumper—and bang, we win. Or, if Vickers missed, we would have Ruland, in my mind the best offensive rebounder in college, grab the carom, stuff it back in—bang, we win. Either way—bang, we win. We're in the Final Sixteen.

Sure enough, Shelton missed.

The problem with our plan was that when Vickers came down the floor and beat his man, Ruland was also wide open under the basket. I still to this day think that the doubt in Glenn's mind about whether to shoot or pass to his teammate caused him to miss the shot. Still, if Vickers' miss had bounded off left, Ruland would have been able to snatch it and pound it back in anyway. As it was, it bounced off to the right side and we lost the game.

In the emotional wreckage that followed in the locker room, Glenn had a very simple explanation. It all had to do with the clock: "Coach, I just wasn't sure we had enough time left," he said. Vickers wanted to let me know he had seen Ruland, but didn't think there was enough time to dump off the ball to him. Then he went outside and gave the press the most memorable line I have ever heard from a college kid after losing such a big game.

Four years before when I was recruiting Glenn to come to Iona and help us put the school on the map, I used to tell him that one day he would have the ball in his hands with the clock winding down and that he would hit a shot to put Iona in the national finals. That must have stuck with him, because when the reporters asked him why he hadn't passed off, Glenn Vickers said: "Because I was recruited to take that shot."

If loyalty such as this didn't result in some tears from this wonderful kid's defeated coach, I'd hardly be human.

And it was *such* a defeat! Probably the most devastating one I'd experienced up to that time. I would learn later in my career that there were a lot of defeats like this, when you thought you were the better team and should have won the big game. At the next level up on the college scene, those games happen weekly. But on the Iona level, this was a new experience for us. It had been such a journey—for me, thirteen years. I knew Vickers and Hamilton and Palma would all be gone the following year, and this might have been our one, great shot.

In order to think about all this, I just started walking. Didn't take the bus home with the team. Didn't drive home with my wife. Me and Richie Petriccione, the Iona manager, simply walked and walked all over Providence. All over New England, for all I knew. No luggage. No other clothes. No toothbrush. Just us. I think we must have walked all night. The next morning we hopped a train to New York, then to New Rochelle. I know a coach is supposed to keep perspective about losing, but this was pure hell, nearly death. I couldn't imagine anything worse. Lombardi talked about "lying exhausted in defeat" as the second-best feeling? Right then I figured I had to talk to ol' Vince about that quote.

Back at Iona, even with the defeat, even after the disappointment, I knew that there would be some kind of new job offers. In the business there are keeper jobs and stepping-stone jobs. As much as I loved Iona and never thought of it as merely a stop in a career, in the back of my mind I realized I couldn't be satisfied with anything short of the highest level of college ball.

In my five years at Iona I had interviewed for several other coaching jobs and always felt it to be a positive experience. I used to tell all my assistant coaches that if they had the opportunity to find out about other programs in an interview, to jump at it. Interviews showed you about life somewhere else, but more important, they let you know how you felt about your current job and how it stacked up. Were you happy where you were? Did you feel an inkling of wanting to be someplace else? What were the salaries, the recruiting budgets, the perks out there in other positions?

There's also the fear a lot of coaches have of going for a job and not getting it, and in the coaching business, interviews inevitably result in a strange little mating dance in the media. No school ever wants to admit it offered a guy its coaching job and he turned it down. No coach wants to admit he wanted a job but didn't get the offer.

Okay, so here's my history on that. I interviewed at Columbia and didn't get it—Tom Penders did. I interviewed at Jacksonville and didn't get it—Tates Locke did. I interviewed at Penn State and didn't get it—Dick Harter did. I interviewed at St. Louis U., got it—didn't take it. I interviewed at Providence and . . .

Here was one of those mating-dance situations. One of those in-betweens. I had a great relationship with Dave Gavitt, who was resigning at Providence to become athletic director at the school (and later to invent the Big East). Gavitt, remember, was a disciple of one of my mentors, Dee Rowe. Through Dee, I considered Dave a friend. The Providence job was a big-time plum. Moreover, Dave told me that the Big East was inevitable, that Providence would be a big part of the league, and that Eastern basketball would never be the same. The obvious inference was that schools like Iona would be dwarfed in the process. We talked for a long time about the situation, about me succeeding him. Dave, of course, was a legend in Providence. Then, the minuet. Would I take the job if it was offered?

Well, that's the trick, isn't it? Providence was not offering me the job unless I would accept it. This is a situation that puts pressure on both sides. This was the year before Ruland's junior season, the season I knew we'd have a chance to win the national championship. My family wanted me to stay. But I was looking down the road too, and the Big East fascinated me. In the end, I "withdrew my name from the running"—the standard, graceful way most coaches depart the job hunt—but some newspapers wrote that I said I had turned down the job, which I had never said. Naturally, when Gavitt got wind of that he was furious. You try to maintain the dignity of both parties and then something like this happens. Yeah, I blamed the media, because it was its fault. I wrote a letter to Dave explaining my position, and luckily he understood, and he remains a friend today.

My Penn State experience was something else. I think I might have bolted to Penn State, actually, what with the name and the tradition and the glamour of working with Joe Paterno. But when I went for the interview, I somehow knew it wouldn't work out. Mainly because I used to wear open-neck shirts and turtleneck sweaters.

If that seems odd, you don't realize the importance of the Nittany Lion image. They don't wear those old, black football shoes and uniforms without names at State College, Pennsylvania for nothing. It seems when I sat down to be interviewed by the Penn State athletic board, they had seen press clippings with my, uh, unorthodox haberdashery, and were duly unimpressed.

"Mr. Valvano, you're kind of loose, aren't you?" asked one Penn State blue blazer.

"Yes, I guess I'm loose. But don't mistake that for being undisciplined," I said.

"We have a dress code. Don't you have a dress code?" said the blazer.

"Oh, yes, sir. When we're on the road, all of our players must wear clothes," I replied.

(There it was again; Jimmy the class clown couldn't resist. Think I had a good shot at Penn State now?)

"Mr. Valvano, are you being facetious?" said the blazer.

"No, I'm not," I said. "I thought we went through all this before. I thought that's what the sixties were all about. A whole decade about not judging people by their clothes or their hair. Sure, I'm jesting. But at Iona we respect certain freedoms."

"Young man, a dress code is not an attack on freedom," said the blazer. "Mr. Valvano, you went to Rutgers, I believe. When Penn State plays Rutgers in football, I know automatically we will win. Why? Because Penn State is wearing coats and ties and Rutgers is not. That's important."

"Ah, it's the jackets and ties," I said. "And does that work for basketball as well as football? I believe your basketball team last year was, what, eight and *nineteen?*"

Obviously, I was not on the same wavelength with the Penn State athletic board, and we made an amicable parting.

During that last year at Iona, Brother Driscoll had discussed with me a long-term contract, renewable every year, as both athletic director and coach, with the understanding that I could step down from coaching when I wished. We had just signed it, when I received a call from a "Roylene Thompson," who said she was calling from North Carolina State University.

Usually, when a coach gets called up about a job interview, there's some banter and small talk, coddling and wooing and the like. "Hey, Jim, how you doing? Congratulations on a fine season. Great year you had. Listen, our coach just left. Did a great job. We were wondering if you'd . . ." Stuff like that. This time, uh-uh.

"Coach Valvano. I've got Willis Casey, the athletic director at North Carolina State University, on the line," said Roylene Thompson.

"Jim? I'm Willis Casey. You want to come down for an interview about our head coaching job? If you do, talk to Roylene here," said Willis Casey.

"Coach, there's a flight getting in to Raleigh at eleven tomorrow morning. See you then," said Roylene.

And boom, that was it. Unbelievable! I hardly had time to catch my breath. My assistant, Pat Kennedy, came in later, and when I told him I was going to interview at N.C. State, he had the same eighteen thousand questions I had. "Wow! Who'd you talk to? What did he say? What about recruiting? Are they really interested? Who else are they interviewing? How many years? How much money?" I had to tell Pat that all I knew was that Roylene Thompson, whoever she was, had a fairly thick Southern accent.

With the same kind of rushed timing and lack of details, my leaving Iona for N.C. State unfolded. Driscoll was disappointed that I would even want to go for the interview. I told him I wouldn't go if he didn't want me to, but because of the kind of man he is, he let me do it. In his heart, he knew as I did that this job was on a different level from any of the others that I had considered in the past. A long time ago, when I was at Connecticut, I had driven to North Carolina for a coaches' clinic,

visited the campuses at Duke and Chapel Hill, and talked to a bunch people about the ACC. There would always be a part of me that wou wonder if I could cut it at such a high level.

My first meeting at the Capitol City Club in Raleigh included Will Casey, former N.C. State star Ron Shavlik, the chancellor, Joab Thoma —who would wind up leaving the school and is now ironically th president of Penn State (I wonder if jackets and ties still decide games there)—and some others. I handled it just like I had most interviews, at least to the point where they started talking contract and money.

I've always believed that in the matter of contracts the important one is the second contract, not the first. You make yourself dispensable or indispensable by performance. Later, as athletic director at N.C. State, this view would be reinforced by many people I interviewed for jobs in the department who, before they even got the job, would inquire about benefits, vacations and the like. Wait a minute! If a job is open, shouldn't applicants interview for it based on what they would bring to the position, about their hopes and dreams and goals, rather than about the medical plan? One job applicant asked me if N.C. State had a dental plan. I said sure, we had a dental plan. If we lost, the alumni kicked our teeth in. My god! What was the guy worried about? Were his teeth that bad?

Willis Casey, though, was one of the toughest, shrewdest, smartest administrators I ever met. He totally outfoxed me in these negotiations. Outfoxed me, outfought me, every step of the way.

As I said, I believe if you're good at what you do, you don't want a contract to start with. If you're good, don't worry about it. They're going to take care of you *and* your teeth. And if you're not good, they're going to get rid of you whether you have a three-year, four-year, or whatever. At Johns Hopkins I had worried about money because I was broke. But everywhere else, if I got the chance to prove myself, I had been taken care of. For example, I had an excellent contract at Iona. A lot of benefits. They had bought our house; they were very good to me. My family and I were at a point in our lives when money was not a tremendous issue. So the perception that I left Iona to come to the big-time N.C. State for loads more money is totally nuts.

Anyway, Casey began discussions by coming right to the point and asking me why I wanted the job. I told him because I wanted to win the national championship.

"Do you think you can do that here?" he said.

"You guys have done it before. I would think you can do it again," I said.

When Casey asked me about a contract, I said that wasn't important. And money wasn't important either. "The only thing important to me is

the opportunity," I said. (By that same token, I've never taken a job without being told what the contract and money would be. To my eternal surprise, Willis took me at face value at this first tête-à-tête and didn't say anything more on the subject.)

"What do you need to win?" somebody asked.

"I need players," I said.

"No. What about facilities and things like that."

"Facilities?" I said. "Check out where I've been in my career. All I really need is enough money in the budget to recruit where I want to recruit. Other than that, you've got the gym and the balls. We can play with anyone." It was a nice, cordial meeting, and later I found out that Casey had said he liked me, and that I reminded him of Lou Holtz, whom he also had hired for N.C. State when Holtz was head coach at William and Mary.

It all happened so fast that obviously I thought there'd be another few follow-up calls, maybe another trip to Carolina . . . and that's if Casey and the board were even serious. But about a week later I was having dinner in New York City with my lawyer-friend Bill Madden when I got paged. It was Willis Casey! He had called my house and Pam had told him where I was. So he had called me at a bar. Simple as that. "Jim? You want to change your address?" he said. "We'd like you to be our next basketball coach."

Just in time before I collapsed from shock I managed to blurt out to Willis that umm, ah, umm, Pam hadn't even seen the place and I hadn't had much time to think about it and . . . I was fumbling and trying to compose myself.

"Jim? What happened to the guy who just wanted the opportunity? The guy who didn't care about a contract or money? I'm giving you the opportunity," Casey said.

He was so smart. He had called my bluff and we both knew it. I tried to prolong the situation and beg for some time. But Casey would have none of that. "Jim, we're having a press conference tomorrow at two P.M.," Casey said. "We're either going to introduce you as our next basketball coach, or somebody else who really wants the job." He didn't mention a contract or anything. And he said he wanted to know either way by eleven P.M. that night.

My immediate move was to call Pam. "What's the salary?" she said. Don't know.

"What kind of contract is it? How many years?"

Don't know.

"Where are we going to live? Where will the girls go to school? What else can you tell me?"

Don't know. Don't know. Nuthin'.

"Great. As I understand this," said my understanding wife, "you want to leave a place where everybody loves you, you and the president are very close, you've had a great team, financially we're well off, you've got the long-term contract . . . and you want to move where you don't know how much money you'll be making, or how long you'll be making it? Sounds like sound business sense to me."

Of course I talked to Bill Madden. Of course I listened to Pam. Of course I knew all the ramifications. But I couldn't afford to turn this down. The biggest problem of all was that I had no time to talk to my players. None. I barely had time to contact Brother Driscoll. It was probably the roughest four or five hours of my life. But the clincher was that I kept thinking back to that Georgetown game in the NCAA's. If you figure a coach has twenty-five years as a head man in Division I, that's a whole lot. That means twenty-five chances to win the national championship. I was thirty-four at the time. What I'm saying is I thought I had maybe fifteen or twenty years left in me. At some schools you might have a chance every other year to win it all. But only at certain schools do you have the big shot every single year. And N.C. State was such a school. I wanted to chase that dream.

When I called Casey back at eleven, I told him I accepted. But I asked him, in order to make my wife feel better, to tell me about the contract and what I would expect to be paid. He said between $40,000 and $45,000. "I'm not sure of the length," my new boss said. "It may be five years, but don't worry. We'll talk about that when you get here."

That money wasn't close to what I was making, when I combined my Iona salary with my house and car, the dough I earned from summer camps and my weekly cable TV show. And I had no idea if I could cash in on those things in Raleigh. So, financially, this move was a gamble.

Actually, Casey did wind up giving me an extra day to clear the boards at Iona, and I was able to meet with Driscoll. He was very disappointed, of course. He was so close to my family, he lived right around the corner, he came to dinner often. When I first told him of my decision, in fact, he asked me to leave and come back later after he had collected himself. Ultimately, he knew leaving for State was the only choice I had, and he gave me his blessing. He also agreed with me that moving Pat Kennedy up as the head coach was the one way to keep the program in place.

However, I couldn't get in touch with the Iona players in time. I didn't want to tell them over the phone, one by one. I wanted to have a meeting with them as a group and explain my decision face to face. But coming as it did right after the season, everyone was scattered, some even on spring vacation far away.

It wasn't until a team dinner a few weeks later that I was able to talk to the team. The city of New Rochelle put on the spread, but Brother

Driscoll at first thought I shouldn't come. A lot of people were still upset at my leaving, especially at the way I'd left. Driscoll was hurt, and I think he feared my showing up at the dinner would upstage Pat as the new head coach. But there was no way I'd miss that dinner. And it turned out to be a wonderful evening, very emotional but very cleansing as well. Pat was great. The players were understanding. There were hugs and tears all around.

Jeff Ruland, especially, seemed to have resigned himself to the situation. I knew he was angry and bitter at first, but that night he forgave me, and we hugged. "We'll be all right," Jeff said. "Good luck to you, but just remember we'll have to kick your ass next season when we play you."

In light of that night, the events that followed over the next few weeks became so perplexing. First, Ruland held a press conference to announce that he was staying at Iona rather than turning pro. But a day later, after it came out that he had signed a contract and accepted money from a man named Paul Corvino, making him his agent, Jeff had to apply for hardship. His connection with Corvino made him ineligible under NCAA rules.

The saddest part of all this for me was that Ruland thought that I had something to do with Corvino. What is worse, he felt that I, knowing about their relationship and that Jeff would ultimately be declared ineligible, had split for greener pastures in Raleigh. Nothing could be further from the truth. A month or so earlier, Corvino had called me to inquire if I would do a commercial with one of his clients, the former middle-weight champion Rocky Graziano, for Lenny's Clam Bar. I met with Corvino a couple of times for lunch so that he could show me some brochures he had put together for his clients, but that was the extent of it. He never mentioned Ruland. After I took the job at North Carolina State, I had to call Corvino and Graziano and bow out of the commercial.

I had started my new job when the Ruland-Corvino story broke in New York. What made me angry was that Corvino called me in North Carolina and said he had employed Jeff to do some house-painting for which he got paid. He also said Jeff had signed something indicating a player-agent relationship. "The kid is trying to back out, but I have a signed contract," Corvino said. "Ruland won't even talk to me, but you tell him he'd better. If he doesn't want me to represent him, that's fine, too. But he owes me some money, and we have to talk."

When I called Jeff to urge him to talk to Corvino and get the thing ironed out, he simply blew up. "You want me to talk to him?" Ruland screamed at me on the phone. "I get it all now. You're in it with him. You knew this was going to happen. That's why you left. That's why you bolted so fast without even talking to me." And then he hung up on me.

It took the better part of ten long years, until Jeff Ruland had gone on to stardom in the NBA, before he would talk to me again. It's still one of the saddest episodes in my life, and I wish it had never happened. I can't help but think it wouldn't have happened if I had just had enough time when I made the decision to leave Iona to talk to Ruland and the team. That would have resolved a lot of things. But since I didn't, there was always suspicion about my motives.

The fact that the NCAA came in and conducted a full-scale investigation of Iona just after I left didn't really clear the air. Even though the school was given a complete bill of health, I was absolved of any wrongdoing and no sanctions of any kind were handed out, relations between the Iona administration and myself became extremely strained. Brother Driscoll stopped talking to me because of the perception of collusion. In an NCAA probe—take it from me, I've been there—a siege mentality takes over, wherein every day you're defending yourself and your integrity. In the Iona probe, the best thing for all concerned was not to talk to me unless the NCAA directed that that be done.

The Ruland thing, however, overshadowed all. It's been one of the greatest disappointments of my life that Jeff and I never got our relationship back to the way it used to be. Jeff was a young man whose broken foot I had bathed, who sat at our kitchen table and was beloved by our daughters, who was one of the best friends my family could have. And then for nearly ten years, not only would he not talk to me, he would turn away and ignore me whenever I tried to say hello at NBA games.

The wounds healed a bit a couple of years ago, when Alex Middleton, a former player, and Jeff Ruland suddenly showed up at an N.C. State practice and we had a wonderful, emotional reunion. It was great to see them again and talk over old times; Jeff and I vowed to keep in touch. But then my controversies began piling up and a certain estrangement occurred again.

Jeff's back at Iona, finally finishing up his degree. We've hurt each other enough over the years. I'm looking forward to a final reconciliation.

Chapter Nine

PIG-PICKIN'S IS WHAT IT'S ALL ABOUT

THE BIG TIME. YOU'D THINK A GUY BORN AND BRED A NOOYAWKER WOULD know from the Big Time, but I could tell from the very first press conference in Raleigh that North Carolina State and ACC basketball was going to be different from anything else I had experienced so far. There were so many reporters and microphones and cameras, it was like Hog Heaven to the stand-up comedian in me. I also got a sense, halfway through, that the audience was not used to coaches who laughed and joked and enjoyed themselves much. Right away, of course, the media tried to build up something between Dean Smith and me: "How do you expect to beat the Dean?" Questions like that. I told them I didn't expect to beat him, I expected to outlive him.

Later, I would polish my Dean routine when Tar Heel fans would show up at N.C. State booster gatherings. I'm serious. There were so many Carolina people in the state that I think the authorities must have designated certain ones to come to our meetings. I was never at an N.C. State gathering where there weren't at least a few Tar Heels. I think, at least I hope, that I established a fun relationship with the Heels. I told them I knew why they were there, because Dean wouldn't talk to them. I said I'd never, ever seen Dean Smith outdoors. No, actually, I played golf with him just the other day when Dean hit it in the water on number eight. I was laughing like hell until he walked right across and picked up the ball.

But seriously, folks. The second-class citizen status in the state of North Carolina wasn't about to bother me. I had read where people like Norm Sloan at State and Bill Foster at Duke had been frustrated with all the attention and notoriety accorded Dean Smith and the Heels, that they had been "driven out" of the ACC by it. Hey, I had played and coached at Rutgers, with Princeton right up the road. I had coached at Iona, with St. John's right down the parkway. Second citizen? I was the second son, wearing hand-me-downs all my life. I was even my wife's second choice. This second-place stuff would be nice and easy for me.

Moreover, I was genuinely touched right away by the people's love for their state university, whatever branch it was. In the North there's not that same feeling. I mean, Rutgers is the state university of New Jersey, an outstanding institution, but like most other state schools up there it's a place for kids who can't afford the private schools like Princeton. In New England, the prestige schools are Yale, Harvard, Brown, Dartmouth, places like that. Then come the state schools: Connecticut, U. Mass, New Hampshire. There isn't the passion for old State U. that I found in North Carolina.

When a kid got accepted to U.N.C. at Chapel Hill or to N.C. State, it was the ultimate. The love for these schools across the state was palpable, and I felt a part of that immediately. As the basketball coach at such a tradition-bound place, I came to realize I was caretaker of something very special. Naturally, everybody was predisposed to liking me just because I was the guy sitting in the red chair.

As a result, from the beginning it was a tremendous high being the N.C. State coach. With Pam pregnant back on Long Island with our third daughter, Lee Ann—ironically, a little Southern romance in Myrtle Beach, South Carolina had set that up; I told Pam if the baby was a girl we should name her Myrtle—I was on my own that first spring. I felt like I was back in college myself.

I had a small room in the College Inn, which was a former motel where N.C. State housed some of its athletes. I did my own laundry at the Glamorama. I ate pizza and burgers and fries. I had an absolute ball. Then there were my visits to all the "Wolfpack Clubs" around the state—one hundred counties in North Carolina; one hundred Wolfpack Clubs. Charlie Bryant, the Wolfpack Club director in Raleigh, told me my first speaking engagement would be in Greenville.

First, I had to dress the part. Wolfpack Clubbers always wear their red blazers. So Dorsey Poole, the equipment man, fixed me up with a red blazer that must have been one-size-fits-all. I mean, this thing was so wrinkle-free it had to have been made out of polyester and steel wool! Get hit by a truck . . . I could brush this sucker off and be on my merry way. Bright red. Wide lapels. A big "N.C. State Basketball" embroidered in gold on the pocket. Then there was the tie. We're talking wide tie here, with huge red wolves on it. When I wore this tie, I really didn't need to wear a shirt. The material was so thick, no matter how tight I pulled it, the knot was as big as my fist, and the collar would stand up. I looked like the Flying Nun.

Was I ready? Not just yet. To complete the outfit, I learned I had to break out those thoroughly nifty pants dominated by *red checks.* Now very rarely on a Sunday would any of the Valvano family of Queens, New York get up and don their red-checked pants. But in Raleigh I would and did. "Now you're a good-looking Eye-talian," said Charles Bryant.

I knew the first Wolfpack Club meeting was an important one, because Charlie told me so. At the time there were no pro sports in North Carolina, and college basketball was the biggest thing going. Not that it isn't still, but this was *May,* for goodness' sake. Charlie said I'd better be inspirational and motivational. "If you're good, the word will spread about our new Eye-talian coach," Charlie said.

I was back in Myrtle Beach attending the ACC meetings when I started the tour. Made my own reservations. Changed into my red jacket and red-checked pants. Hopped on the plane. "Are you the coach at N.C. State?" a woman sitting next to me asked.

"Yes I am. Are you a State fan?" I said.

"No, I'm not," she said.

"I'll make you one," I said.

"No, you won't," she said.

When we landed, the guy at the luggage racks asked me if I was the new coach at N.C. State. "And proud of it," I said. "Are you a fan?"

"No, I'm not," he said.

"I'll convert you," I said.

"No, you won't," he said.

Whooaa, I thought to myself, this is a tough group we got here. I was supposed to be picked up at 5:30. An hour later—half the people in the airport had been waving at me, the other half giving me strange looks—I heard myself being paged. It was Charlie Bryant. "What the hell are you doing there?" he said.

"I'm in Greenville," I said.

"You're in the wrong *state,"* Charlie said.

Nice start to a career. For the most important speech of my new life I had dressed up like Bozo the Clown and flown to the wrong state. Everybody was staring as I walked back to the ticket counter. But before I did that, of course, I whipped off my red blazer and tried to hide it when I talked to the airline guy.

"Excuse me," I said. "I didn't know there was a Greenville in North Carolina *and* South Carolina."

The guy turned and called back to his office, "Hey, Burt. I *told* you this guy had no idea." Then he gave me some advice. "Coach, you're getting into a tough enough league as it is," he said. "If you don't know what state you're in, ol' Dean is going to beat yo' ass, regular."

So, the South was different. But do you know what? I learned very quickly that people are people, actually pretty much the same wherever you go. If you like people, they'll like you. And if you're honest and sincere, no matter how different the language and culture and food, people will understand you. What struck me was not the difference between me and the natives, but the similarities. Warm, family ties were all-important. Not just the symbol of the family but the closeness, the affection. That's how I grew up, with touching and loving. We hugged and kissed all the time. And when I went to these Wolfpack Club meetings around the state of North (not South) Carolina, the audience would be packed with families, their youngsters, their relatives. And I could sense how everyone was caught up in this warm, sharing atmosphere.

I think I went to thirty-two different meetings—lunches or dinners or speeches—in May alone. And talk about barbecue! Back in New York, barbecue was burgers or dogs on a grill. In North Carolina they introduced barbecue to me like this: "You're goin' to a pig-pickin'." I told them, hey, in college they used to have these at dances all the time, only we didn't advertise it. But they said no, they were really going to roast and pick a real pig. At my first one, everybody stood around watching the Eye-talian kid take his first bite. I felt like Mikey in that TV commercial: "Mikey! He likes it!"

Actually, I loved barbecue. And everybody loved me. That's the way it always is for a coach in that Love Interim (L.I.), the time between his hiring and his team's first loss. Everything he does and says is perfect. Everyone he recruits is great. His wife is beautiful, his family a dream, all his stories are unbelievably hilarious. Even if he is an Eye-talian from Nooyawk.

After my first couple of months in the L.I., everybody was offering me two new experiences besides barbecue: fishing and hunting. But I tried to tell the folks I'd never had much luck at either. I'd never been fishing a day in my life; it's tough to fly-cast into a fire hydrant. And as far as hunting goes, up in New York we never went hunting, we went following. If I wanted to catch something that flew through the sky, I didn't need to shoot it. I just followed it for awhile and the air was so bad it usually dropped dead at my feet. Still, everybody wanted me to go duck-hunting. What was the big deal about duck-hunting? A guy explained it to me. You get up at 4:00 in the morning, sometimes 3:30, and you go sit in a duck blind, which is actually in the water so that you're freezing cold. Now you sit in the freezing cold water and wait for the ducks to come out so that you can shoot them, but most of the time you miss anyway. Hey, I said, that sounds like a marvelous time. Why haven't I gotten into this duck-hunting before? Some of my new friends actually made up T-shirts that said: "Mama V's little boy never went fishing," with a picture of me fly-casting into a fire hydrant. They may still be working on the duck-hunting T-shirt.

I thought it was important to try to create some of this North-South combination flavor in the makeup of my coaching staff. As a result, I retained Marty Fletcher, who was a holdover from Norm Sloan's regime in Raleigh; and I hired Ray Martin, a former player at Notre Dame whom I remembered from his high-school playing days in New York. Martin was black, and I was personally committed to getting at least one black assistant. When the Egg Man elected to stay in New York, I chose Martin, who had been an assistant coach at Harvard. Martin had gone into the banking business in Boston, then worked for Pony, the shoe company, then decided he wanted to get back into coaching. For an impressive background and training, I knew I couldn't beat this guy.

As a hang-around, coffee-drinking buddy, I also had the baseball coach at State, Sam Esposito, the former Chicago White Sox infielder. Sam had been a high-school All-American in football, basketball, and baseball and a college star at Indiana University. Sam was my sounding board and my guru. He was a wonderful companion who kept me in stitches— especially when he helped run my basketball camp. Anyone who has ever had to put up with screaming monsters away from their mother and father for a week at summer camp could sympathize with the situation Sam found himself in one day, when confronted by me and a pair of angry parents.

"Uh, Sam," I said. "This is Mr. and Mrs. Blankenship, and these folks have come to see me about little Johnny and little Joey, who may have a problem. It seems Johnny and Joey think you don't like them."

"Listen, Mr. and Mrs. Blankships or whatever your name is," Sam growled through his ubiquitous cigar smoke, "I have enough trouble liking my own kids, much less yours."

It was the classic camp director's thought, if not the standard reply. But I was so dumbfounded, I could only stammer and try to think of something to lighten the mood. "Uh . . . uh, yeah," I said to the Blankenships. "How about a refund?"

Practicing every day in Reynolds Coliseum on the Raleigh campus, it didn't take long to realize I was no longer in the Have-Not mode. Some coaches in a new job automatically talk about doing everything different from the last guy. But State had such a great program, with Everett Case followed by Press Maravich followed by Sloan, that I didn't talk about change. I stressed how our staff had been handed the baton. State had won eight ACC championships and one national championship. I formulated some goals based on that: I wanted to be the seventh school to win two national championships. I knew that UCLA, Kentucky and Indiana were the only schools to win more than two. I wanted to be the fourth school to do that, as well.

At Hopkins, Bucknell and Iona I always had the safety net of not having to win. I could build; I could have a year of 10 wins, then 12, then 15, and so on. Here I was faced with the 20-victory plateau. If I didn't win 20, I wasn't doing the job. Talk about hyper. I would stand in the Coliseum with all those ACC and Dixie Classic banners hanging from the rafters and I would practically shake. Or I would walk around our offices in the Everett Case Athletic Center with the old N.C. State coach's picture staring down, and I swear Case's eyes would follow me wherever I walked.

For about a decade prior to television's interest in college ball, N.C. State led the nation in attendance. *Life* magazine once had a spread on Everett Case. Case was responsible for the old Dixie Classic tournaments. Case was responsible for North Carolina hiring Frank McGuire; the Tar Heels had to get somebody to compete with Case. One of Case's players was Vic Bubas, who would build the program at Duke. If Case begot Bubas and McGuire, who begot Dean Smith, then we're talking about the coach who virtually invented ACC basketball.

Was I going to measure up? Was I going to get it done? In reading the history of the ACC, I knew how many losses I should avoid. I knew the records of all the coaches. I knew that no one in the history of the ACC had not experienced at least one losing season. Despite all of that, I didn't ever want to lose, especially to the Polish National Team in our very first exhibition game.

In the locker room before the contest, I tried to low-key it. I knew the Poles weren't any good. I knew it was only an Exo. But I was a madman. *"This is what it's all about!"* I kept screaming. I'll always remember the first game. I paced. I sweated. *"This is what it's all about!"* I yelled at my team. I told them that we were in the famous Reynolds Coliseum; told 'em about tradition and banners and championships; told 'em about Everett Case. They must have thought: "Who is this maniac? We'd better grab him quick before he flips!"

I must have done thirty minutes of this. I was like a boxer before his big championship bout. And every time they'd start to run out, I'd stop them and say, *"This is what it's all about!"*

We beat the Poles by 50. They couldn't play at all. After the game, their poor coach, who hardly spoke any English, came up to me and said: "Run good. You team. Run good."

And I said, "You bet your sweet ass, we run good."

Holy smokes. What had I turned into? I mean, this guy had a bunch of stiffs and I was out there trying to crush the daylights out of them. I was trying to convince everybody we were 1–0 already and the game didn't even *count.*

Sam Esposito tried to warn me. He tried to tell me this was a different level now. I had to pace myself and my team much better. "Hey, V, take it easy," Sam said. "Those were foreigners. You were supposed to beat those guys. The real games don't start for a while."

But I was like that for every game. Back then we had a little tournament in December called the Big Four: Carolina, us, Duke, and Wake Forest. It wasn't enough to play each other twice in the regular season and maybe once in the ACC tournament. Oh no. We had to play each other another time. My first Big Four game at State was against Wake Forest in the Greensboro Coliseum, over 15,000 on hand. I went out to look at the crowd and . . . this is what it was all about!

I went back in the locker room and told the kids there were 15,000 out there waiting for them. I was pacing all over the place and screaming again. I was ready. On that team I had a 7'5" guy named Chuck Nevitt, who would later play in the NBA for quite a few seasons. However, he didn't start until his senior year.

"Look at Chuck, you guys," I said before that game with Wake. "Here's a guy who isn't starting this year. But he's ready. Like me. He knows what it's all about. Right? Right, Chuck? You know what it's all about. Chuck?"

I never heard the guy talk. "Chuck? Chuck? Are you nervous, Chuck?"

"No," he said.

"What do you mean, no?" I said.

"I'm not nervous about the game," he said.

"Well, Chuck. What are you nervous about?" I said.

"My sister is going to have a baby. It's her first. I'm nervous whether it'll be a boy or girl," he said.

"What's the difference, Chuck?" I said.

"I want to know whether I'm going to be an aunt or uncle," he said.

Well, the kid had reeled in the coach, and then hooked him. Those are the fishing terms, aren't they? Everybody laughed, including me, and we went out sky-high and opened up a quick lead. We were rollin'.

Wake Forest won 87–57.

It's called peaking too soon. I mean, this was a total burial. Talk about being knocked off a cloud. "Welcome to the ACC, Valvano," more than a few of those 15,000 screamed as I was leaving the floor. I was fortunate nobody shouted, *"This is what it's all about!"*

If anything, that blowout might have helped me as a coach. I was embarrassed, but I finally relaxed and stayed off the players' backs. The next night, in fact, we beat Duke.

My first team at State was young, but I loved our speed and quickness and we played a transition game about as well as it could be played. Moreover—and I've always said this—that first team was one of the best I had in Raleigh. Captain Queeg just didn't do a very good job coaching it. If I had had that team at the end of my career rather than at the beginning, we would have won 25 games. Teams would have been hard-pressed to beat us. I still use a tape of that team—the young Sidney Lowe and Dereck Whittenburg running the break—to demonstrate exactly how the transition game should work.

But the game that changed our first season came early: Maryland at Maryland, our first ACC road game. I've always believed the easiest road game to win is your first one. The players, especially if they're young, don't know yet that they're not supposed to win away from home. Sometimes you can sneak in and steal a victory. And that's what I thought we could do at College Park against the Buck Williams/Albert King Terps, who were ranked number three in the country.

Remember, a lot of our kids were from the Washington, D.C. area— Lowe and Whittenburg, plus Thurl Bailey and Kenny Matthews. And I knew they'd play well in front of all their home folks. There was no clock back then, so when we took a 10-point lead late and went to the passing game, there was no way Maryland could get the ball away from us. Our three guards up top were just too good a bunch of ball handlers.

Maryland's only chance was to foul, and sure enough, we started missing free throws. They cut our lead to eight, to six. Lowe got called for a travel. Sidney was in a double team, he stepped through it, held to make a pass—and they called him for walking. It looked bad, but it wasn't a walk. They called him for it anyway. Maryland scored to cut the margin to four points, then stole our inbounds pass to make it two. We had an easy dunk the next time down the floor, but instead of dunking it our man just went for the lay-up, and Buck Williams, out of nowhere, soared in and fouled our man. He made one free throw for a three-point State lead.

We exchanged baskets and it was still a three-pointer. Maryland ball, with about thirty-five seconds left. The game was a lock. We were going to upset the Terps and be on our way. In the huddle during the time-out I began to talk, when I remembered something Abe Lemons, the old Oklahoma City humorist/philosopher once said at a coaching clinic. He said never tell your team what *not* to do. Never, ever. Because that's exactly what they *will* do. Never suggest the negative, because that's what will happen. To illustrate this, Abe would tell a group at a clinic not to think about black cows. Then he'd say, "I bet every one of you has a picture of a black cow in your mind." And he was right.

I remembered what Abe said—but I didn't take his advice. "Don't foul," I said. "Don't foul don't foul don't for god sakes foul." I said other things like: We were going to play straight man defense; no easy shots; when their shot goes up, get to the board; traditional stuff like that. But my key strategy was . . . you guessed it . . . *don't foul.*

So, sure enough, after Maryland came downcourt and ran a simply horrible play, Albert King taking an off-balance jumper from way out of range, the ball hit the backboard and bounced off to the right where my man, Craig Watts, had tremendous position. But sure enough, here came Buck Williams again flying down the rim, skying his brains out to grab the ball away from Watts, come down, lift off right away gain and float in another soft shot. No problem, right?

Sorry. Does the "black cow" image ring a bell? I can still see it in slow motion: Buck with the ball. Buck rising. Watts jumping with him. Hah! As if that was possible. Watts chesting Buck. *Tweeeet!* And the foul was on State. To make a tragic story short, Williams converted the three-point play, the game went into overtime and we got drowned by seven points.

That was one of those games where there's no way we lose, and then somebody fouls the sonofabitch. Coaching death. It was also a game where afterward I looked at the schedule and saw Iona and maybe St. John's coming up at the Holiday Festival in Madison Square Garden, then all those road games in the ACC. I longed for the days when I padded—uh, made—my own schedules at Iona, and could be assured of some easy marks.

Going down his season schedule, a coach usually figures out the W's and L's before they happen to him. If I was trying to win 20 games and my team only played 27 . . . heck, I don't have a lot of leeway, do I? If we lost those games in the Garden, that would be four L's already. Then we've got six more road games to try for upsets in the ACC—beating anybody in the league at their place is an upset—which makes ten. That's 17–10, and I should be feeling good. Except 17–10 doesn't cut cheese at N.C. State. So where does that leave me? It left me realizing the difficulty of playing in our league, of playing in any league like ours where every conference game is a big game.

I should point out here that to a coach, every game is a Big Game, period. But to players, there are big games and there are Big Games. There are big games you have to win to get a championship or get to a tournament. Then there are Big Games because you're playing Big Names like Kentucky or Indiana. Here was an example: Iona at Madison

Square Garden was not that big a deal to the N.C. State players. *I* was going back to play against my former team and players and friends, but to the Wolfpack, the game was small change. Now I understood how those other teams felt playing us when I was at Iona: Nothing to gain, everything to lose.

Though the crowd was on my rear the entire time, we managed to hang on for dear life and beat Iona 61–58. The fans were so enamored of me, they booed during the introductions. And that was just the first night. During the finals against St. John's, they never let up. My father was at the game, and he couldn't understand why anybody would boo his son. He kept coming up behind the bench and saying: "Shove it up their . . . Jimmy. Give 'em what for." And I'd say: "Yeah, Pop. Thanks."

As if the Redmen of St. John's and my father weren't enough to occupy me, we went ahead by ten points late in the game and here came Frank Weedon, an assistant athletic director at State. Frank loves State and loves every sport at State, but he gets so nervous at games, it's hard to deal with. Since Frank's a statistical whiz and keeps all the numbers, he's the kind of guy who would come up to me after a game and let me know that, hey, the Pack didn't score from 7:32 left in the game until 2:15 left, and did I know that and what was wrong and where do we fix that and what about it?

On this night against St. John's—God love him—there was Frank right next to our bench. I could hear him as we went into the passing game: "Remember Maryland. Remember Maryland."

So here I am fighting for my life with my team in the finals of the Holiday Festival. On one side, I've got Rocco Valvano screaming, "Shove it up their . . . ," and on the other side Frank Weedon's chanting, "Just like Maryland." I felt like shouting at everybody to just *shut up*. Luckily, Lowe made about six free throws in a row down the stretch and we won by nine points.

The next morning, the *New York Daily News* had a picture of me cutting down the nets at the Garden. What I recall best, though, was me draping the nets around Weedon's head and handing him the trophy. "Remember Maryland," I told Frank. "I think we did it," I told my father.

My god. I had gone through the Polish fiasco, the Wake Forest pounding, we had come back to upset Duke, there'd been the Maryland disaster and the incredible emotional wringer in New York and the season wasn't to the halfway mark yet! That's when I think I learned about coaching—essentially, the numbers in coaching.

As I discovered all too quickly, the ACC was a great conference to be in, but you had to pace yourself. There seemed to be all sorts of numerical ways to lose your coaching job on the court, forget about off the court, and it wasn't just the overall record I was talking about.

First, a coach had better be winning 20 overall because that's the standard. Once you win 20, people say, well, everyone wins 20 in this conference. What's he done in his team's *conference games,* where it's not so easy to maintain a winning record, not to mention a good one? For example, it's difficult to go above 7–7 in the regular season. Then, once you rise above that, maybe once in five years you can get to 9–5 or something. Now, they'll say, sure, but what's his record in the ACC tournament? That's the third record they measure you by. And you find out soon that it's not easy to win a game in that baby either; for example, Terry Holland's ACC tournament record: 14–16. Lefty Driesell's is 17–16; mine is 9–8. It's hard to stay at .500. And it's even more difficult to win the thing outright. For instance, the great Maryland coach, Lefty Driesell, only won one in seventeen years. Now, how's the coach's record in NCAA play? Oh, he lost first round? Can't even get into the regionals? What a stupid shnook! Then if you're as good as Dean Smith, it'll be: Oh, seven times in the Final Four? Great, but how many national championships? Or like Mike Krzyzewski: Oh, four out of five Final Fours? Any championships? And that's not all. When you finally think you're through being measured by different records, everybody wants to know how you did against Deano and the Tar Heels. There is even a guy in North Carolina named Barry Jacobs who puts out an ACC yearbook every year. He'll tell you that your record on every other Valentine's Day, when it occurs on Wednesday in years divisible by three, is 2–5. That's if it's not snowing. And if the kids got all the Valentines they hoped for. Unbelievable, the numbers you've got to deal with in the ACC!

So, that first year we were 13–12 with one game left. We wound up 14–13. Paying attention? Hah! You forgot the ACC tournament. I wish I could have. After we ended the regular season, beating Wake Forest 66–65 in my famous "mathematically impossible" game, we lost our first game in the tournament—to North Carolina. That was three defeats to the Tar Heels (who three weeks later would finish national runners-up to Indiana) by three, by three, and by, uh, fifteen. Zero and three to the Deano Derby numbers. By tournament time I was totally drained, tapped out. If a coach doesn't pace himself, the ACC will rip him apart every time.

I mentioned the Wake game. I had a classic coaching line in that one. We had somehow gone ahead by 22 points with only six or seven minutes left; the score was something like 55–33, so I was confident. "Fellas," I told the team, "as long as we continue to play offensively, if we can score 10 points the rest of the way and get to 65, they'll have to get 33 in that time just to tie us. Mathematically, the game is over . . . as soon as we score 10 more." Of course, no sooner had I said that than Wake Forest went absolutely berserk, we broke down and the lead was cut to one as we gasped for breath.

Wake had the ball and held for the last shot, but Alvis Rogers missed as my guts multiplied and divided themselves somewhere in the pit of my stomach. I was right, they didn't quite catch us. But mathematically, I knew better than to ever say that again.

The Carolina losses in the regular season were two more examples of prime gut-wrenchers. I talk about Big Games. Holy God, we went into Chapel Hill and this seemed Bigger than a Big Game. Played our hearts out, too. Came down to the end, we were one point down, they had the ball and their guy knocked Kenny Matthews right on his ass! This was in the final seconds, and if it had been called a charge, then Kenny, a helluva free-throw shooter, would have had two from the line and we would have gotten out of there with a win on my very first visit. But, surprise! They called it a block. And they got the two free throws.

In the rematch, we were down by one point again with twelve seconds left. Carolina had the ball, but our Scott Parzych stripped the ball from Sam Perkins. Parzych hit Lowe in the middle of the floor, who passed to Matthews for the shot that would have won the game. Kenny didn't drive, though. He stopped and shot. *Kaaaang!* They got the rebound, we fouled and they won by three again.

At times the press can be so difficult, and this was one of those times. All the writers wanted to know why Matthews took the last shot. I knew he had had an awful game. I knew he had been in a slump.

"Uh, you guys have a problem with Matthews on that shot?" I said.

"He was four-for-seventeen up to then," they said.

"Four-for-seventeen?" I said. "Well, you know, I better go ask him about that." And I did. "Kenny, about the last shot. Didn't you know you had missed a bunch in a row? Why did you take that shot?" I said.

"I was due, coach," Matthews said. "I was due."

The fan mail that came after we lost to Carolina for the second time was incredible. One letter-writer obviously had been following my career. "Coach V, you don't seem to get the hang of this thing down here," he wrote. "First, you fly to the wrong state. Okay, we can tolerate that. But then you lose to those blue bellies in Chapel Hill and you come back to Raleigh and lose to them again. That's twice in the same season by a few points. We can't tolerate that. I'm telling you I know where you live and I'm coming to Raleigh to shoot your dog."

My God, what a letter! Now this wasn't on sanitarium stationery or anything. I don't think this was a crazy guy. There was a business address, a picture in the corner, references listed on the back. It was then

VALVANO

I realized that they really took this rivalry seriously down here. So I wrote back and told my pen pal that I didn't like to lose to Carolina either and I didn't plan on doing it too long, but that we didn't need fans like him; we needed people to support us, win or lose, and maybe he should root for somebody else. Then I wrote, "P.S. I hate to spoil your day, but the Valvano family doesn't even have a dog."

Two weeks later a UPS truck drove up to our house and the driver delivered a package to our front door. Inside was the cutest little pooch. He had a note around his neck. It said: "Coach, don't get too attached."

Chapter Ten

SEVEN AND SEVEN, GO TO HEAVEN . . . BUT DON'T GO TO THE CORNER

MOVING RIGHT ALONG . . .

I firmly believe stories like that helped to diffuse some of the bitterness in the rivalry between the sister schools in my newly adopted state. Over the next two seasons, as the record books show, North Carolina and North Carolina State took personal possession of the national championship, back-to-back, and I continued to get valuable mileage out of tales about the rivalry.

I respected Dean Smith so much that I didn't go for barbs, just benign yuks. I used to mention Dean's luck, for instance. When we both were recruiting a tall center prospect from Texas named John Brownlee, the kid flew in to visit Chapel Hill first, then came over to Raleigh and our campus. "How have you liked it here in the state, John?" I asked Brownlee. Fine. "What brought you to consider these schools?" Well, when his father went to the University of Kansas he had a roommate named Dean Smith. "Oh, really?" I said. "Excuse me just a minute." I stepped outside, grabbed both my assistants and went crazy. How do you like this? Dean doesn't have enough players; oh no. Now his college roommate winds up having a 6'10" son! The next day I called Bob Lloyd, my old roomie from Rutgers. "How you doin', Rooms? Uh, about that boy of yours. What's he up to these days? Oh? Great. Hairdressers' school? You must be very proud."

The best one was the time I went into the barbershop, Sam and Bill's place, in Raleigh. The guy sitting in the next chair recognized me.

"You're the coach at State, aren't you?" he said. "Boy, what a tough job. I don't envy you at all."

"Well, I really like it. I think we're going to have some really good teams," I said.

"Yeah, but having to beat Dean . . . that's not so easy. I want you to know I'm a Carolina fan and Dean Smith is one great coach. He's put out some great teams."

"You can say that again," I said, "but we've had some pretty fair teams over here too. Norm Sloan did a great job. Norm won a national championship one year. And what about the year before that? The Pack went undefeated, 27–0."

"Yeah, that was a heckuva season," the guy said. "But just think what Dean could have done with that team."

Is it any wonder that, by the time my second season at N.C. State began, I had a new philosophy, Seven-seven and Go to Heaven? Looking back over the history of the conference, I figured out that since the NCAA expanded the tournament to sixty-four teams, allowing more than one representative from a conference, every ACC team that had split its games 7–7 in ACC competition automatically made it to Heaven—the NCAA tournament.

So, rather than peak for the opener against Belgrade Red Star, our goal would be to win 7 in-league games and 20 overall. Our next goal would be to win the conference championship. Who is the conference champion? Not the winner of the regular season. No, it's the winner of the ACC tournament. So our goal was to win 20, win the ACC tournament, and then win the NCAA tournament. Survive and Advance became the code.

Except for my very last season, the 1981–82 season probably was the toughest year of all for me as a coach. It was the last year college basketball went without a clock, remember, so everybody held the ball. I mean, everybody. If you didn't think you were as good as the other guy, you held it. If he didn't think he was as good as you, *he* held it. The fourth game of the season: N.C. State 44, St. Peter's 33.

St. Peter's? The tenth game of the season, finals of the Rainbow Classic in Honolulu: Rice 51, N.C. State 47. *Rice?* The ACC got blamed for this mess when Carolina and Virginia, numbers one and two in America, played that showdown championship game in the ACC tournament. But the style was prevalent all over America.

The thing that made me so mad in Hawaii was that by beating Rice, we could have been 10–0 coming out of Christmas break, as well as the talk of college basketball. I was running hard with the program, trying to live up to its past, bringing it back, the whole shebang. We had opened the ACC season by blowing Maryland out, after which the team threw me into the shower. It had to be the earliest a coach had been heaved into the shower on record. We had also just soundly beaten two fine teams in the

Rainbow, Michigan State and Wichita State. The Spartans had future pros Kevin Willis and Sam Vincent. Wichita State, with Antoine Carr and Cliff Levingston, was ranked third in the country at the time, but we pounded them, too.

There was a Japanese contingent in Hawaii looking for some teams to come play in Tokyo the next year. They were offering a super guarantee: tours, meals, gifts, all kinds of treats. So, figuring how I could improve my chances of being invited, I went up and introduced myself as Dean Smith of North Carolina. Needless to say, it didn't work.

Prior to the championship game, the highlight of the tournament was one of the greatest coaching moves I have ever seen. It was made in the first round by Dick Versace, then the coach at Bradley.

Bradley was leading favored San Francisco by a bunch with time running; but then on consecutive trips down the court, Versace's team was called for traveling, a three-second violation, an offensive foul, the works. Versace was fit to be tied, and so was the game.

Then, in the final seconds, a Bradley player got absolutely mugged— just like he was on the New York subway. There was no call, and the final buzzer sounded: overtime. Except here came Versace, enraged. He went positively bananas at midcourt. Tweet! One technical. Tweet! Two techs. Tweet! Three. Now Versace reared back and just as he was about to punch the ref, he thought better of it, grabbed the guy's whistle and threw it high up in the stands! Right, so now the guy couldn't blow it any more. But it was too late. The ref gave him a couple more techs, and San Francisco had about twelve free throws to shoot. The Dons had to go oh-for-twelve for Bradley to get into overtime. Never happened.

Afterward, the press asked me what I thought about that referee. Would I mind having him? "Why not? He can't hurt me. He ain't got a damn whistle."

Scouting San Francisco playing Rice, I knew as a coach the Dons had the far superior talent. But I'd rather play them than Rice, any day; just as, when the NCAA tournament pairings are announced each season, every coach in America gets down on his knees and prays to the basketball gods that they don't draw Princeton. It's true; nobody wants to play against that deliberate style of Pete Carril's. We don't want to play Princeton. Or a team with a dash in its name. Or what we used to call a directional school. We want to play *whole* states, like Iowa or Iowa State. But not Northeast Iowa. Like Missouri, but not Southwest Missouri. Like Alabama, but not Alabama-Birmingham.

San Francisco had so much talent out there, they didn't have enough basketballs for it all. But that's the squad I wanted to play. Not Rice, whose coach, Tommy Suitts, was in his first year and just happy to be there. At the pretournament dinner, Suitts had gotten up and said exactly that. And he really meant it. He really was just happy to be there. He also introduced his wife, the children, his athletic director and his . . . mom! He was playing in Hawaii, and he knew what he was supposed to do. He was *supposed* to lose—but he didn't.

The game between two teams of such starkly different styles was no fun at all. Rice ran what is affectionately known in the trade as "the flex," which simply meant "we ain't going to shoot it." So they went side to side, side to side before a kid named Ricky Pierce got a good shot. Pierce—you may have heard of him after he moved from Rice, ultimately to the Milwaukee Bucks; he's just about the best sixth man in the NBA since John Havlicek played for the Celtics—got enough good ones to score 23 points.

So we were 9–1, and nobody could console me. Know the difference between 10–0 and 9–1 at the end of December? Only this. Hardly anybody's 10–0 and there are about *thirty f-----g thousand teams who are nine-and-one!*

That was my mood on the long plane ride back to Raleigh. We had a wonderful group of Wolfpack Club members with us, boosters who supported us win or lose, and it was New Year's Eve, a day before my wife's birthday. I think that our crossing one of those time lines meant she had her birthday twice or something. Whatever the case, I just wanted to be left alone.

To a coach, winning is not so much exultation as it is relief. You're happy if you win a particular game or even a conference championship, but most of all you're relieved. The only ultimate exultation is winning that last game, that national championship. Now I was looking ahead at the schedule, and I saw Clemson, Southern Mississippi, and Georgia Tech. In those days, a coach called up Georgia Tech to make sure they knew what time the game was. You sent the bus for them, if necessary. If they didn't want to play at your place, you got in a cab and paid full fare to go play at their place. Anything to get on the court with Georgia Tech and get the easy W. Of course, Bobby Cremins has changed all that.

So, my God, we would have been looking at 13–0 if we had beaten Rice. Thirteen-and-oh, playing North Carolina at home. I mean, isn't that exactly what I had given up Iona for? I don't recall what our ranking was, but the Tar Heels were right around number one and two all season, and we had a great shot at them. Even if we were only 12–1.

The game was close all the way to about the eight-minute mark. Then they got a two-point lead, spread the court, went into the four corners and held the ball. I'll never forget it. Some guy by the name of Jordan, I think his first name was Mitch or Mickey, went back-door a couple of times, and before I knew it we were chasing them all over the court, the lead was up to 10 points and for all practical purposes, the game was over. We wound up losing 61–41.

It was an aberrational score for that season. Before that, we beat Southern Miss 46–45, and Georgia Tech 55–49. Afterwards, we beat Wake Forest 52–50, and lost to Duke 49–48. You thought I was kidding! Every night was Ulcersville. Every game was pulse-pounding. I'd never seen anything like it. After the Duke game, Willis Casey called me into his office for the first Coach-to-AD talk I'd received from an athletic director. We had gone into Duke and run up a 12-point lead on what was a very bad team. Mike Krzyzewski had the Blue Devils packed back in a zone defense, that's how bad Duke was. And yet we wound up losing. Casey wanted to know why I didn't bring them out of the zone when we had the lead. He thought we should have won the game. He thought it would be a good idea to win that kind of game.

I agreed that it would be a good idea. But the next time we played North Carolina, we never had a chance for the lead. Though the score was closer (58–44), there wasn't much tension in the air; it was as if the Tar Heels were just putting in another work night. James Worthy. Sam Perkins. Michael—yeah, I remember now—Michael Jordan. You could see that really was a special team.

Finally, we got our shot at Virginia. Our place, February 10, our time. The Cavs were number two, but we had a way to stop Ralph Sampson and beat them. My philosophy always was to stop the other team's best player. Let the secondary guys beat you. If they had two great players, try to stop them both. Box and one. Triangle and two. Doubling down all over. If you had three greats, there was nothing we could do.

Our defense on Sampson was a 7'5" center, Chuck Nevitt. Everybody else was helping out. We wanted full coverage on Ralph; we wanted to Velcro him. I didn't want to make it too technical, so I told our guys we wanted a guy on the ball, two guys on the wing, a guy in front of Ralph, and Nevitt behind him. "Don't go to the corner," I told everybody. "Let their outside guys beat us from there if they can. I want Sampson doubled at all times. Velcroed. Don't go to the corner." We also knew that if the game was close, nobody would want to take that shot from the corner.

Now, this was the opposite of what we did most of the time. It was usually the wings guys' jobs to go to the corner and contest the ball when it went there. So this was a departure. In fact, it was *so* different that Scott Parzych *refused* to stay away from the corner.

In the locker room before the game, I acknowledged that Parzych had been attacking the ball in the corner all season. But I told him that, for this game tonight, our plan had changed.

Didn't matter: Parzych kept going to the corner. At least, what the rest of the team was doing was working. The final score was going to be in the thirties, which was our plan. But by halftime, we still had to keep reiterating to Parzych not to go to the corner. Every possession was tense, every pass meaningful. It was one of those nights. Then Scotty went cornersward one more time, they dumped it inside and Sampson scored. I went nuts. They did it twice, a third time. A foul was called. I roared up the sideline and called Parzych over.

"What in the hell are you doing?" I screamed. *"I told you, don't go to the damn corner!"* My veins were popping, I was so hot. *"Do you understand? Don't go to the corner!"*

But Parzych was equally emotional. *"Coach,"* he bellowed, *"I* have *to go to the corner! I* have *to go!"*

Can you believe it? People wonder why coaches end up on loony farms. I walked back to the bench like a whipped puppy. Marty Fletcher, my assistant, said, "Coach, what did Scott say?"

"He said he *has* to go to the corner," I said.

"Well, what did you say?" Fletcher asked.

"What else? I said go ahead and go."

I often wonder what the players who aren't playing in the game must have thought of their coach, when they look back on these things. Everybody thinks the benchwarmers are sitting there on the edge of their seats all tense and caught up in the excitement. Sometimes that's true, but other times I think three guys are checking the house for girls and the other three are playing Password. They're not even in the game, and yet they're the ones we all scream at. "See that? See that? Parzych won't stay out of the corner. Goddammit, you guys! *You see that? You guys better stay out of the corner!"* Then they see Parzych yelling at me. I can just imagine the conversation on the bench:

Scotty told V he's got to go to the corner. What did V say?

He said go ahead and go.

Despite Parzych going to the corner, the game was a war the whole night long. We'd be up a point and hold it, then score to make the lead three points. They'd come down, pass it around and score to cut it back to one. 3–1, 3–1, that's how it would rotate, until finally we had possession with less than thirty seconds left. We ran the passing game well with our quick little guards; the one weakness Virginia had was a lack of quickness. So you know what I was going to do: I was going to hold it. And you know what Terry Holland was going to do: The Virginia coach was going to signal his team to foul. In fact, he was standing up waving the foul signal. Everybody in the place—and all the ships at sea—knew that Virginia was going to foul. Everybody in the world but one guy: the referee.

I mean, Whittenburg was at halfcourt just bracing himself for the foul. And sure enough, here came Jeff Jones running at him for one reason and one reason only: to foul and stop the clock. Jones tackled him, he mugged him. A Virginia gentleman like that! A future Virginia coach, in fact; Jeff took over for Holland this past season. It was unbelievable! What Jones did to Whittenburg would have been a crime in at least three states. Imagine, Virginia fouling deliberately like that! Why, Whit was almost embarrassed to go to the line and shoot the clinching free throws.

He never got the chance. The referee blew his whistle and called . . . a jump ball. *Jump ball!* The alternate possession was not yet in effect then, so there really would be a jump. But I didn't care. I was out on the floor; way out there. I should have been kicked out of the game, I was so far out. It was one of those times when you suddenly realize something's awry, you look down and you're the only one around without short pants on. You know you're in serious trouble. It's also one of those times when the referee comes over and is about to hit you with a technical foul until you say: "Hold it. I'm not going to say anything. I'm not going to say one bad thing. Not anything bad. But it's okay if I'm thinking something, right? It's all right if I'm thinking something bad?" The ref says, "Sure, you can think whatever you want. I don't care what you think."

"Good. I think *you suck!*"

That didn't happen on this occasion, but it would have. I was out there on the floor, though, spread-eagled, laid out. I couldn't believe it. On the jump ball, Whittenburg was so enraged that he back-tapped the ball. He slammed that sucker so hard, it flew over our two back guys' heads, and Virginia got an easy lay-up. The Cavaliers got another couple of free throws in the dying seconds and won 39–36.

Whoa boy! This was one of those postgame times that you did not want to get anywhere near Mama Valvano's thoroughly enraged little boy. My wife and daughters would tell you: Everybody thinks I'm so great after a loss, but they don't see me behind closed doors. Even in the locker room afterward I was pretty good at keeping my composure.

"How about the call?" the press might ask.

"Oh, well, yeah. We might have a little difference of opinion on that one," I might say. "Jeff Jones says he didn't touch him? Well, I thought he might have caught him just a touch, you know? But who knows. Heh-heh. All in the game. Better luck next time."

But after the last media person had left the sanctuary of the locker room, I closed the door and became a stark . . . raving . . . mad . . . *lunatic.*

After a game like that, Pam and the girls knew better than to speak to me at home. They would open the front door for me and make no eye contact at all. It's like walking the sidewalks in New York. Rule number one in the Valvano household after such a defeat: No eye contact. That night I went right from the front door to my office at home. And started throwing things all over my office. I wrecked the room that night, totally totaled it. I would have turned my desk over but it was too heavy.

Heh-heh, boys. All in the game.

We won a rematch with Duke and lost a rematch with Virginia. One of our very Big Games was at Notre Dame. I should say that was one of those Big Names, not Big Games, because Digger Phelps was having his problems during that time. Still, it was Notre Dame, and I felt I had to shake the team up a little. We needed to relax more for the stretch run. We needed a laugh. Fortunately, I soon found an opportunity. We had a walk-on kid named Quinton Leonard, a transfer from a junior college in Louisburg, North Carolina. The night before the game in South Bend, we practiced before heading back to the hotel. When we got back, Quinton was asleep on the bus. You guessed it, we didn't wake him up. We all just filed out quietly and left him there. Fact is, we even told the bus driver to drive down the street further away from the hotel and park. Which he did, so that when Quinton woke up he had no idea where he was.

And people think coaches aren't solid, mature citizens? Hey, anything to loosen us up. It must have worked. The next day we beat Notre Dame by twenty.

Postseason, our goal in the ACC tournament was to get past the first round. The previous year when we lost out of the gate, I saw how unhappy all the State fans who had come to the party were. The ACC's are such a big social event that if you lose your first game, it spoils the festivities for everybody. They act like, "What have you done to us?"

Fortunately we drew Maryland—a team we beat twice in the regular season—in the first game. Then it looked like we would play North Carolina again. But even if we lost to the Tar Heels, we would wind up with 22 wins and an easy invitation to the NCAA tournament. That would give us nine defeats for the season, three of them to the number one team in the land. Which is exactly what happened.

Still, I must mention the real landmark of that tournament: our 40–28 victory over the Terps. Maybe the worst game ever played in the ACC. Maybe the worst postseason game in *history*. The only game in all the years of that tournament to my knowledge where both teams were booed throughout. We were bad enough; Maryland was worse. After a while even Lefty Driesell couldn't stand it anymore. He kicked a chair, booted it a good several yards. In fact, Lefty had to pay for the breakage, and that chair sits today in the office of the manager of the Radisson Hotel in Raleigh.

Seven and Seven, Go to Heaven . . .

They say the Carolina-Virginia ACC final, two days later, brought the shot clock to college basketball. But our game put everybody in the mood for that final. So who's the unsung hero of the clock after all? Thankyouverymuch.

My first opponent as the N.C. State coach in the NCAA tournament violated all my principles of whom to avoid in such circumstances. We didn't play Tennessee. We didn't play an entire state. Oh, no. We played a team with a dash. Tennessee Dash Chattanooga; the Moccasins. And they beat us 58-51.

But what I learned from that game directly affected the next year and became a huge factor in how we scheduled, prepared and advanced through the tournament to win the championship. That loss convinced me that the NCAA's were so humongous that the first-round games were both the least exciting and most dangerous of all. The atmosphere, for one thing, can be just stultifying; not even close to that of an ACC tournament or even any regular-season game in our conference.

I say this because all season you're used to playing with bands and cheerleaders and tremendous crowd noise, and then you get somebody like Tennessee Dash Chattanooga . . . at Indianapolis . . . maybe on a Thursday . . . and maybe with an 11:40 A.M. starting time! I mean, in the locker room there was no excitement, no anticipation, no readiness at all. There may have been eight or ten thousand people out in the arena sitting on their hands, and we didn't recognize anybody. Even the media aren't into these first-round games, they're supposed to be such routs. You look over at the press tables or up into the stands and you don't recognize a soul! The real advantage goes to the team that's not in the tournament every year, and doesn't care what the environment is; to whom merely playing in the NCAA tournament is the ultimate.

Of course, it should have been that way for us. When I was at Iona, we could have played the thing in an alley and we would have been psyched. But I guess, having just played all season in that dynamic ACC atmosphere, it just wasn't the same. It's the same reason the Princetons and Murray States and Sienas and Cleveland States (not a dash in there anywhere) are such threats in the tournament. Don't get me wrong— these are good teams. It's just that they tend to be more ready than the so-called big-name schools.

It's the coach's responsibility to get his team ready for just such a letdown, but I wasn't ready for it. The players were flat, and we fell behind the Moccasins by 20 points just like that. We couldn't even bring the ball in bounds. We turned the ball over twice by stepping across the line trying to in-bounds the pass. We did that a couple of times. The second half we made a great comeback, but it was too late.

What formulated in my mind, however, was that next season I had to teach the team how to play in a big game in a neutral environment. That was something I had to get done. For 1982–83, we strengthened our schedule with games against Louisville and Missouri on their home courts, but the game that may have been the key was, strangely enough, West Virginia at the New Jersey Meadowlands. Big name, neutral court, and we played it three days after Christmas. Little did we know how much it would prepare us for another Christmas-style celebration three months later in Albuquerque, New Mexico.

Chapter Eleven

SURVIVE AND ADVANCE

T HE REASON I WAS SO CONFIDENT GOING INTO THE SEASON OF 1982–83 HAD nothing to do with how good I thought our team might be on the court, but it had everything to do with what had happened off it. I loved our personnel; I figured Lowe and Whittenburg would be one of the best guard combinations in the country. We also had a little mad bomber in Terry Gannon and a very talented freshman scorer in Ernie Myers. That backcourt would be simply terrific. Up front, Thurl Bailey was just coming into his own as a senior; he was a late developer who would go on to have an illustrious career at Utah in the NBA. This was our nucleus of veterans. But we also had in two younger players, "Co and Lo" (Cozell McQueen and Lorenzo Charles), something we really had been missing in the past two years: a center who could neutralize the middle and a crunching power forward to muscle the boards.

The ACC was going to be a briarpatch of a league. Carolina was the defending national champion; Virginia had Ralph Sampson back for his senior year. Wake Forest was coming off two 20-victory seasons and would also be very tough. The fact that we survived this deathtrap and came out on top probably was a result of our coaches' meetings in Myrtle Beach, South Carolina. That previous spring, we voted to recommend to our athletic directors that the ACC institute the three-point shot and the 30-second clock. This came about after some long and, shall we say, vociferous infighting among those present.

The year before, remember, the college game had become ultimately boring. The games were slow and low-scoring, and then there was the Carolina-Virginia fiasco which set the whole country howling. I felt that the clock and the three-pointer would be good for the game, but by the

113

same token I had a team that was not suited for an up-tempo contest. In addition, we were one of the biggest culprits in stall ball. I had to do what was best for my ball club. I had a hard time explaining my contradictory thoughts on the subject. I did know this: If I went through another year of coaching like the last one, I would blow my brains out.

Ours had become a game of coaches, not players. We had taken a beautiful, action-packed thing and made it into a chess match. It took about as long as a game of chess, and about as many points were scored. It was ridiculous and horrible. The players all wanted to play, not hang back. The fans wanted it; everybody wanted it.

Yet we had huge battles about the proposed rules changes in our meetings. Terry Holland of Virginia didn't care either way, but if there was to be a clock, he wanted it as short as possible and kept on for the whole game. Mike Krzyzewski at Duke wanted to leave the game the way it was, except that he would go for the three-point shot if he had to opt for one rule. Bobby Cremins at Georgia Tech didn't want to change, either. His team was pretty bad, and he figured he couldn't be competitive with the new rules. Carl Tacy at Wake wanted the three-point line back further, and Dean Smith wanted a closer shot, one that would be part of the offense at all times. Lefty Driesell and Dean went at each other pretty hard over the distance. As for the clock, Mike wanted something longer than 30 seconds. Most of us wanted it shorter. I knew our offense was going to change. With a three-guard set, we were going to run and gun. I wanted the clock at about 12 seconds. I wanted the rule to be that after two passes you had to shoot.

The meetings were so long and involved, we had to meet again at Duke later in the summer, where they measured out different shot lines on the court for us with masking tape. Picture this: a bunch of middle-aged men in their coats and ties out on the floor taking J's from all over, doing something that would change college basketball forever. Most of us couldn't shoot, anyway.

Twelve other conferences would legislate new rules over the summer; we were the catalyst for the whole country. And we wanted to make a bold statement—even though we'd have to adjust back to the old rules during the NCAA tournament, and we knew that might hurt our teams. We ended up with the shortest clock and the shortest distance. The game in the ACC was the most fun in all of college. And a blast for North Carolina State.

The changes helped us win the national championship, to be precise.

I kept thinking about how the '82–'83 Wolfpack could combine the best of our first two years in Raleigh. My first season we ran well, but we didn't have a good halfcourt offense. The second year we played excellent defense; we ranked second in points allowed and fourth in defensive field-goal percentage in the nation. But we didn't run at all. That's when I first put together my plan for two different styles of ball on the same team. With a three-guard lineup, we could press and run. I also had the personnel for a power lineup that could be deliberate and pound it inside.

Our formula for making it to the NCAA tournament was a bit skewed this year. In ACC play, it was no longer 7–7, get to heaven; it was 9–5, stay alive. We told the kids, given the ability of Carolina and Virginia, that we needed a 9–5 in the league to get third place and a guaranteed bid. We had seven nonconference home games that were a must to win. We had six huge contests of national importance: Michigan State, Louisville, West Virginia, Missouri, Notre Dame and Memphis State. We ended up winning two of them. So much for tough scheduling.

The first big game for us was Michigan State at home. I knew the Spartans would spread the court and slow the tempo. Our new rules only applied to league games, unless the opponent agreed to them. Jud Heathcote, the Michigan State coach, didn't. So it was a game like the year before, and they had three future pros, Sam Vincent, Kevin Willis and Scott Skiles, playing it.

It turned out to be a heck of a game with a great ending. We were ahead by two points with 17 seconds left, when Michigan State called time-out with the ball. Vincent had been killing us all night, so we decided to go with a 1–3 zone and a chaser. But who would chase Sam?

We had a guy named Harold Thompson who had earned his scholarship every year by winning a game for us defensively. He was the obvious choice, but Harold had only played a few seconds in the game. What happened if they shot early, missed, then fouled Harold? What if he missed and they got another chance? What if? What if? Our entire defense would be based on Harold's ability to stop Vincent. This was risky, which is what bench coaching is all about. If it works, you're smart. If it doesn't, you're a bum.

What happened? Harold stole the in-bounds pass, Thurl hit a couple of foul shots, we won 45–41 and I avoided being a bum for another day. Although every decision I made that season didn't turn out right, this win foreshadowed a stretch late in the year when it seemed everything I did turned to gold.

We were 4–0 then, but I still didn't know how good we were. It took our reaching 4–1 before I realized that we were *very* good. Some defeats are like that: You come away feeling down, but knowing there's hope. For us the true test came at Louisville, a team which had been in the Final Four the previous year—and to whom we lost by five.

Christmas came between Louisville and our trip to the Meadowlands to play West Virginia. West Virginia had won 27 games the year before, including its first-round game in the NCAA's. Remember, this was the game I deliberately scheduled to get a tough opponent in a neutral environment. Being from the Eastern Athletic Association, West Virginia played with a 40-second clock and a three-point shot from the top of the key, as opposed to our 30 seconds and 17'9" three-pointer. So we compromised and played the game using their shot and a 35-second clock.

What this game did was to solidify our feeling that we would be helped by the new rules. We won, 67–59.

At this point, we played a series of games under both the new and old rules: winning against Clemson 76–70 under the new; losing to Missouri under the old; and losing to Sampson and the Cavs 88–80 in a heartbreaking game in which Dereck Whittenburg broke his foot.

Starting with Georgia Tech in Raleigh (whom we blew away) and ending with Duke in Durham (whom we also blew away), there was a 14-game stretch which I have always referred to as our season-within-a-season. Obviously, we had to start all over. What style do we play? What kind of defense? What's the rotation on substitutions? We thought Whittenburg was gone for the season, when in actuality he did return after those 14 games. But it was a different team he returned to, a better team, a team that had found itself, a team that would go on to win the national championship. And that season-within-a-season was the foundation.

I still think it's the best coaching job our staff ever did. We started out 2–4, then won seven of our next eight games. Had it not been for a one-point loss to Notre Dame, we'd have nailed all eight. And the unsung hero was Ernie Myers.

Ernie started off by scoring 27 points against Georgia Tech. That was great. But the education of our new team started in a beating by North Carolina. Before the game, I showed Ernie the backdoor play Carolina likes to run. I told the staff he'd get beat the first time they tried it, and sure enough, Michael Jordan whipped by him right away. Ernie looked over at me on the bench and just shook his head.

That was all right. Even the 18-point licking was all right. What I couldn't stand was that for the first time, I felt the team didn't believe me. They didn't believe we could get the job done without Whitt. I ripped into them in the locker room. "If you guys don't believe, if any of you can't have the same dream I do, then get the hell out of here because I don't want you around. If it's three or five or whatever, we'll go on without you. We lost a player, but that's over with. I didn't promise it would be easy. It's a long, hard struggle. But we will get this thing done with or without you."

After that, we had some incredibly tough games. Wake Forest blew us away by 18; then we had two nationally televised games against Memphis

Here I am, aged 3, with my brother Nick, getting ready for our beloved Yankees.

Jim of all trades, master of none—Seaford High School.

My biggest thrill—playing at the Garden. Looks like
an air ball to me.

Here's the real coach in the family—my dad.

The world's best mom with me and my brother, Bob.

The Rat was getting more ink than I was—but then again, he's better looking. Chris Sheridan

Happy times with two of Iona's best—Glenn Vickers and Jeff Ruland.

The dunk heard 'round the world: N.C. State beats Houston. Simon C. Griffiths

I finally found a hug after the Championship game.
Andy Hayt/Sports Illustrated

The happiest day of my professional life.
Copyright © 1983, E. J. Attayek

Here I am with Al McGuire, after another win in Reynolds.
Simon C. Griffiths

My reaction during our '87 ACC Championship— a special win over the Tar Heels. Simon C. Griffiths

Making history with the last shot in Carmichael. Simon C. Griffiths

My last game in Reynolds. Simon C. Griffiths

At least one of us has
aged beautifully.

Believe me, girls are harder
to raise than boys.

Talkin' b-ball with hoop junkie John Saunders on ESPN.
Copyright © 1990 Rick LaBranche Images

The veteran and the rookie on ABC.
Copyright © 1990 Capital Cities/ABC Inc.

State (57–53) and Notre Dame (43–42). We lost both games down the stretch—games in which I felt we played not to lose, instead of playing to win.

Incidentally, I feel that "playing not to lose" has resulted in our poor performance in international competition. Since the 30-second clock and the three-point shot have been standard for international teams, they can take full advantage of this. Since most U.S. coaches grew up without the clock or the shot, our coaching tends to be conservative and we lose in international games. However, I think American basketball is evolving and we are learning how to play in a style more similar to other countries'.

Back then, there was no clock and no three-point shot. But right after the Memphis and Notre Dame games, I decided that from now on, we would play to win.

So, after the Memphis game, here I was 8–6, my best player had a broken foot, and Carolina had beaten us seven times in a row, when I got a call from Willis Casey. Many thoughts went through my mind on the way to his office. I was pleasantly surprised when Willis informed me that, not only was he pleased with my performance, but he wanted to discuss a long-term contract. Dean Smith had recently signed a 10-year contract at Chapel Hill, and Willis felt that the basketball coach at State should have the same. Considering that Dean had won a national championship, an Olympic gold medal, and was one of the winningest coaches in the history of the game—my being 8–6, I thought it was a fair offer. I always felt that Willis' confidence in me was one of the things that enabled me to coach the team to a national championship.

We went on to a 14–8 record. Coming into the season, there was a lot of talk about our losing six straight to Carolina, but I felt we had played a great team every time. I mean, they were national runners-up and national champions in two consecutive years, so we weren't exactly alone when it came to getting beat by the Tar Heels. When we had played them a month earlier and lost by three touchdowns, it was exactly a week after Dereck went down and they moved to number one in the country. For the rematch they had dropped down to number three. They still had Jordan, Perkins and the boys. We still were without Whittenburg. And I don't suppose our 14–8 record struck too much fear into the visitors, either.

Among other things, coaches are basically schizophrenic. We are pessimistic to the press and among fellow coaches, but to our teams, we are the eternal optimists. This was true for the Carolina game, as well. The closer we got to this one, I talked publicly about how great the Heels were and how many things could go wrong for us. It was all negative. In the locker room, however, I was extremely positive to the team, telling

117

them how well we'd prepared and practiced. "We're ready, gentlemen," I said. "There is no way you can lose this one tonight." Then, after they'd left, I turned to my staff and said: "No shot. Geez, these poor kids could get absolutely killed."

However, this time we played a strong game from start to finish. Two technical fouls on Carolina in the first half may have been the key. Gannon hit four free throws, and we led at the half, 37–36. We built the lead to seven points late in the game before our foul shooting went south. Then, we missed three straight one-and-ones and I started panicking on the bench. "Can't anyone make a damn free throw?" I screamed.

"I can," said a voice from down the bench. It was none other than Cozell McQueen, who was not famous for his pinpoint foul shooting. What the heck, I thought, nobody else could make them. Immediately, Carolina fouled McQueen and with 17 seconds left and N.C. State leading by 66–63, he calmly hit two big ones to clinch our victory over the Heels.

This was the game where Michael Jordan scored 17 points and Gannon scored 15. It was the game Lowe finished off by bounce-passing through his legs to Bailey for a game-ending dunk. It was the game after which the State kids cut the nets down. Late in the game, Dean came over to say he was happy for me, and I believe he was sincere. How could anybody *not* be happy for me? Dean had won only eight thousand games; gimme one or two somewhere.

It had been quite a while since State had beaten Carolina in football or basketball, and our fans celebrated in Reynolds for more than an hour. No one would leave. The rush of emotion made me so giddy—we had played with the clock, beaten a great team, gone up and down with them and actually won—that I felt we could beat anybody. At one time, amid all the celebration, Whittenburg himself was sitting up on the goal, dressed in street clothes. If that wasn't a true vision of the future, I don't know what was. One week and one day later Whitt was back in the N.C. State lineup.

For all the decisions I keep saying a coach has to make, sometimes they must be made based on emotion more than anything else. When we got the stunning news that Whittenburg was able to rejoin the team in time for the rematch with—who else?—Virginia, I had to make one of the hardest decisions of all. We were 9–5 without Whitt. In his place, Myers had come into his own, averaging 18 points. Our team had learned to play together and we were on a pretty good roll. Our record was 16–8 with three games remaining. Do I start Dereck and put Ernie back on the bench? My decision was yes, I do.

Whittenburg, the senior, had maybe four games left in his entire college career. I couldn't take those games away from him. Myers, who had proven he could play in the league, had the rest of his college years ahead; he accepted the decision like a trooper and became a strong cheerleader for Dereck. Although Whitt rejoined the team, we now had to adjust to his presence, and in fact, we lost to Virginia and then to Maryland.

After the Maryland game, I was very disappointed. I thought our tenth loss had critically hurt our NCAA chances. Everybody was talking about us going NIT now. But then came Senior Day against Wake Forest, the final home game in Reynolds, and the team exploded for 130 points, the highest total of any team in the conference that season. Whitt had 25, Myers had 13, Gannon had 25. Threes? Try sixteen three-pointers for the Wolfpack. I think Mama Valvano could have hit a couple of threes that afternoon.

It was precisely the way we were playing nearly two months before, when Whittenburg broke his foot. The ironic thing was that I feared we still could get left out of the NCAA bids unless we won the ACC tournament. I felt that three bids were locks from the ACC—Carolina, Virginia and Maryland—and the fourth would be between us and Wake Forest. And, to boot, our first-round game in the ACC's was against Wake, the team we had just destroyed by 41 points.

You think I'm crazy, right? Well, in Atlanta at the ACC's, Wake cut the deficit by a cool 40. That's right, we won by the skin of our wolf-teeth, 71–70, and only because Danny Young barely missed a shot from halfcourt at the gun. Looking back, the significant decision came with about 20 seconds left when Wake called time-out with the score tied at 70. Unlike what we later did all through the NCAA tournament, this time we elected not to foul. I didn't want them on the line. I just felt we could make a defensive play, so I told our guys to get in their faces, *make* them beat us. If we were going to lose, lose aggressively. Sure enough, Lowe made a steal, giving us the ball. After our own time-out, Charles was fouled and made the winning free throw.

Game number two in the ACC tournament was against North Carolina. As if this clash wasn't emotional enough, in my first year we had lost to the Heels in the first round of the tournament; my second year, we had lost to them in the second round.

The game was strange. We led by five late in the second half, but Carolina came back to tie. We had the last shot, but Lowe got stripped and Carolina got the final try instead, a 30-footer by Sam Perkins that just missed. I watched that baby from an angle and it looked in all the way. I think it took five minutes to get there. I *know* it took five minutes off my life. Actually, the ball did go in. Then it came out. In the overtime, the Heels mirrored that shot. They were in, then out. Carolina seemed to have the game locked up with a six-point lead and 2:13 left, but then we resorted to the strategy that we would use throughout our journey to the NCAA championship the next month. How can I put this in the simplest way? Okay; we fouled.

Sonofagun. Deano was way ahead of me here, too. My staff had always discussed a special strategy where if we had a lead late in the game and the other team was fouling us and we made our two free throws, why not foul them back? The best they can do is make their two, you get the ball and the situation is the same. Even if you miss yours, foul the other team's worst shooter. He may miss and you lose nothing. That's in lieu of letting the other team shoot the three and go ahead and maybe beat you. Well, that's exactly what Dean did in this game. Rather than permit us to foul, have the Heels shoot one-and-ones and then have us look for the three-point bombs, Dean fouled us back to put the pressure on us. I recall shouting, "They're fouling *us!*" more than a few times. It was a gutsy strategy.

Luckily for us, though, we made our free throws and the Heels missed theirs. We cut the lead to four, Whittenburg swished a three-pointer and later drove the baseline for a score. Held in check through regulation, Dereck scored 11 points in the overtime and we won 91–84.

Now we were finally in the ACC finals, on the cusp of one of my fondest dreams, winning the ACC title. I still laugh when I read that because the ACC tournament no longer decides the only NCAA representative, the intensity and desire to win it are diminished. What a crock! I'll tell you one thing: We were fairly fired up. We were about to play Virginia, the best college team over the past four years, with the nation's premier player in Sampson and with a winning streak of three YEARS against us. We were probably as emotional for that game as any in my entire tenure in Raleigh.

We came out smoking, and led 12–1. Remember, we had been ahead of these guys by 16 points back in January, so we knew they could be had. As seemed to happened every game, though, we couldn't stand prosperity. Virginia came back and led by eight: 59–51, with about eleven minutes left in the game. We had been behind Wake by seven, Carolina by six and now Virginia by eight. But there was plenty of time left. Another terrific State comeback—we went ahead by nine points—only enabled us to withstand still another embarrassing drought from the foul line. We kept missing free throws, and the clock didn't seem to move.

Our lead was still three points when the littlest player in the game made the biggest play. As Sampson went up for a shot on the inside, Gannon stripped him clean. Ralph had 24 points and 12 rebounds, but Bailey matched Sampson's points and Charles matched his rebounds for us. Nevertheless, if Sampson had scored there and maybe gotten fouled, the game might have been tied.

As it was, we kept our three-point lead until there were six seconds left, Virginia ball. We had decided to try to keep the ball from Othell Wilson. In fact, we were successful in doing this, and Doug Newburg, not nearly as quick as Wilson, was forced to dribble up the court and make the play. Our pressure was successful; Newburg finally passed off, but the shot came after the buzzer. We were the new ACC champions.

Of course, I cried. Standing there watching the joy on all our players' faces, I couldn't imagine feeling any better or more fulfilled. After that, there was partying back in Raleigh on Hillsborough Street and at the Brick Yard all night, with welcoming groups at the airport and the campus. When we were on the plane coming into Raleigh, there were rumors that a large crowd had gathered. Somebody suggested we land on an outer runway and sneak away so we wouldn't have to deal with the mobs. Uh, just a moment. I had another suggestion. How about if you strap a parachute on me so I can *dive* into the crowd? What, are you kidding me? We win the ACC's and the guy suggested we sneak away! Who does this guy's PR, I wondered, Howard Hughes? When we bussed back to the campus, I felt like I had when I'd returned to Rutgers as a player; I wanted to get back on the bus and climb off to another ovation. From that night on through the rest of March Madness, the crowds greeting our successes were phenomenal. It seemed like we became a professional pep rally school. But this initial ACC victory was such an absolute shock that the campus and town simply flipped out.

What a difference a year made. While the past year, we were apprehensive about who and where we'd play in the NCAA's, this time when the bids came out there was no partying, no phone calls all around. Instead, it was just: Let's roll up our sleeves and go after it. A team with a cause and a dream is a very dangerous customer, and we knew we were that team.

People who don't coach for a living, who don't go through the seven months of a team's working and playing and fighting with each other, can't know how important that old cliché of "togetherness" is. N.C. State had far more talented teams a few years down the road. But this team was so happy, so secure in themselves. And a coach can tell. There was something special going on here.

Then came the NCAA draw. And, sonofagun, if they didn't do it to us again. Did we get Kansas, or Alabama or Seton Hall or some school anybody had ever heard of? No. They came up with Pepperdine, a toothpaste. Those were the jokes, of course. I knew who Pepperdine was. I knew they were an outstanding team. I knew the coach, Jim Harrick (who has gone on to resurrect the UCLA program where other "name" guys have failed). I knew they'd be licking their chops for us: "Bring on the ACC. We're going to kick some high-profile butt." Stuff like that.

They probably high-fived themselves all the way to practice each day. Not to mention, we would have to travel to Corvallis, Oregon to play the first round. We were the ACC champs, and we had to go to the end of the world to play. Well, maybe it wasn't the end, but I'd been there. And you can *see* the end of the world from Corvallis.

In truth, it may have been a blessing for us. It gave me a chance to use that wonderful coaching word, "focus." We were going to be able to "focus" on the game because there wasn't much else to "focus" on in Corvallis.

So I knew if nobody else did that, Pepsodent—er, Pepperdine—wasn't going to roll over for us. All the same, when we tipped off, it seemed like a repeat of our first-round game the previous year against Chattanooga. We played awful, missed our first 12 shots, and didn't score for over five minutes. There was a difference from the last time, though. We were a team with a lot of character and with a cause. Most of all, we could play defense. Our defense had kept us in many games, and it did again. Also—a big factor—Pepperdine played as lousy as we did. Friends back East told me that the game was so bad, when we fell behind by eight points late, everybody turned the TV sets off and went to bed. Okay, so it was about two A.M. Trust me, the game was that bad.

In fact, when I go back and run the tapes of that championship season, this game is where I stop the machine and ask myself: How could we possibly have won this thing?

The regulation game ended 47–all after Pepperdine missed two crucial foul shots. In the first overtime, we were down 57–51 with 1:10 to play. To make matters worse, Lowe fouled out with 45 seconds left. At :29 we were behind 59–55. Playing catch-up the whole night, we couldn't quite catch up.

Then we had to foul Dane Suttle, the Waves' best player and an 84-percent free-throw shooter. That's about the time you tell the bus driver to rev the engines. We're goin' home, Jack; it was nice while it lasted. You don't tell the kids that—you still coach the hell out of the contest. But in the back of your mind, you're thinking of the off-season and how it will be unpacking the woods and irons.

But Suttle missed! George McClain, a sub guard who earlier in the season had been hospitalized for spinal meningitis, had just come in for Lowe. He took the outlet pass from Charles and threw the best pass he would ever throw at State to Bailey roaring down the middle. Bang, a dunk! We fouled immediately. Suttle, again. We had to. We wanted him to feel the pressure from that first miss.

The kid missed again. Now we came down with the ball, and Pepperdine fouled Whittenburg with nine seconds to go. At this point I sent in McQueen, a lefty with the dangling arms of an octopus on hormone pills, for a better chance to tap the rebound back out to our guys in case Dereck missed. It was one of those spot decisions that worked out, although it didn't look too snappy at the time. Sure enough, Lo and Co began arguing over who should take the second spot along the lane. I had to holler at Charles to get out of there.

What happened next defied logic, again: Whitt did miss. And McQueen was there for the tap-back, a play made famous, incidentally, by Dean Smith at Carolina. Steal from the best, I always say. But instead of tapping the ball back as I had hoped, Cozell caught the ball and went back up to shoot himself. Oh no! *Ohhhh . . . yes!* The ball bounced over every inch of that rim before falling through.

Pepperdine didn't call time-out; I think they were too shell-shocked. They ran it up the side, took a long shot and missed. Double overtime!

We knew we would win now. Pepperdine had gone from high-fiving and celebrating on the bench to looking hopelessly lost on the court. Most people believe our run to the NCAA title started in the ACC tournament. But I've always known our "Team of Destiny" tag began with that shot by McQueen against Pepperdine. We won after the second OT, 69–67.

Before the game I had told Frankie Dascenzo of the *Durham Sun* that if we got by Pepperdine, we could go all the way and win the whole thing. I really believed that. I honestly felt that if we could just get over that first giant hurdle, we had the type of team to win the championship. In the locker room afterward, I told the guys exactly that. We were in the hands of Fate now. A different guy each night was going to come through for us. We were going to win every game from here to the end of the tournament.

Each year going into the NCAA's there seems to be a tendency to look only at a team's win and loss record. But once a team gets hot and is on a roll, you should forget the numbers. People had forgotten about us, but we had great confidence from beating Carolina twice and Virginia. We knew, absolutely, that those two were as good as any teams in the country. What did that make us?

We had motivated ourselves for this first NCAA victory. Motivation for our second game came from the opponent, UNLV, when Vegas' star forward Sidney Green said he was "not impressed" with Thurl Bailey. "He didn't show me very much," Green said. You think I didn't Xerox that baby a few times and put it up in the locker room?

It's a cliché, but believe it: We coaches will use anything for an edge, a psych tool, a mind ploy. Bailey would end up just about matching Green—25 points and nine rebounds to 27 and 10—and our team played great. The problem was, so did Vegas.

As a team moves through the tournament, the competition obviously becomes better and better. Well, Vegas might have been as talented a team as Houston. I know Jerry Tarkanian's club was the best defensively. Now it became a battle of wills, of execution, of who was the healthiest, deepest, most fit; who had the most nerves and guts.

With over eight minutes to go against Las Vegas, we were behind by 12 points. But we'd been behind before; we were used to being behind. I had always told the kids: "Let's just get in position to win." That was a coach's job, to get his team in position. It sounds like a simple thing, but in fact, a few years later, I read that a successful CEO who was giving a speech to a management seminar told *them* their jobs were to put their people in position to win. And he told them he had taken that philosophy from the 1983 North Carolina State basketball team!

The score and time always dictated how we positioned ourselves; since we always seemed to be behind, that dictated press and foul. Rush the ball up the floor, score, time-out, foul. After we fought back against Vegas to within three points, 67–70; after Bailey hit a jumper with 37 seconds left to make it 69–70; after we called time-out and elected to foul UNLV; after the Rebels' Eldridge (El Cid) Hudson, a 68-percent free-throw shooter, missed—we were in position to win again. This time, we didn't call time-out. Instead, we rushed down the floor, hoping to catch Vegas off guard.

I remember what happened next in slow motion. I even remember what we called the play: 5-play. Whittenburg started a drive to the basket with eight seconds to go, but he was cut off and let loose a 20-footer. The ball glanced off the front of the rim, where Bailey was there to tap it back, but that missed too. In the scramble, three Vegas guys should have gotten the ball, but they didn't; they bumbled. Thurl came up with it one more time. Slo-mo. Slo-mo. Off-balance, falling, Thurl tried a banker from the sharp angle . . . Good!

Holy God! We rushed onto the court, thinking the game was over, but Vegas still had three seconds to make something happen. Their last play didn't come close; the shot went over the backboard. We won 71–70.

In the last nine minutes, Bailey had scored 16 points, most on turn-around jumpers at critical times, including the game-winning ones. I didn't ask Sidney Green if he was impressed.

Following our fourth victory over a Top Five team in the past month, we left Corvallis for Ogden, Utah and the West Regional, knowing there was something Very Special at hand. We were confident. We were excited. Nobody was going to beat us now. I was so sure of all this, Pam and I took a detour to San Francisco for some serious R and R.

In the first place, because the Regionals were all in the West, we figured it was useless to return to Raleigh, where the players wouldn't be able to get anything done in school, much less on the court. We were getting video tapes from home in the mail, showing one pep rally after another. We thought it better to stay away from all the pep.

Nevertheless, at the San Francisco airport, our own personal pep rally ensued when a singing and dancing messenger greeted us by plopping a party hat on my head. This was the artful work of none other than my old college roomie, Bob Lloyd, and his wife, Kay, who were our hosts for a welcome day of vacation.

Later, by the time we had toasted State's victories at Bob's house in the Los Altos Hills, I was barely able to walk. I do remember being forced to watch ancient tapes of the 1967 NIT featuring a Rutgers backcourt that seemed so slow, I kept asking Bob to "speed up the tape." The next day, the Lloyds carried me onto a flight to Utah to join the team for the next rounds.

At a press conference in Ogden, somebody asked what the team was doing with our free time. "Mostly we eat and meet," I said. "In the morning, we have a staff meeting to see what time we should get the guys up to eat. Then we have a premeeting meeting to plan the next meeting. At our meeting, we discuss when we will eat next and what we will eat and what time the next meeting will be after the next meal. In the evenings, we meet to watch tapes of ourselves eating."

In Ogden, all the teams were in the same hotel—Virginia, Boston College and us—except the home team, Utah. The University of Utah is in Salt Lake City, an hour away from Ogden, but you get the picture. First, we had to play a couple of Western teams on the West Coast. Now we got to play Utah in Utah. Nice, huh? Think we had Rodney Dangerfield's problem?

It's interesting how viewpoints change. In Ogden, all the officials and reporters and hotel and restaurant people remarked upon how loose the Wolfpack players were in comparison to Virginia, whose players seemed tight and nervous. Several years later—try my last season at State—the N.C. State coach took heavy heat for promoting such an "unstructured" environment; a loose, open, laissez-faire program. Back then, the way we did things seemed appealing to folks. Not to mention that it won a national championship. That last year . . . Hmmmmm.

Utah had gained the regional with an emotional upset victory over UCLA, and I knew the Utes' coach, Jerry Pimm, would have them prepared. They played very tough defense until we kept moving back further out and taking those three-pointers we had learned to shoot in the ACC. They didn't count for three points now—and Pimm told his team at halftime: "Don't worry. They can't keep shooting that way" (i.e.,

59 percent). He was right. In the second half, we shot 78.9 percent, and won 75–56. Virginia beat BC in the other game, so the West Regional final would be a repeat of the ACC final.

I knew that in a Big Game, playing another team from our conference would be easier than playing a stranger. It's called Familiarity. It doesn't breed contempt so much as a sense of confidence that you *can* play with the other guys. There's no fear, no ascribing to them a higher rating than they deserve. This may sound self-serving, but that is precisely why I've always felt our victory over Houston in the championship game in '83 was a bigger upset than Villanova's over Georgetown two years later. The 'Nova kids had played Georgetown twice already; they were not in awe of Patrick Ewing. (We had the same feeling for Ralph Sampson.) On the other hand, when we played Houston, they had won 26 straight games, they were ranked number one, had just blown away powerful Louisville, and Akeem Olajuwon . . . well, Akeem wasn't Sidney Green. We had no reason to think we could play with them.

But I'm getting ahead of myself. Against Virginia, as big a game as it would turn out to be, I knew we would be relaxed and play up to the level of the game.

It was a great regional final. Virginia skipped out ahead by seven points, but we came back and it was virtually nip and tuck to the wire. Sampson slammed in a dunk with about a minute and a half to play, to give the Cavaliers a 61–59 lead. But then Whittenburg arched in a 22-footer. We decided—one more time—to make them win the game from the foul line. We chose to foul our old pal, Othell Wilson. Wilson made the first but missed the second, so we were in a position to win again: down 62–61, with possession of the ball.

This time we decided not to wait for the last shot; we were going to take the first available opportunity to score. Whittenburg drove the lane and dished off to Charles, who went up hard for the basket. Bop! he was fouled by Sampson. Lo was going to the foul line with two shots and 23 seconds left.

During the time-out, all I talked about was what we were going to do after Lorenzo made *both* shots. This time I remembered Abe Lemons' advice; I didn't want any black cows in this huddle. No negatives. I focused only on the positive. "Lo, Baby," I told Charles, "this is it. We've come this far. Team of Destiny. The Pack. The Cardiac Pack. It's on you. Knock them both down. When you do, we're calling time-out again. Then we'll talk about defense. But there is no defense now, baby, because you are the man. Brooklyn, New York's own Lorenzo Charles. The guy from the Big Apple. My guy, Lo. Do it, baby."

Oh, was I positive. I was so positive, I made myself sick. That time-out never seemed to end. I wanted it to end, because I didn't have anything more to say. At least I didn't want to say anything else. As the seconds ticked off, I kept encouraging Lo. I had to practically bite my tongue off to keep myself from screaming anything else. Like . . . *This is what the hell we're going to do when this S.O.B. misses both of these &*%$# free throws!*

As soon as the horn went off and the team started out on the floor, I grabbed Sidney Lowe and told him what to do if Lo missed.

Lorenzo, however, truly my guy, knocked in both shots, and Terry Holland called time-out for Virginia. There were seventeen seconds left. Our defensive strategy was simple. It was the same we had played the whole game: one man on Othell, one man on Ralph, and then a triangle zone around Ralph. We wanted anybody but those two to shoot the ball. We had Sampson surrounded, and the criticism that Holland got later about not getting the ball to his 7'4" center was totally improper. Plain and simple, Virginia couldn't because we wouldn't let them.

Our defense was no surprise to Virginia. Terry knew me well enough to know that my teams tried to stop the opposition's best players. He had to know I was going to guard Sampson and Wilson. Because if Wilson had beat us, I would have screamed into the night about what I should have done to keep the ball out of his hands; if Sampson had beat us, I would have gone out and put a bullet in my brain. But if some other Cavalier got lucky and hit the open shot that we were giving him, I could go home and sleep like a baby.

Bottom line, this was one of those times when everything a coach planned came out the way he planned it. On that occasion—and there have been a couple more like it—it was as if God was paying me back for twenty years of having Harvey Carter shake me, of losing at Syracuse by 57, of watching the Iona last-ditch chances fall away. All of a sudden all those stored-up atrocities were paid back. Because what happened in Ogden was that Tim Mullen of Virginia, who hadn't scored all night, who *hadn't even taken one shot* all night, got the open 18-footer—and missed it. After the ball bounced off the rim, Wilson got the rebound. But his attempt got nothing but air and fell way short; I'm not sure if Othell was trying a lob pass to Ralph or a shot, but it didn't matter.

A lot of people have since criticized Ralph Sampson for the style of his game, for his personality, for the way he ended his college career. I don't know about him as a pro, but I do know he was a great college athlete. He was an unselfish player who played within the framework of his team. In his four years at Virginia, the Cavs were ranked number one and won 112 games, more than any other team during that period. I'm not sure what else he could have done except win the national championship. I am still proud I was a part of his career and his final game.

Not that I thought much about that at the time. The arena at Ogden was circular; long into the night after the game, I remember simply walking around it. Around and around. Had it finally happened? Yes, we were going to the Final Four! I opened the door to the outside during one of my circular walks and there were some fans out there. "Do you believe it?" I said. "We're going to the Final Four." Anybody who says anticipation is greater than realization has never made it to basketball's biggest event.

We finally came home to Raleigh because we ran out of underwear, but our pre–Final Four practices were ridiculous. I opened them up to the public, so we had about four to five thousand people there every afternoon. We got nothing done. People would just stand and cheer for every little move we made. Actually, I would have preferred for the season to have ended right there. We wouldn't play any more games; we'd just continue practicing and have the multitudes come and cheer us. We'd sign autographs and pose for pictures and that would be it.

During a telephone-hookup press conference for the Final Four coaches between Houston, Louisville, Athens, Georgia, and Raleigh, I couldn't resist poking a little fun. When the reporters were asked if they had any questions, from the different cities came this: "Houston passes . . . Louisville passes . . ." I broke in: "Raleigh bids three spades."

Pam, meanwhile, was bidding to make the All-Superstitious Team, Lifetime. As if most of our Wolfpack club members weren't superstitious enough—they all seemed to have the same assigned seats, not to mention assigned clothing—Pam wore this ceramic wolf pin, and at every game two thousand people used to come up and touch it for good luck.

"What are all those people doing to you?" I once asked her.

"They're rubbing my wolf," she said.

"I beg your pardon?"

And not only that. At the three-minute mark of every game, Pam had to get up and leave. She started doing this a long while ago, and we had won. So it got to be that if she forgot at any N.C. State game with three minutes to go, an entire section might stand up, point their fingers toward the exit and say: "Pam, out."

We left for Albuquerque, the site of the Final Four, a day early, and we had an absolute ball. I knew this was the basketball moment of my life, but I wasn't about to let that detain me from having a fun week. I had looked it up: There had been a ton of great coaches who had never won the championship, who had never been to the Final Four. Only twenty-seven men in history had coached a national champion. I told our team: "We've had a lot of big wins. We've had a lot of fun. This is the ultimate, and we may never get back here again. But let's not make this life or death. Let's continue to have fun."

Our first practice in Albuquerque was in a high-school gym where the baskets were fine, the floor was fine, the hospitality was great, everything was super except somebody had forgotten the basketballs. So we threw some socks around.

That night the staff and I went to a local disco called The Hungry Bear and the next day it came out that I had won second prize in a dance contest. Actually, I hadn't, but the story grew out of an incident where two patrons presented me with a napkin proclaiming me a runner-up in the dance finals. No, Pam hadn't arrived yet. When she did, and read about my exploits in the newspaper, she was nonplussed. "Really getting ready for this one, huh? Really hitting those game tapes," she said.

"The VCR's haven't arrived yet," I replied.

I was having the time of my life. If there was a newspaper writer who wanted to talk, I talked. If there was a TV camera crew that wanted me to pose, I posed. If you were a photographer and ran out of film, I bought you some film.

I'll never forget the Friday-afternoon practice when we came onto the floor of the University of New Mexico's "Pit." There were nearly twelve thousand people in the stands, about half of them coaches. Every year the coaches' national convention is held in conjunction with the Final Four, so the four mentors of the lucky teams are always under the surveillance of their peers. It was intimidating, to say the least. All we did was two-line lay-up drills; somehow I felt we should be doing cartwheels over the hoop. The first time I saw all those people up there I wanted to go up in the stands, shake their hands and say: "Thanks for coming, we'll have a drawing later."

My whole coaching career raced through my mind during practice that day: My first Final Four at College Park, Maryland, when I was a coach at Johns Hopkins and sat smack in the middle of the New Mexico State band. The time at the Final Four when I saw John Wooden getting off an elevator and he actually *spoke* to me. He remembered meeting me at a summer camp years before and he asked me how I was. My shocked answer was, precisely: "Hub . . . b . . . b . . . Hub . . . b . . . b." Sitting in the cheap seats at the old Madison Square Garden. Watching Adolph Rupp at one of the coaches' dinners telling the dinner organizer he didn't like peas and he didn't want peas . . . so the organizer changed the menu and didn't serve peas. That's coaching power! All this stuff came back to me as we practiced. I made up my mind that we couldn't lose the semifinal game. It was important we make it to the final.

In the postpractice press conference, Rick Brewer, the sports publicist at Chapel Hill, got in his annual dig. "Time for one last question for Coach Valvano," he said. "I know there's one more answer."

Something of importance did come out of that day, though. I told the team that I had spoken at a lot of annual business conventions where there's a keynote speaker, and that this Final Four would have its keynote speakers as well. There'd be two of them, the two winners on Saturday. I think we started winning our semifinal game against Georgia right then, a day early.

The fact that the Bulldogs had beaten North Carolina in a stunning upset in the East Regional helped get our players' attention, believe me. Still, we knew everybody considered ours the consolation game, that Houston-Louisville was the heavyweight division and the survivor of that game would undoubtedly win the championship. I called the doubleheader "the A-game and the Jayvees."

We were worried about Georgia's speed and offensive rebounding, but right away their terrible shooting neutralized the Dogs. We led 33–22 at halftime after Georgia began the game by missing 19 of its first 23 shots. We pushed the lead to 59–41 with about six minutes to play. The mistake I made came then, ironically the same error Houston Coach Guy Lewis would get crucified for two nights later in the championship game. We spread the court and held the ball; I figured State being an agricultural school, we should have been able to milk a lead. Wrong. We ended up struggling to the finish and won 67–60.

Actually, one of the features of the first game was when the Houston Phi Slamma Jammas entered the arena in their workclothes, all ready for battle, and sat right behind our bench. The crowd went wild. Of course, the Houstons couldn't hear the noise. Most of the Cougars still had their Walkmans strapped around their heads.

When I returned to the Pit floor, the Houston-Louisville game was at halftime. Later I wished I had missed the second half too, for what transpired before my eyes was incredible. Louisville was playing high above the rims early in the second half and seemed to be in control with an eight-point lead, but then Houston started stealing, blocking and dunking everything in sight. Women and children were not safe. Brent Musburger and Billy Packer were not safe. In a few seconds, Houston went from eight behind to eight ahead, with as fearsome an explosion as I have ever seen. One steal, breakaway and dunk by Houston's Benny Anders was so invigorating, a good part of the Cougar bench got up and huddled around a nearby TV monitor so they could watch the instant replay.

Myself, I was excited and depressed at the same time. I knew that everybody was going to root for us, but that nobody thought we could win. That was the exciting part. The depressing part was, I thought they might be right. This could be a 50-pointer.

As expected, nobody gave us a chance on Monday night. The commentators and columnists were fairly brutal in describing what a horrendous mismatch the championship game would be. I particularly recall *The*

Washington Post's Dave Kindred's line: "Trees will tap dance, elephants will ride in the Indianapolis 500, and Orson Welles will skip breakfast, lunch and dinner before State finds a way to beat Houston."

Well, the staff and I spent all day and night Sunday and all day again Monday figuring out how to enter Babar at Indy. Our team certainly didn't believe what was being written. We didn't beat the numbers five, four, three and two teams in the country by giving up. People had also forgotten that we had played nine games against teams ranked number one that year.

Another wit wrote: "Rain would make it perfect. It always rains at an execution." Even I said things like, "We'll hold the ball till Tuesday." Except that I remembered a couple of things. Houston lost to Virginia early in the season, a Virginia *without* Sampson. And Houston couldn't shoot free throws. Boiiiiing!

Our decisions were fairly simple. We would set the tempo: When we wanted to run, we would run; if we wanted to slow down, we'd do that too. We never wanted Houston to get out on the break. Another part of our plan was not to allow any dunks, practically the *raison d'être* of the Phi Slamma Jamma. We were going with the three-guard offense to draw them away from the basket. We wanted to get Akeem in foul trouble. We had to shoot well. And the game had to be in the 50's for us to have a chance to win.

I gave one of the best pregame talks of my life. It wasn't one of those out of Drawer 26, Speech #23. It was very sincere, and it took a lot longer than our normal meeting. We went over everything about the game, from halfcourt to full-court sets, rebounding positioning, out-of-bounds plays, last-second deals. I bet we stayed in there a full hour.

Sure, I'm a seat-of-the-pants coach. We've never been a system team. Against Georgia we played a certain way, and against Houston we were going to play a different way. I think what I do and what we've always done is change things during a game, adapt, adjust. I think I'm good at that. We had tremendous confidence for this championship game. Can you imagine what it was like to get the ultimate challenge against the number one team in America—with the entire basketball world thinking you had no chance? With a club that has just won nine straight games, beaten numbers four, three and two . . . without a clock . . . without a three-pointer? And we're going against a team that only plays zone? Some teams have a smaller margin of error than others; Houston's was very small. Force them out of their transition game, and they could get very frustrated.

"Now I want to tell you guys something," I began in the locker room before the game of our lives. "I've waited all my career to be in this position, to be playing on the last day, to be playing for the national championship. And I'm telling you this. Everybody in America thinks we're holding the ball. Houston thinks we're holding. But we're not. They're all wrong. We're going to go out there and shove it right down their throats."

I was a Rat again, and every last one of these guys, my guys at N.C. State, was a Rat. I got right up in the faces of the whole starting team:

"You, Sidney Lowe! This is your last game ever. You're the finest point guard I've ever coached and tonight you are going to play flawlessly. You are going to go out and handle and dish and play the game of your life and lead us to the national championship.

"And you, Dereck Whittenburg! You've come back from the dead. They said you'd never play again. You're going to get those passes from Sid and hit those downtown J's from all over the gym and lead us to the national championship.

"And you, Cozell McQueen! You're getting every rebound there is tonight. You're going against Akeem the Dream and you're going to do a job on him and lead us to the national championship.

"And Lorenzo Charles! You're going to get inside position and power for points and rebounds and lead us to the national championship.

"And Thurl Bailey! You're going to hit jumpers. And grab rebounds. And block shots. And dunk the dunkers. You're going to jump and bang and control the glass and lead us to the national championship!"

I told them we were going to go when we wanted to and stop when we wanted to, and that not only were they going to play the game of their lives, but I was going to coach the game of my life, too.

"We're going to leave this locker room and we're going to knock Houston right on their asses," I shouted.

The place erupted. The team ran out of that locker room sky-high. I think we could have destroyed some small nations, we were so hyper. We started out with a dunk (by Bailey) and took 18 shots in the first five minutes of the game. Houston took six. The only problem was, we didn't make many of those 18. I was a maniac, of course, but that didn't seem to matter. N.C. State played just about as perfect a half as we could. We got four fouls on Clyde Drexler. We held Houston to 25 points. We led 33–25, showing everybody that we could play with the vaunted favorites. Our defense was solid, and Houston wasn't doing things at will on the offensive boards either.

At halftime I became very selfish because I wanted to win so badly. To have come that far with an eight-point lead and then lose the national championship would have broken my heart. I told the kids they had 20 minutes to make their mark on history. I said: "Please believe this. Never, ever, for the rest of your life in whatever you do—insurance,

selling cars, teaching, television, banking, anything—never will you have
the feeling that will come when that final horn blows and you have won
this game. Should we lose, it will haunt you the rest of your days. You will
ask yourself why, what could you have done? I'm not telling you now to
remember what a wonderful journey it's been and just go out there and
have fun and do the best you can. No. It's too close. I'm saying, let's go
out and win the national championship. There's no reason not to now."

All my fears came to fruition at the beginning of the second half. We
were drained emotionally, flat. And Houston was too great a team not to
make a run at us. We scored only two points in the first ten minutes,
Houston scored 17, and suddenly it was 42–35 for the Black Hats. Still,
we weren't getting beat by dunks or rebounds or because we were getting
run out of the gym. Houston was romping because we couldn't score.

With just under ten minutes to play, Cougar Coach Guy V. Lewis gave
us the break we needed. Houston slowed the tempo and went into its
infamous delay game, the Locomotion. I know why Lewis did it. Let's
face it, we all do it. I'd done it against Georgia two days earlier and it
almost cost us the game. It's just general game maintenance. Where it
failed Houston, though, was that they were such a poor free-throw
shooting team, 60.9 percent on the season, 57.3 percent during the
tournament, and (as it turned out) only 10 of 19 in this championship
game. Lewis tried to eat a little clock, and the only reason that was wrong
is because it didn't work.

Also, it was wrong because fouling is what we did. We fouled as a
strategy. I wasn't going to get to the final game and let the clock go when I
was losing. If we were going to lose, I didn't care if the margin was by 20
or by one. We were going to determine the outcome of the game. They
would have to hit their free throws to beat us.

We tried fouling Drexler first. He knocked in two, so we didn't touch
him again. We fouled other people. We had clawed back to within 52–48
when Whittenburg hit two baskets to tie the score at 52. (The N.C. State
team hit six of our last seven outside shots in the game.) When the clock
got down close to a minute, we wanted to foul their freshman point
guard, Alvin Franklin. We did this with 1:05 remaining, Whitt doing the
hacking honors.

I don't necessarily think players choke, not players who help teams win
26 straight. What they do is miss. Just as when a batter strikes out or a
running back fumbles or a golfer misses a five-foot putt. The pressure of
making free throws late in a championship game is immense. Franklin
just missed.

When we got the rebound, I knew we would win the game. It's that
simple. It had happened so many times before. We called a time-out with
44 seconds left to set up exactly what we wanted to do, a play we had used

all year: Lowe in the middle with the ball, making something happen. As soon as the clock got under 10 seconds, Sidney was supposed to go for the basket. If they came at him from Gannon's side, the dish would be to Terry for the shot. If they sent help from Whittenburg's side, Dereck would get the ball. If they stayed tight, Lowe was to continue penetrating and see what happened underneath.

Give credit to Houston: They knew we wanted the last shot. They knew we weren't going to take just anything quick; we wanted to win the game or go into overtime. The Cougars played a good halfcourt trap stopping all penetration. A couple of times we got bent out of shape, and Houston almost stole the ball. Exerting tremendous pressure, the Cougars forced Bailey in the corner to throw a sloppy pass out to Whitt. Anders came this close to intercepting, which would have been good-night because he had clear sailing for a breakaway dunk that would have won the game.

My heart went into my throat as Whittenburg barely controlled, searched for the basket and the clock at the same time and hurled up his final 30-footer. The amazing irony was that Charles, on the opposite side of the basket, saw the ball falling short, and Olajuwon, in textbook rebounding position facing the basket, did not. Akeem never even jumped. Lorenzo did, grabbed the ball with both hands and smashed it home. North Carolina State had won the national championship!

And there I was searching for someone to hug. I had told Lo in the huddle to make believe anything near the rim was a hubcap, but this was ridiculous. People were running every which way, everybody was hugging everybody, I knew the TV cameras were on me, and yet I couldn't find one person to hug! Where was I running? I was running around looking for Dereck because I had dreamed of this moment all my life and I knew I was only the 28th coach in history to win the NCAA title and that sixty million people were watching and I had been hugging Whitt after all our games because he was my designated hugger and I thought I'd be making history myself here.

Every weekend of my life I had tuned in "Wide World of Sports" and heard about the Thrill of Victory and the Agony of Defeat and watched that skier come down the mountain—boom, schuss, boom, splat—while somewhere in France, some poor woman is going, "Look Pierre, here comes *ton père!*" I felt as if all they had ever had to show on "Wide World" was the Agony of Defeat, and now I, Jim Valvano, would be the Thrill of Victory. I imagined that the cameras would be zeroing in on me running slo-mo and the crowd would be roaring *aaahhhhh* and I would be running and Whitt would be running and "Chariots of Fire" would be playing in the background and it was going to be History! Me! Whitt! Slo-Mo! Thrill of Victory! History! Me! Whitt! Together! Hug! Chariots of Fire! And I would be on TV forever.

Then I got out in the middle of nowhere, and there's Whitt . . . hugging somebody else!

So I ran left, looking for somebody else to hug. Everybody was hugging somebody else. I ran right, looking. Everybody was hugging. There was nobody left to hug! I had just won it all: history, 28th coach, sixty million watching—and I had nobody to hug! Where was I running? I finally found my athletic director, Willis Casey, my boss, a bit old and out of shape but a very nice man. He gave me my break. He grabbed me. He hugged me. Wonderful! Great! Finally, a hug! He wasn't Whitt, but a hug's a hug. Slo-mo, "Chariots of Fire" hug. And then Willis Casey kissed me square on the mouth!

I had just won the national championship, 28th all-time to do it . . . sixty million have watched me running around like a maniac . . . and then I fell into the arms of a sixty-five-year-old, out-of-shape old man who kissed me square on the mouth! The guy watching in Dubuque must have thrown down his beer and said: "Mabel, come look at this." I felt the Thrill of Victory and the Agony of Defeat all at the same time.

But I did recover long enough to tell everybody how much I loved Albuquerque, "the greatest city the Lord ever made," I said. "My wife is going to be pregnant—she doesn't know this yet—and I'm going to name the kid Al B. Querque."

Chapter Twelve

THE GIFT MY FATHER GAVE ME

F OLLOWING THE NATIONAL CHAMPIONSHIP, THE DEMANDS ON MY TIME increased to the point where it was hard to find a minute to just sit back, relax and enjoy it. I guess I never realized how much a stirring athletic event could touch multitudes of people until I had been part of one. The numbers of letters we received just blew my mind. They usually came in three categories. First, from friends, relatives, colleagues, and people in the basketball world. Second, from successful people in other walks of life such as business, the arts, even politics. Successful people simply like to associate themselves with other successful endeavors. The final grouping of letters was the significant one. These were from people who had found hope and inspiration from our quest. Their letters were incredible. They ran the gamut from folks who were out of work or in total despair to terminally ill people in hospitals. Everyone seemed to get a spiritual lift from what we had accomplished.

One example of this came when I had to go into the hospital for a minor operation. The treatment I got there amazed me—special food, visits from fans, cards and letters and flowers from all over. During my stay, one of the nurses came in to see me, and said that there was a woman down the hall who was terminally ill with cancer, whom I should go to visit. She said that the woman wouldn't even let her husband and daughter come to see her, she was so depressed. I said, "I'd be glad to, but what good can I do?" She said, "She's a Pack fan. You could cheer her up." And the nurse sent one of the hospice people in to talk to me, to explain their goal of trying to make a patient want to live, rather than to wait for death.

Well, I began having lunch with this woman, who was indeed very depressed and ill. Then I started having breakfast and lunch with her every day. I gave her Wolfpack hats and shirts, and we talked a lot. I kept telling her she ought to let her husband and daughter come to see her, but she kept saying she didn't want them to see her looking so bad. On my last night there, I came to tell her good-bye, and said again that she should allow her family to visit. Again, she said no. But the next morning, as I was leaving, the nurse found me and said, "Come here." I went to the woman's room, and there she was with her husband and daughter, all wearing the shirts I'd given her. She'd finally let them come. We all cried.

A few months later, I got a letter from her husband. He said he wanted me to know that last week, the Lord took his wife. "But," he said, "because of your interest in her, she decided to come home and live with us. In fact, the last week of her life was a happy one." I was glad to know that I'd been able to do some good for her and her family.

Requests for speaking engagements proliferated; they came from areas out of the realm of mere sports. All of a sudden Corporate America came calling, asking me to business meetings and conventions and such. They wanted to know what it took to get ahead and reach the top of a profession.

I had never given it that much thought, but in devising an outline for a speech, I looked back at my own life as an example of how athletics could shape a kid and take a larger role in his life than anyone might imagine. I came up with a formula, which I described as: You plus Motivation equals Success. This was something I got a long time ago out of a speech by the Reverend Bob Richards at a basketball camp.

Richards had told several stories with the theme of "Who Would You Rather Be?" They were always about the kid who didn't have much, but made it to the top anyway. As a sixteen-year-old, I was very moved by these stories. Richards told everyone in those audiences to know that God must love ordinary people because he had made so many of us ordinary. But in every walk of life (and he used sports as an example), ordinary people do extraordinary things. In later years, I would use that as a cornerstone of my own speech, explaining that the way to make ordinary people extraordinary is through motivation. To me, motivation is a three-pronged attack.

The first part is enthusiasm. Remember, I always thought the only thing that got me a place on that first team way back at Rutgers was my hustle and diving on the floor. My enthusiasm. Whether you're selling groceries or teaching school or running the corporation, enthusiasm has to be a constant.

The second important part of motivation is dreams. I was an un-abashed dreamer, from dreaming of playing in Madison Square Garden to coaching in the Final Four.

Finally, the work ethic. The relationship between work and success is not that direct. It's not: If you work hard, you'll be successful. The thing to remember is that if you *don't* work hard, you *can't* be successful. That opens up the fear of failure, which may be the strongest motivator of all.

If you can accept the idea that with motivation, dreams, enthusiasm and hard work, ordinary people can do extraordinary things, I think you're on the way to success. Then the key becomes how to live your life each day. I told everyone that my life had been filled with laughter, with thought, and with emotion. Simply stated, at the end of each day, you should attempt to laugh, to think, and to cry.

I then related several humorous anecdotes from my career, as I traveled from Rutgers to the pinnacle of my success in the '83 National Championship. We all should be able to laugh about our shortcomings. However, in order to reach our goals, I feel that it is important to spend time improving our minds.

I always discussed the importance of improving oneself by reading. George Raveling, the coach at Southern Cal, once told me that if you read five books a year, you were in the top five percent of all people who read in the United States. I try to make it a habit to read 70 pages a day, seven days a week. That's 490 pages a week, 52 books a year. My goal is to read 100 books a year. I read books on communications, on business, on success. I read the trade publications. I read books by other basketball coaches.

In the last part of my speech, I talked about the importance of emotion, of tears, of crying. More and more in the years after the championship, I talked about my father, Rocco, and the understanding and care he showed me growing up.

When I first began coaching, I told my father that I wanted to win the national championship. He said very simply: "You will."

I told him this was going to be very hard. He said, "I know you will."

It took me eight years even to make it to the tournament. When I finally got my first bid while I was coach at Iona, we celebrated at my parents' home. After dinner, my dad told me that he had his suitcase packed. I said, "Where are you going?" He said he was going to the NCAA championships to see me win the national title. And that became our little joke every season: Dad saying, "My bags are packed; I'll see you in the championship game." And then his son's team would get knocked out of the tournament in the early round.

Then, the night we won the whole thing in Albuquerque, one of my fondest memories is of my dad hugging me at center court. Dad was at the back of my press conference following the game, and a reporter asked him to describe his feelings. "I feel great," he said. "Other than the day I married my wife, this is the happiest night of my life. Tonight I watched my son's dream come true."

That night, while celebrating in Albuquerque, my father called me into his room and said how proud he was of me. He also asked, "What are you going to do now, big shot?" I told him it was so much fun the first time, we were going to win it again. He said that his bags were packed, and he'd be there when we did it. I told him, "Hey, Pop, it's really hard to do again!" He said, "Don't worry, you will. I know you will."

The following year, I didn't even make the tournament, but two years later, we did. We beat Nevada–Reno, Texas–El Paso (UTEP), and Alabama, putting us in the Regional Finals against St. John's. Unfortunately, we lost to the Redmen in the last few minutes of play. I was very depressed when I spoke to my father on the phone that night. Sensing my mood, my dad ripped into me for not being thankful for all the accomplishments of the season, and for not realizing the great opportunity I had in the upcoming years. He also said that being depressed was not very productive, and that if I ever expected to be back in the Final Four again, I'd better get off this self-pitying trip. My spirits were immediately lifted, and before we hung up, I said, "You know something, Dad, you're really unbelievable. I just want you to know: Dad, I love you."

Those were the last four words I said to my father. The next night, he had a heart attack and died.

I lost one of the best friends I've ever had. In the next few months, I was not very enthusiastic, I didn't have many dreams, and I wasn't working very hard. And my performance in my professional and personal life slipped. Those of you who have lost someone you love might recognize the feeling. There was something missing, and I didn't know what it was. It took a while until I got the answer. My father gave me something that we don't give to each other very often. In fact, I now call it "the gift my father gave me." It's simple, and yet the most powerful gift a person can give to someone else. The incredible gift my father gave me was that he believed in me. He believed in me when I was wrong, when I failed, when I didn't live up to the standards that were set for me, or that I set for myself. No matter what happened, my father could look me in the eye and say, "Son, my bags are packed for you. I know you'll get the job done."

I guess I'm a little more emotional about my dad since he's no longer here, but my mom was just as much a part of any success I've ever had as anyone else. In fact, Mom was always the one who kept the entire family together. My dad was gone a lot, and my mother was really the backbone of the Valvano clan. Her belief and confidence in her sons was no less than my dad's. And she was a better cook than he was, too.

I have been giving speeches for the last twenty years, and as my life has evolved, so too have my speeches. And yet, I feel more strongly now than I ever have that to be successful in the competitive environment in which we live, and to be able to overcome adversity in both our business and personal lives—an ordinary person who is motivated, enthusiastic, who has dreams, and who works hard; who has the ability to laugh, to think, to cry; and who can give the gift of belief to other people can accomplish anything.

Most of the people who hire motivational speakers want you for about forty minutes. I tell them I can't do forty. I've got to have a full hour or they can get somebody else. For the first thirty minutes, I'm so busy laughing and having fun and trying to get people to enjoy themselves, that when I get to the motivational part, the time is up. I even have a story about my father's death that I don't hesitate to use. It really helps to take the edge off my loss, and it's more a reminder of his full life than it is of his death.

Just as he was for a good portion of the human race, Joe DiMaggio was always my father's idol. He thought the sun rose and set on Joe D. I grew up loving Mickey Mantle, of course, but Dad always made me aware that the Mick couldn't carry DiMag's jock. We used to argue all the time. My father followed Joe's every game. He took me to Joe's last game in Yankee Stadium. Dad had never met DiMag, but he drank an awful lot of cups from Mr. Coffee.

Anyway, following N.C. State's loss to St. John's in the 1985 West Regional final, my mother flew back to New York where Dad picked her up at LaGuardia Airport. Remember, my father only came to the tournament if we were in the Final Four. When he met my mother, he was as giddy as a little schoolgirl. "I can't believe it," he said. It seems that while he was waiting for the plane, he looked over and there was Joe DiMaggio standing a few feet away! Well, naturally, my father went up and introduced himself. Being the proud father he is, he also had to say that Joe must know his son, the basketball coach who won the national championship a few years earlier.

My dad told my mother that he went on and on about how he admired DiMaggio and enjoyed watching him play. My father had the biggest grin on his face. I laugh even now, thinking about the seventy-year-old Rocco Valvano fawning all over Joe DiMaggio. After they went home, the very next night, my father was standing at the top of the stairs when he suffered his fatal heart attack. He had been in such fine health, and then this. At least, he died having just come face to face with one of the heroes of his life.

It was just a year later that I was playing in the Crosby golf tournament in Winston-Salem, North Carolina. Between rounds, Pam and I went through the buffet line in the clubhouse, where, sure enough, I looked up and there he was: Joe DiMaggio. This was the first time I had ever seen him in person, except for his last game in New York. I had to say hello.

It was an awkward moment, to say the least. I didn't know how to approach him or what to say. Joe was filling up on the shrimp and roast beef and salads and so forth. He was struggling with both hands full of food. Bread and rolls were falling off the plates; it was one of those Buffet Moments. I wanted to say just the right thing, but I knew I had to be quick, Joe was concentrating so hard on balancing his dinner. Finally, I just blurted it out.

"Mr. DiMaggio, my name is Jim Valvano," I said. "I'm the basketball coach at N.C. State." Joe was struggling now, the lettuce and cold cuts going every which way. But I kept plowing forward. "And my father . . . uh, you were his idol. He thought the world of you . . ."

"That's very nice," DiMag said.

"Yes," I said, "and you probably don't remember this, but he shook your hand at LaGuardia airport one day and . . . and . . . and then he died."

Oh, God! There I did it again. It was of those—as soon as it came out, I wanted it back remarks. Joe DiMaggio must have thought I was some deranged whacko who had been living with this pent-up anger and now wanted to avenge his father. I'm stunned he didn't call for the security police right then. Oh, the look on his face! And then I couldn't get anything else to come out of my mouth. I didn't know what else to say; Joe didn't know what else to say. I'm sure he thought I was some lunatic about to choke him.

Ultimately, I just said thank you, and walked back to my table. Pam asked me how my conversation went. "I think I just told Joe DiMaggio that he killed my old man," I said.

Playing in golf tournaments like the Crosby, joining the Washington Speakers' Bureau, appearing on the "CBS Morning News," even later hosting "The Lighter Side of Sports" on ESPN—all these "celebrity ops" arose out of our winning the national championship. But it wasn't as if my extracurricular career was born in March of 1983; I had done speeches and TV shows and product endorsements long before that. I took a lot of criticism for doing so many things other than coaching over the next several years, and the people who knocked me were right. I *did* do too much. There was no reason to get involved with all those things except simply that they were fun.

When somebody asked me to do a commercial, I thought, great, I'd like to see how a commercial gets done. When I had an opportunity to do the weekly gig for CBS, that was fun, too. Limos, makeup rooms, working with Phyllis George, all fun. To do that, I flew to New York each week on a Sunday night, did the show early Monday morning and was back in the basketball office in Raleigh not long before noon the same day. To say I ever shirked my duties as basketball coach during this period is simply not correct.

I did regional commercials for Hardee's and Mountain Dew. I represented an insurance company. I did commercials for a local car dealer. I got a truly lucrative contract with the Nike shoe people. I had a sports clothing line of my own—shirts and pants with a little "V" inscription—at Belk's department stores. Back at Iona, I had founded a company called JTV Enterprises. In North Carolina, I hired a local TV sports announcer named Don Shea to run it for me. Dick Stewart, my old teammate from Rutgers, came on board as a personal business manager.

JTV did all kinds of unique things. We marketed everything from huge college sports yearbooks—thick, thorough magazine and newspaper records of a college team's year, which would be bound and placed in a library—to kids' rocking chairs monogrammed with the school's logo. We were involved in the statue business. A sculptor did original, gorgeous life-size sports figures for us, and we made hundreds of copies for patrons around the country.

We had statues of Julius Erving and Walter Payton and Aristides, the first horse to win the Kentucky Derby. That likeness of Dr. J outside the Spectrum in Philadelphia? That's our original. The Payton statue is in the Chicago Sports Hall of Fame, right next to Mike Ditka's restaurant, downtown. Aristides is at Churchill Downs. Our art company was called Senter Vitale Associates Fine Art Reproductions and Sculpture (Vitale after my mother's maiden name). I didn't use my own name because I was starting to get heavily criticized for all this. Our original name was "Championship Art," but we couldn't get into fine art galleries with that name. Jim Valvano from Championship Art meant Jock Pictures. I couldn't get a Double Bubble card as Championship Art. But if I was Mr. James from Senter Vitale Associates, I could get into the Louvre. Unbelievable!

The thing is, these ideas had been in my head for years. It was winning the national championship that made them viable. I remember flying to the little town of Hickory, North Carolina, up in the mountains, and there were five thousand people waiting to get autographs. Sure, all of this activity took huge chunks out of my family time. But it was never at the expense of my job. Coaches play golf, tennis, do a lot of things in the off-season. I was doing this. And time wasn't the biggest sacrifice, it was energy. I was using up a lot of that. But then, coaches think they can go on forever, too.

While our student bookstore sold something like $500,000 worth of goods related to the national championship, there was nothing done of supreme quality. I happen to love art. I think it goes back to my art appreciation course at Rutgers. My idea was to hire an artist to paint an original portrait of the national championship game. I would make one thousand limited edition prints, sell the prints to the alumni, boosters, townspeople, food chains, anybody in the general interest area of the national champion. The payoff would be an elegant black-tie banquet to which all the owners of the prints would be invited and where I would unveil the original and donate it to the school. Also at the banquet we would have a drawing for a brand new Mercedes in the school color. The proceeds from the banquet would go to a scholarship program at the university.

My first choice for the artist on this project was Claude Monet, but he was unavailable. So we got in touch with LeRoy Neiman, who wanted to charge us around $5,000 a print. Hey, that wasn't going to work.

At the '86 Final Four, I thought the idea had come to fruition. We had the artist, the sales brochures, the commitments from almost everybody. Then Tom Butters, the athletic director at Duke, said his school was not interested.

I had gone to all four schools involved in the finals in Dallas— Louisville, Duke, LSU, and Kansas—and thought they had all agreed that whoever won the championship would participate with us in this venture and would get a ton of money in scholarships, besides. I had over $50,000 invested in the idea myself. On the Monday afternoon of the final game between Duke and Louisville, Butters told me his school would not do it. Boy, you talk about rooting. Duke's Coach, Mike Krzyzewski, was a good friend of mine, and the Blue Devils were conference blood brothers. But it was Go, Cardinals! all the way. Thank goodness, Louisville won the game. We gave the school the painting, they had a big dinner down there, but ultimately we didn't have the manpower to carry out the whole thing.

Woman power? I had that about covered too. In fact, if another idea of mine had gone over, there might not have been that huge controversy over female reporters in the locker rooms. I noticed a long time ago how embarrassed our players were talking to the women of the media right after games. So, my company marketed a school body towel, an extra-long towel in all colors and logos so schools could buy them in bulk.

Look, all of these ideas were dynamite, if you ask me. After all was said and done, I think my experiences in the fine art business ended up making me nearly a million dollars. That was the good news. The bad news was, they cost me about 1.2 million. Later on, the Raleigh newspapers would be upset because I wouldn't give out the JTV conglomerate figures. The facts were, we didn't make a dime on the clothes or the towels. The statue business lost money. I wound up losing several hundred thousand dollars on everything combined. So there was this misconception about how "rich" I was getting, on or off the court.

I'll admit that I probably should have avoided a lot of this stuff. When I first came to N.C. State, I did a mattress advertisement, a takeoff on Joey Heatherton and the Serta commercials. Me lying on a mattress in a furniture showroom. Now that . . . okay, that should have been avoided. But another of my early commercials I will never slander: Ronzoni. *"Ronzoni sono buoni,"* which means, for those of you who are either non-Italian (and I realize there are a few out there) or who have never turned on a TV in New York City, "Ronzoni is so good."

I grew up eating Ronzoni-brand pasta. That's all my mother ever cooked. She loved it; the family loved it; I absolutely adored it. My family was in the same parish as the Ronzonis. My brother Nick went to school with Ron Ronzoni. The Ronzoni factory was right next to Shea Stadium. You can imagine how excited I was when I was contacted to be a spokesman for Ronzoni. General Foods had purchased the brand, and wanted to get a foothold in the South, so they called me. Geez, I mean, I couldn't believe it. This was like a mission; spread the word about Ronzoni throughout the region. Just wait until my mother hears about this.

Whoops. "The noodles aren't any good any more," my mother said.

"Whadda ya mean, Ma? Not any good. We're talking about Ronzoni here," I said. *"Ronzoni. Sono buoni."*

"They changed their noodles," she said. "They don't make the same noodles."

Damn if my mother wasn't right! I called up Ron Ronzoni and asked him if it was true he had changed his noodle, and he said it was, that they had gone to some different recipe, it didn't work out, and now they were going back to making the noodles the old way. I said Hallelujah! to that.

The bottom line is, I went to tour the Ronzoni factory to see how the noodles were made, while Ron sent an entire shipment of Ronzoni products to my mother to check out. We all agreed that she would do her own taste test—she and her sisters would make the noodles and the sauce and the spaghetti and all the stuff—and if it passed, I would agree to be the spokesman. There I was waiting at the corporate headquarters, holding the telephone while my mother did the testing.

Sure enough, it was the old noodle. She did like it. So we ended up basing all the commercials around my mother. I'd get on the radio and

The Gift My Father Gave Me

say how I ate Ronzoni as a kid and now they were going to have it in North Carolina, so the viewers should rush right out and buy it. Why? Because my mother says it's the best noodle. I'd go to shopping malls and make Fettucini Alfredo with Ronzoni. I went to Atlanta Fulton County Stadium where they had Ronzoni Day, featuring guest artist Tom Lasorda, naturally. I even co-authored a cookbook with all my mother's recipes in it.

Don't get the idea I'm some kind of philanthropist or anything, but Ronzoni also pledged $25,000 to N.C. State over two years for scholarships. And the company furnished the food when the school started a Senior Dinner for everybody in the senior class. Who did the University ask to host the dinner so they could draw a crowd? Right. *Moi.* And what happened? Typical. They held the dinner at the student center, and more seniors showed up than they expected. They hadn't asked Ronzoni for enough pasta and ran out of food, forcing long lines of seniors to go completely hungry. Of course, who got ripped in the newspaper the next day? Right. *Moi.* I told the kids the night before, though: "Cheer up. This is part of the learning process. You're finally learning about the Real World. And let this be your first, most important lesson: Don't be last in line."

Meanwhile, back on the basketball court . . . I felt wonderful about the national championship, not the least because I had vindicated my university for giving me that ten-year contract in the middle of the 1982–83 season. Not to steal from Frank Sinatra, but we had won it my way, laughing and tap-dancing our philosophy to the top of the rankings. It was a whole different mind-set from that which people used to think was needed to win. Moreover, I had established my own credibility as a coach and leader. I think I had finally risen from the level of being just a wise-cracking clown to a coach people could take seriously for his knowledge.

When we hung that national championship banner in Reynolds Coliseum, I felt I really belonged. Remember, at that point, only a few of us had won ACC titles. Dean, of course; and Terry Holland. But only Dean and I had won national championships. Since Carolina and State had won the last two NCAA's, there were a large number of articles written comparing the styles of the two programs, the monies spent, the philosophies, etc. I remember one story comparing the Tar Heels' caste system, where the freshmen carried the bags and balls and the tape machine on trips, to our more loose program. Eventually, all of the stories got down to comparing the two coaches. Then that led to gossip, at times true but mostly untrue, escaping from behind closed doors. And that led to Dean and myself having our differences as to what we supposedly said and felt about each other.

145

I hate to disappoint a lot of people, but Dean Smith and I happen to be good friends. I have the utmost respect for Dean—for the man and his accomplishments. But what would a book by someone who had been an N.C. State basketball coach be, without some stories about the Dean?

At the coaches' meetings, Dean always came prepared with newspaper clippings in which we had been quoted. He always underlined the quotes. "Did you actually say this?" he'd ask. Well, yes, Dean, I did. But they were harmless, joking things. The quote about the Brownlee kid whose father was Dean's roommate? He had that underlined one day. Not that he didn't get us all back. After our championship season, he always kidded me about "Jim's foul-line defense. I'm anxious to talk to Jim and ask him how all those shooters missed from the free-throw line," he'd say.

Dean's position in the game has now become so venerated—and rightfully so—that his coaching is virtually inviolate. In the same year that I took all the press heat for Kenny Matthews taking that bad shot at the end of a game, the Heels blew a big lead against Virginia after they went to the four corners. I remember this so well because I thought, aha, the master is going to get ripped now. I believe the dialogue went something like this:

Reporter: "I know this has nothing to do with the defeat, but did you go to the four corners too soon?"

Dean: "Definitely not. A fine Virginia team scored 1.4 points per possession in those last few minutes, the highest number anybody has ever scored against us."

Reporter: "Oh. Thank you."

Or how about the play that won the Tar Heels Dean's national championship? They talk about the Wolfpack miracle in '83 . . .

I used to tell audiences that I had called time-out specifically to map out that lot-pass play from Whittenburg to Charles for the victory in '83. Everybody would laugh because nobody believed me. So now here's the difference between Dean Smith and me. Tar Heel fans are convinced that when Freddie Brown of Georgetown threw that pass to James Worthy of Carolina at the end of that '82 championship game . . . why, Dean had to call that play from the bench!

No kidding. I was sitting up in the stands in the New Orleans Superdome that night . . . Carolina possession . . . time running out . . . Michael Jordan about to score his famous basket. Some Carolina fans turned to me and said no matter what happened, Dean would outsmart John Thompson. They asked me if the Tar Heels scored, what would John Thompson do? I didn't know, I said, but he had three options. Brown driving the lane and looking to dish. Hit Sleepy Floyd coming off a pick. Or get the ball to Patrick Ewing and let him go to the hole.

146

Suddenly, Jordan fired the bomb. Brown raced down the floor. He stopped, looked, passed to . . . Worthy! Geez. I didn't realize there was a fourth option. "See," my Carolina fans reminded me. "Told you Dean would outsmart him."

The rivalry between State and Carolina was so intense that sometimes it adversely affected situations it shouldn't have. I think Dean felt we were even employing *spies* one year because after Terry Gannon got out of school and was first starting his telecasting career, Raycom Sports sent him to Chapel Hill to do a game. Dean wouldn't even let him into the building for some interviews. Finally, somebody convinced Dean that Terry was there only in his capacity as a television announcer and not as a North Carolina State espionage agent, and he was allowed to do the game.

Dean makes it difficult for everybody in the ACC simply because his teams have gone out and beaten us so much. Carolina is the Yankees, the role model, the measure; everybody would rather whip the Heels than anybody else in the conference. So automatically he's everyone's biggest conference rival as well.

Lefty Driesell felt this rivalry intensely. The comparisons, the images, his Maryland teams' losing records against Dean, just drove Lefty bat-crazy. And oh, did they clash, believe me. In one particular coaches' meeting, we were discussing some new rules and how they might affect recruiting, when Dean made some innocuous comment to the effect that "We don't all have the same problems; we recruit different kids."

Lefty slammed his fist down on the table. "Aww come on now, Dean. Don't give us that bull . . . We all recruit the same kids. You just don't git all of them. What about Moses (Malone)? You damn *know* you would have taken Moses if you could have damn git him."

There weren't many players Carolina didn't "git" over the years I coached in the league. And Dean didn't win eight thousand million games—has he passed Adolph Rupp yet? I've lost track—by missing any tricks, either.

At one ACC coaches' meeting a few years ago, we were sitting around discussing getting referees for our preseason scrimmages. Fred Barakat, the supervisor of officials for the conference, suggested it would be nice to give the refs a couple of tickets for the home football games on those weekends they came for the scrimmages. Then Fred went around the room, asking each coach what we provided for the refs in our intra-squad scrimmages. Most coaches said they gave the refs meals and tickets to the football games. Imagine our surprise when Dean said that he was amazed that that was all we did, since for a long time he had been feeding them meals *and* paying them to make the trip to Chapel Hill.

Whoooa. I mean, the only things all the other coaches gave the refs for those Saturday preseason gigs was a sandwich or something. I would give them ham on rye, maybe some other coach would come up with tuna fish. But *paying* them? You can imagine, Lefty went absolutely nuts! The rest of us weren't exactly happy to find out that Carolina—which got every other edge known to man—seemed to be getting a leg up in the preseason as well. Not only was Dean beating us on the court; now he was outsmarting us off the court, too. We quickly came up with a policy whereby all the schools would pay a set fee to the refs for the scrimmages.

Since we're on the subject of officials, here's another story. When I first got in the league, coaches could actually blackball officials. We'd sit in Myrtle Beach and bring up an official's name, and all you had to have was just one coach who said, "I hate that guy, I don't want him to ref any more," and he'd be out. If you had a good record with an official—say, you had a guy ten times and you won eight—you'd want him in.

Later, Fred Barakat was brought in to be the supervisor of officials, and after that, a single coach couldn't blackball an official anymore. After that, you really needed five or six of the guys in the league to dislike someone before you'd have a chance to influence Fred.

Anyway, here we were sitting in Myrtle Beach again, voting on refs, and of course Dean Smith was present. Now, Dean Smith has been so successful; the man is in the Hall of Fame already, he's got a building named after him, he's got a bronze bust. And when a guy like Dean wins so much and is so revered, it's just more fun to beat him. So, whenever Dean would say he didn't like a particular ref, and we'd vote, Dean would be the only guy with his hand up. Nobody would vote with him. By the same token, if Dean thought a guy was a great ref, hey, you might have six hands go up to get him out of the league. So Dean had to be very careful about what he said about officials. But in the end it didn't matter, because he'd beat you anyway.

With all the times Dean beat me both on and off the court, I still had a chance to get the last laugh. The final game ever played in Carolina's Carmichael Auditorium was another Carolina victory to the tune of 90–79. While all of the fans were cheering on the night of this hallowed building's closing, I rushed over to shake Dean's hand. After we shook, I took the game ball from him and drove in for a lay-up, making sure that I would forever be the answer to the trivia question: "Who made the last basket in Carmichael Auditorium?"

If I learned anything from coaching in the ACC and from our coaches' meetings in those early days, it was that, competition-wise, the league was an entirely separate planet from any place I'd been before. This was kind of hard to deal with since I consider the guys in my league to be friends. Bobby Cremins was one. In one of my early years, I asked him if he wanted to go to dinner before the game, but I could see his reticence.

Bobby's old mentor, Frank McGuire, had warned him never to get too close to his competitors, and Bobby didn't.

Unfortunately, that happens a lot in a profession when you have to butt heads with people you know so well. The fact is, though, most of us in the league got along. When the dust settled last spring and I was finally on the way out at N.C. State, Dean Smith asked me to call him if he could be of any help. He wrote me a letter this past summer asking when we could get together and play golf.

Other members of the ACC community always seemed to be feuding with Lefty Driesell. But they all showed up for his roasts, usually the tip-off of mutual affection. Terry Holland, who played for Lefty at Davidson, used to joke that when he was recruiting with the Lefthander somewhere out in the deep boonies, Lefty rolled the window down to ask directions and got arrested for mooning. Bill Foster said he talked with Lefty's parents. His mother wanted him to be a doctor and his father wanted him to be a basketball coach and it's a shame they both had to be disappointed.

Similarly, Mike Krzyzewski is a close friend of mine, and we don't hesitate to nail each other. During the '84 Final Four weekend, as the coach of the defending champions, I got to coach the East in the coaches' All Star game. We lost by 43 points. At the banquet that night, Coach K announced to the crowd that despite the outcome, prior to the game he had such faith in me, being in the same league and all, that he had taken the East and 44.

I got him back last summer in several speaking engagements. "You know, Mike had a tough summer, living out that 103–73 Las Vegas victory in the championship game. But I just want Mike to know I was with him all the way, I knew he'd get it done. I had Duke and 31."

Chapter Thirteen

PLANES, TRAINS, HI'S, LO'S, SPUDS, SHACKS, AND TREYS

AFTER THE '83 CHAMPIONSHIP SEASON, ONE OF THE HIGHLIGHTS OF THE year was being invited to visit the president of the United States at the White House, on two occasions. (Back then, NCAA rules prohibited the team from accompanying a coach to the White House; that rule has since been changed.)

It was a great thrill, and quite honestly, I was very excited to meet President Reagan. He's a very warm and friendly person who made me feel right at home. Unfortunately for me, I can never pass up an opportunity for a laugh. When the president asked me how to pronounce my name—Val-vah-no or Val-vane-o—I told him, and then I asked him how he liked his name pronounced: Ray-gun or Ree-gun? We had a good laugh over that one.

On the second visit to the White House, Thurl Bailey, Sidney Lowe, Dereck Whittenburg and I were being honored by the Washington Touchdown Club for our national championship, along with Morgan Wootten, the legendary DeMatha High School basketball coach, who coached both Sidney and Dereck. My sense of humor must have rubbed off on my players. When we toured the White House and were shown the Roosevelt Room, Dereck pointed to a chair and asked whether President Roosevelt sat in it. The guide said he was sure he did. Dereck pulled up the chair, sat in it, and said, "Next time you give a tour, make sure you say 'President Roosevelt *and* Dereck Whittenburg sat here!'"

On the way out, one of the president's aides remarked that I had been there two weeks in a row. I said, "Yeah, it's been great. However, I don't know about the president, but I can't make it next week."

Winning a national championship increased my and the team's

visibility. In addition to my own local TV and radio shows, I worked on the "CBS Morning Show" in New York. The TV exposure helped us broaden our recruiting base and recruit nationally. Actually, we started taking too many big-name guys and not enough role-fillers. I got heady over athletic ability, and we brought in several star-turn youngsters who were unwilling to share playing time. Unhappy campers resulted in unpleasant situations, and serious problems soon were to follow.

Although our '83 NCAA title enabled us to bring many more blue-chippers flocking to Raleigh, it didn't necessarily mean we would sign any.

I'll be honest with you. There are things I certainly do miss about coaching: the excitement and emotion of the locker room; the challenge of preparing a game plan and then going out and trying to execute it; the hugs and the tears and the kisses after victories. I don't miss the tremendous burden that I felt after a defeat. But the one thing that I *really* don't miss—and, to be honest, it's something I was pretty good at—is recruiting.

Without question, recruiting is the most difficult, and probably the most demeaning, aspect of college coaching. It's also the most important aspect, the one on which you spend the most time. Let me give you an idea of what it's like.

First, you have to make lots of phone calls. You have to stay in touch with the kids. And there are so many rules and regulations about when you can call and how many times you can see a player, it's difficult to keep them all straight. But still, you've got to stay in touch. The more contacts you have with a kid—you can only have six in person off-campus, but you can write letters and call—are important. So at least once a week, generally after my Monday night radio show, I'd meet my assistant coaches to make calls. We'd take my office, the secretary's office, and then the other two assistant coaches' offices; we'd have four or five phones going at once. I'd be in there and one assistant coach would say, "Line 1, Coach," and he'd tell me where the kid was from, and then he'd stick a note in front of my face with the youngster's mother's name, father's name, the dog's name, the girlfriend's name—not that I didn't know them, but when you're dealing with so many kids, to remember it all off the top of your head becomes difficult. So I'd take it and then I'd say, "I saw this kid at the Nike camp, didn't I?" Or, "I saw this kid at Garf's camp. Yeah, I remember now. Sure. I saw him play."

Then I'd get on the phone and say, "Hey, Billy, how you doing? How's it going? How's Mom and Dad? How's that dog of yours? How's that girlfriend? How's chemistry class going? You still want to play point guard in college?" And you'd talk. Then you'd say, "Well, we'll see. Hopefully you're going to come for a visit, set that up. Everything's great.

151

Put your mom and dad on, I'd like to talk to them." Then another coach will say, "Line 3, Coach, line 3, it's the center from . . ." Oops, got to get in there and do that. And you'd talk to them and then pick up the next line, on and on.

At times, bizarre situations would occur. Sometimes you'd pick up the wrong phone: "Hi, Billy, how you doing? Oh, it's not Billy, it's Tommy. Sorry, Tommy." One time, the mother answered, and I said, "Gee, how you doing? Is so and so home?" No, he was gone, which happens quite often. I said, Well, how are you? And she said, Well, she shot herself in the foot last week. It's one of those lines that are hard to respond to. Hey, gee, I'm sorry you shot yourself in the foot. You want to say, Why'd you have a gun? So you say, Well, okay, take care of that foot, and keep the safety lock on, take care. Boom.

And in addition to calling the kids, you have to call all the people involved. The closer you get to the possibility of signing a youngster, you've not only got to call the player, you have to call the coach, you have to call the minister or the grandmother . . . whomever it is that is making the decision. It can get a little crazy.

Then, the visits: Every weekend you have the youngsters coming to visit your campus. I've been embarrassed on more than one occasion. One time, we had a kid who kept telling me he was interested in engineering. So, we set up a meeting with the head of our school of engineering. We got in there, and the dean of the school of engineering said, "Why are you interested in engineering?" And the youngster said, Because he liked trains. Right? And then you sit there . . . But you've got to go through all of these things to recruit.

There are a lot of ways to lose a player. There's the story about one of the assistant coaches who had worked all year with a particular guy, and got really close with the kid and the family, and again knew the whole thing, always was sure to ask about the dog, and so on. It got down to the last home visit; the kid was going to make a decision soon. They said good-bye, he tickled the dog good-bye, and then the assistant coach backed the car out of the driveway and ran over the dog. Yep. He didn't get that player, I guarantee you.

Then, too, you come upon serious problems in recruiting. I was in a home once, seeing a youngster to whom we had devoted a lot of time and energy. The kid seemed like a nice young man. We were in his home, getting ready to sign a letter of intent. The youngster signed it three times, and then the mother came in. She looked right at me and said, "What are you going to give me?" And I said, "What do you mean, what am I going to give you?" She said, "The last school said they'd pay our rent for a year. Over my dead body is my son going to your school for nothing." So we just walked out and went about our business. But that's the kind of situation I'm not going to miss.

Another time, we were in a home, again visiting a nice family and a nice young man. The family wanted to come to the school to see some games, and asked where they could stay when they came up; where they could get a meal. Obviously, they were hinting that they wanted us to put them up. We said, We can't do that. They said, We could stay with an alumnus or something. No, you can't, we said. And they said, Well, that makes no sense. They said, There's got to be someplace that will take care of us. And you have those situations, where you walk out knowing you're not getting that kid. And when you see that youngster go to another school, you know what's going on at that place.

Let me clarify one thing about recruiting. I still feel that the majority of the programs in schools are clean, or do everything possible to stay clean. I also think that many of the "holier than thou" programs are fortunate that they're at schools where they don't have to cheat to recruit, because the schools attract the better players. That's not to say that the coach or the program shouldn't be praised. God bless them, that's wonderful. But sometimes we're too quick to jump on another coach and program where it might be a lot more difficult to attract the kind of student athlete they want. Yet that coach is still under the same pressure to win. Until a university can be realistic in its approach to what is required of its coach, you're going to have situations where people are in the last years of their contracts, knowing that if they don't win, they may get fired. These are the people who are going to look the other way and say, Well, this kid may not be able to make it academically, but I need him for a couple of years. Or, the only way I'm going to get this player is if we offer what he's asking for.

I know that there are a lot of people who think there are thousands of horror stories about recruiting. The fact that I don't have a lot of them is because, for ten years, I was in a conference that basically didn't have to recruit illegally. The ACC will attract great basketball players, and for the most part, you're going to see programs that are winning. The ACC has had some problems recently, and we were part of it, but at least we had no recruiting violations whatsoever. One thing that I can say is that we didn't cheat. But I can certainly see the problems that arise in schools that are trying to compete at the highest level, who don't have the same advantages of schools in the bigger conferences. These are the real problems that a coach has with the recruiting of athletes. Recruiting will always be the lifeblood of a successful program, as well as the most difficult aspect of the job.

Of all the fine point guards we went after during our championship run—Pearl Washington, Kenny Smith, Keith Gatlin—we signed precisely none, which is why I found myself at the Raleigh-Durham airport one day waiting for somebody from Midland College in Texas named Anthony Webb. My assistant, Tom Abatemarco, had told me about this kid and how he could jump out of the gym. We were desperate for a point guard anyway, so we had invited him for a visit.

As everybody had already de-planed, imagine my surprise when this young-looking, rather short guy approached me in the airport.

"If this is our point guard, you're fired," I said to Abatemarco.

"Uh, V. I forgot to tell you. His nickname is Spud," said my suddenly not-long-for-this-world assistant coach.

"Coach Valvano?" said the kid, sticking out his hand.

"Unfortunately, yes," I said.

Actually, Spud Webb was five feet, seven inches, 138 pounds of the most amazing, exciting basketball player that I and anybody else in college basketball would see over the next two years. For our first game of the 1983–84 season, we played a rematch against Houston in the Tipoff Classic in Springfield, Massachusetts. This was a game many in the N.C. State camp advised me against playing, for fear we'd get our butts kicked in the way they must have expected we would in the title game six months before. For one thing, Houston had Olajuwon, the best center in basketball, back. And we had lost three fifths of our starting lineup. Yeah, we could have lost. But what could they do—take our championship trophy back?

On the other hand, I pointed out, what if we won?

We won by 12 points. And the MVP of the game was none other than Anthony (Spud) Webb. Spud scored 18 points, had 5 assists, 4 rebounds and 3 steals in the first of many scintillating performances over a season in which: 1) he led the ACC in assists, and 2) I'll be honest, I was quite happy to finish with a 19–14 record. I'll be honest, because several weeks from the end we were 19–7. Actually, I was quite happy to finish the thing *alive.*

I wasn't the only one who realized how heavy a load we had to carry after losing the championship team's senior triumvirate of Thurl Bailey, Sidney Lowe and Dereck Whittenburg. None of the preseason polls had us ranked in the Top Twenty. But after we defeated Houston and then won the Great Alaskan Shootout, beating tenth-ranked Arkansas in the final, we jumped from nowheresville to number seven, causing me to wonder how expert were the experts, including myself.

This was a transition year, and though everybody thought I was being coy when I insisted we were a season away from another national challenge, Virginia Tech wasn't fooled when we played the quick Hokies in the McDonald's Classic in Greensboro. We were 5–0 (15–0 over two years), but Tech exploited our small backcourt and quarter-pounded us, 89–65. Opponents got the "book" on State from that game, and most of the time during the season Lorenzo Charles, our only effective inside scorer, would be surrounded as if he were in a cage. How we won nine games in a row was beyond me.

I should have called off the season when we were 19–7 and given up the quest for the magic 20th victory. Carolina ripped us by 24 points—big surprise, this was Michael Jordan's last team, and maybe Dean Smith's best; the one that was upset by Indiana in the NCAA East Regional. But the game that really turned our season in the direction of the gutter was a 73–70 overtime loss to Duke at our place. Lo was in foul trouble the whole game; he only played 18 minutes. Still, we had a chance to win until Spud missed a shot at the end. After that, it was unbelievable how we just couldn't make any big plays. Not that the schedule was any solace; nineteen of our games turned out to be against NCAA tournament– or NIT–bound teams.

But people wonder why this game destroys your brain? Why, to be a coach, you don't have to be completely nutso, but it helps? Why the sport is a labor of lunacy? After we won those nine straight, we were on such a roll. One more win and we'd be in the NCAA tournament, back to defend our title, this time even more of an underdog than before. One more win. Just one. Then Carolina killed us, Duke edged us. And before you know it, it's that snowball rolling down the mountain. We couldn't stop it.

After we finished the regular season losing to Maryland for the second time in a week, the conversation went something like this:

Anybody: "Do you think you'll get an NIT bid?"

Me: "I hope not."

Fans who think teams want to keep playing when they've lost six in a row and can't get over the hump just aren't thinking straight. In that situation, you just want to pack up the balls and call it a year.

We made it into the NIT anyway. Home game against Florida State. How's this for a finish? One minute six seconds left in the game. We were up by two points with our best free-throw shooter, Terry Gannon, on the line. If he made them, it was over. If he made one, it was probably over. There was no three-point shot in the NIT yet. One free throw, just one. Gannon missed. The Seminoles raced the ball down, scored at the buzzer and beat us in overtime, 74–71.

We had lost seven games in three months, then seven games in about three weeks. And yet we had played so far above what I had expected. The most significant aspect of this first postchampionship season, moreover, was the recruitment of the player who was going to lead us back to another national championship, Chris Washburn.

Any time a coach can get a kid to sign early, it's a plus. When the kid is

6'11", 254 pounds, it's another plus. When the kid was Washburn, the fourth player in history to be named to the *Parade Magazine* All-America team for three straight years—a player sought after by almost every school and coach in America, despite his attending in his last four years Hickory High School (North Carolina), Fork Union Military Academy (Virginia), and Laurinburg Institute (North Carolina)—you can understand why I was ecstatic.

Let me say right here and now that getting Chris Washburn was the start of things going wrong for me. Let me also point out that I had no idea that would be the case. People ask, Why take a player whose academic background was so shaky, whose college board scores were so low? Like the rest of the 250 or so institutions of higher learning who were offering Chris a scholarship, North Carolina State and Jim Valvano both were taking a gamble. Coaches and universities do this all the time, and not only with athletic scholarships. There were darn few schools who were *not* looking at Washburn.

So, if I say N.C. State was okay merely by association, I also want to acknowledge that Chris was a preppy-dressed, polite, likable, seemingly happy kid whose mother worked at Hickory High and told everybody that the goal of her life was seeing her son go to college. I knew that Chris had left two high schools because of disciplinary problems. A coach is often blinded by a kid with this much talent, and thinks he'll be able to change his life. Sometimes that's true, but all too often it doesn't work that way.

Granted, if Washburn wasn't a 6'11", All-American monster talent, we wouldn't have sought him. Nor would anybody else. But it must be understood that most individuals of this athletic caliber who are recruited to play in major college competition are *not* of the academic caliber to qualify under regular admittance procedures. Kids that are below normal admissions levels are called "academic risks."

Fully five percent of the incoming freshmen at N.C. State were "at risk" students, below the standard of admission. This wasn't Jim Valvano's policy, but the university's policy. Remember this, because it's important. Jim Valvano didn't admit anybody. The Admissions Department did all the admitting.

As well-mannered and likable as Washburn was—and the media at the time fell in love with him—Chris was a follower, easily influenced. When you couple that with his academic deficiencies, you have a situation rife with danger. Right away, he got into an argument with a girl on campus and slapped her. Then, he got in trouble over a stereo. College stuff, small potatoes, right? Not exactly.

In cases like this, the downside of being a campus celebrity far outweighs the advantages. If Washburn had been an anonymous 5'9" biology major, the stereo thing would have died down within an hour. As it was, after I got a call that Washburn was suspected of stealing a stereo, I called Chris to my office. He denied it. I and my assistant questioned him for some time, but he was adamant that he didn't steal anything.

Finally, I suggested that if that was the case, he should go down to the police station the next morning to give a statement. Chris willingly agreed.

The next morning, after signing autographs at the station, Chris met alone with the detectives assigned to the case. Forty-five minutes later, an officer came and told me that Washburn had admitted stealing the stereo. In hindsight, I should have recommended that Chris take a lawyer with him. If counsel had been present, who knows? When I got to talk with Washburn, this time he admitted taking the stereo, but insisted it was just a prank, and that he was going to replace it. He said that he was afraid to tell me before. The whole thing, according to Washburn, was a joke that had gotten out of hand.

When the youngster who owned the stereo found out that it was Chris, his high-school classmate, who had taken it, he wanted to drop the charges. But the way the legal system works, once charges were filed, it was up to the District Attorney to decide whether to prosecute, and— you make the call—Chris being an already famous, 6'11" basketball player at N.C. State, no charges were going to be dropped. Oh no. The DA's office went full steam ahead.

Forget about his grades or whether Washburn should have been in school or not; what happened to him from that point on was pure and simple injustice, in addition to being absolutely disastrous to his development as a maturing adult. The national publicity, the shame, the incredible ridicule hurled upon him after the DA insisted that his test scores (which had been private and should have remained so) be put in the public record purely to embarrass the kid, not to mention all of us at State . . . this kind of thing was devastating. Was Ralph Sampson's academic record at Virginia ever revealed? Was Patrick Ewing's at Georgetown? But for this kid, there it was. I believe that the exposure of Washburn's test scores was the real genesis of the national outcry over college athletes' academic performance and, in turn, the cause of Proposition 48.

Ultimately, Washburn was placed in the First Offender program and sentenced to three hundred twenty hours of community service, reports to a probation officer, appointments with a psychiatrist and all the rest. Here it was the beginning of the '84–'85 season, and Chris had played in only seven games as a freshman—his final one a team-leading, 18-point, 9-rebound, 5-assist performance against St. Francis. Now I had to suspend him from the team for the rest of the year, since it would have been impossible for him to practice, play, go to school, and fulfill the court's stipulations. Something had to go, and it was basketball.

The Washburn situation had other ramifications for North Carolina State. While the school had all the highest academic societies in the sciences, math, and engineering, we had never had a chapter of Phi Beta Kappa, which is more associated with the liberal arts. State had been working very hard to get a chapter, and was on the verge of that just as the news of Washburn's academic problems surfaced. At the hearings on State's eligibility for Phi Beta Kappa, a professor from Duke got up and spoke about the Washburn embarrassment, effectively deep-sixing State. Afterward, the academic community felt terrible that all their work had gone down the drain, and of course they blamed me and the athletic department.

I pointed out that N.C. State was nearly one hundred years old, and that Washburn was not responsible for the previous ninety-nine years in which the University had lived without Phi Beta Kappa. But the tension surrounding the incident was palpable, and looking back, I feel that some of the seeds were planted then for what was to take place a few years later between Academe and me.

A word about the Recruiting Jones that had come over Abatemarco and myself. As I said, following the championship, we had much better access getting into the homes of the best blue-chippers in the country. Tommy knew every player in America; he had cauliflower ears from talking on the phones all day. He got up and went to bed recruiting. I still feel that Tommy is the best recruiter in America.

What happened, though, was that we got somewhat eaten up by our own success. In the past, we recruited for holes, for positions, to fill needs. No players left school in those first three or four years. Everybody was happy, mainly because we didn't have any superstars. Lorenzo Charles: It was between us and the Navy, and I don't mean Annapolis. Cozell McQueen: Us and Toledo. But now we simply went out and signed more good players than we knew what to do with. Beginning with Washburn and 6'7" John Thompson, who came from Lawrenceville, Virginia in that same year, we started getting a string of High School All-Americans . . . Charles Shackleford from North Carolina, Walker Lambiotte from Virginia, Andy Kennedy from Mississippi, Sean Green from New York. Some of them worked out, others didn't. And by that I mean that Thompson and Lambiotte and Kennedy and Green just weren't patient enough to wait a few years for their minutes. They got disenchanted with the fact that they didn't play right away. They'd always meet with me to talk about why they weren't playing more. I came to realize the more "meetings" a coach had, the more problems were on the horizon. Chucky Brown . . . Chris Corchiani . . . Rodney Monroe. Starters never have to have meetings; only those guys who didn't get enough PT (playing time) want meetings.

Valvano's coaching tip for the ages: Limit your meetings.

This became more of a unique problem at N.C. State because the school/campus itself was not enough to hold them there. Basketball was not the only reason talented players enrolled at Duke or North Carolina; so that when they sat the bench there, they still wanted to remain at those particular schools, because of the whole package—the academics, the student life and the basketball. The way we recruited at State, we got kids who seemed to have come there only because of the basketball program or the coach. And starting with the '84–'85 team, we got too darned many of them.

Look at that year's roster. Even with Washburn sitting out, we had McQueen, Charles, Thompson, Russell Pierre, Bennie Bolton—five high-quality guys on the inside who needed to play. In backcourt, we had Ernie Myers, Spud Webb and Terry Gannon, with Nate McMillan (now with Seattle in the NBA) in his first year with us after two years at junior college. All in all, it was one of the best teams I had at State, even without Washburn.

We won 20 games during the regular season and opened the NCAA tournament on a for-once friendly court, the Pit in Albuquerque. When we landed there, I got off the plane and, pope-style, kissed the tarmac. We beat Nevada-Reno and UTEP in Albuquerque—I didn't realize how close El Paso was to Aubuquerque until approximately 400 million UTEP fans showed me—and then dumped Alabama the next week at the West Regional in Denver. That qualified us to play St. John's for a spot in the Final Four.

We had lost early in the season to the Johnnies, 66–56, in the finals of the Holiday Festival in New York. With Chris Mullin and Walter Berry, they were awfully tough to handle. And yet I thought we could beat them. (With a maturing Washburn, I felt all season that we could have beaten anybody, even Ewing's Georgetown.)

A big, big situation. Late in the game against St. John's, we were down by three points when McQueen drove to the bucket, scored, and a foul was called. I figured the worst we could be was down one with a charge on Cozell. Silly me. The call was no basket and a charge. At the other end, I had Spud guard Mullin. I knew St. John's would try to post up Mullin, but I figured my guy would get in front of him, do some harassing, may-be steal the ball. Again, silly me. Chris controlled the ball easily, scored, got fouled and made the free throw. In a matter of seconds, we had gone from one point behind to six behind. Ball game. We lost 69–60. Whereas in '83 every decision I made in the tournament worked, in '85, this decision to play Spud on Mullin was fatefully wrong. With Washburn around, of course, we would have been able to play our big zones, and the game may have turned out differently.

Knowing we'd get Wash back the next year, that McMillan would be our glue, that Shackleford was coming in, I didn't feel that badly about the defeat. But as soon as I got back to Raleigh, my mother—having flown home to New York from Denver—called with the news that my father had died of a heart attack.

All the pluses in my life left me for several months after Rocco Valvano died. Enthusiasm, work, play, dreams, laughter. I did not deal with his passing well. I wasn't happy. I questioned myself. And then I realized that the gift he gave me was this unshakable belief in myself, and that if I lost that, I would have lost everything. I also realized the importance of trying to give that gift to other people. Eventually, I snapped out of my funk and vowed to work toward that goal.

Not that the '85–'86 team had to be told to believe in themselves. That group was the quintessential example of overrecruiting. No, that's not the proper term; "improper blending" is more accurate. We had the same number of fourteen players, but they were all stars. Or former stars. Even a guy whom I thought might never make it, sophomore Vinny Del Negro, was progressing to the point where he would be an important contributor.

We were a huge question mark in the league in that we had lost our top three scorers, and our preseason roster was made up of seven untested bodies—including five freshmen—whom we would be counting on. The thing was, almost the entire squad expected to be playing, and that's where the grumbling started. Despite all this, we managed to make it to the final eight in the NCAA tournament for the second straight year.

Five games into the season, however, a situation occurred which turned out to be another watershed in my career at State. The name of the watershed was Charles Shackleford.

Shack was 6′10″, 222 pounds, the North Carolina high-school player of the year at Kinston, an angular, slippery, slashing-type player with size 19 feet and a thousand moves, most of them unorthodox. If you thought a Shack basket was, to put it mildly, interesting, stay tuned. The next Shack basket would be totally different.

Shackleford was an academic qualifier—Proposition 48 had not been instituted, although it was being talked about—both by NCAA and N.C. State standards. But because he had scored less than 700 on the college boards and had struggled in the classroom, Chancellor Bruce Poulton thought it best that he attend summer school prior to enrolling with the freshman class. In addition to that, the Academic Skills Program people felt that Shack would become more acclimated to his studies if he sat out a while and just concentrated on his grades. It was agreed that we would give him an incentive. We had a big game coming on December 7 in the Greensboro Coliseum, against Kansas. It was decided that if Shackleford made the mandatory progress—which ultimately he did—that would be his coming-out game at N.C. State.

As an aside, it has been my experience that kids to whom academics are not that important need some kind of carrot to succeed. There are also certain athletes who play only as hard as the competition warrants; there are tenfold as many students who study only as much as they have to. If they know they've got to make a 1.6 to qualify, they'll make a 1.6. If they know they've got to make a 2.0, they'll make the 2.0.

Well, with the attendant hullabaloo over the decision to play Shackleford, you would have thought I had grabbed a bucketful of grenades and rushed the hallowed halls of Academic Integrity! The presumption was that the kid had been "ineligible" all along—which was not the case—and that we were breaking our own rules because it was a big game. That simply was not true. No matter what school we were playing on December 7, Shack would have played. However, the fact that it was a nationally televised game, against a national power, gave Shack even more incentive to try to do well academically.

It was a situation where perception again superceded reality. The truth was that we had made a decision based on academics at the beginning of the school year in order to help Shack. Now it had become a sinister plot to trash the system. Sometimes, I felt I just couldn't win.

Under the attendant media hype—it was also the homecoming game in Greensboro for Kansas' Danny Manning; if Larry Brown had not taken the coaching job in Lawrence and had not hired Danny's father, Ed, as an assistant coach, we always felt we would have had a great shot at getting Manning—a shaky Shackleford, nervous and scared, threw up an airball on his first free throw. He wound up with nine points and five rebounds, and though Manning didn't play as well as he could, Kansas won 71–56.

How did the development of the rookie Shackleford affect our team? Well he developed, all right. In our last six games of the season against Oklahoma, Virginia, Iowa, Arkansas-Little Rock, Iowa State and, ahem, Kansas again, Shackleford accumulated these points/rebounds: 14/11, 12/8, 10/8, 15/11, 22/7, and 20/6. Meanwhile, Washburn, although a sophomore eligibility-wise, was playing his first season on the varsity as well. In those games his stats were: 22/9, 19/6, 18/9, 22/7, 20/6 and 17/5.

I belabor all these numbers only to show that in the next few seasons, N.C. State seemed to be set with the finest young front-court tandem in the land.

Little did I know, back on December 7 of that season, that three and a half months later we would face Kansas again, this time the prize being a trip to the Final Four; and that I should have treasured those days of wine and roses to the hilt. It was not only the first time Shack and Wash would be so young, great and naïve together, it was the last.

If the Kansas games were the bookends of our season, in between came a set of four weekends in which we glowed in a stretch of national TV games that was probably the finest consistent basketball my teams ever played at State. February 2—we beat Kentucky 54–51 with a box zone and chaser on Kenny Walker. Kentucky went on to a 32–4 record and Eddie Sutton was coach of the year. February 8—we beat Louisville 76–64, the last time the Cardinals would lose all season. They went on to win the national championship.

Before the Louisville game, it was announced that I would be the new athletic director at State. A while before, all of the coaches had gotten together and signed petitions which they sent to the chancellor, supporting me for the job. However, when the chancellor offered me the job, he said I had to quit coaching. I said I don't want to do that, so the discussion stopped. Then after that, a number of coaches went over to ask the chancellor just to let me do the job, because they wanted to work for me. The chancellor decided to let me coach, and that we would evaluate the situation every year, and if it got to be too much, I'd stop doing it.

Now, I took no money for the job. In fact, when I first took the job and I got the letter of appointment, they said my salary would be $77,000. At the time, I was making $84,000 as the basketball coach. So I had to call the chancellor to say, I'll tell you what, let me just get paid as the coach and forget about the AD's job salary, because it was one thing to work for free, but it was another thing to take a $7,000 pay cut for the job! The chancellor got a good chuckle out of it, and then they sent me a letter stating that I'd be paid the basketball coach's salary. I did the job because I was asked to do it, and because I enjoyed the relationship with the other coaches.

Funny thing: After it was announced that I would be the new athletic director at State, Denny Crum, the Louisville coach, said he didn't think anyone could handle both jobs. I said, That's why we didn't interview Denny. Funny thing number two: Crum has won two NCAA titles, and in both those years I was lucky enough to coach the last team to beat his champs.

February 15—we lost to would-be national finalist Duke 72–70, after leading by two with under a minute to play and Shackleford on the line! I'll never forget it. Shack missed and they scored to tie it. Then Washburn missed an easy dunk! And our Nate McMillan got called for fouling Johnny Dawkins deep in the corner at the buzzer. Dawkins threw up an air ball, we would have been in overtime, yet they still blew the whistle. Arrggghhh! (Do I need to recount that Dawkins made both free throws? Or that after we came down for one last shot, Washburn got absolutely hammered and nothing was called? Arrrggghh!)

Where was I? Oh yeah. February 23, we beat North Carolina—Brad Daugherty, Kenny Smith, Joe Wolf, Jeff Lebo, all the usual suspects—76–65.

In terms of sheer talent, though young, this may have been the best team I ever had. In the NCAA tournament we beat Iowa at Minneapolis —again, my acumen in geography prevented me from realizing how much a "visiting" team we'd be, like 30,000-strong to zero—despite my initiating a tournament-long habit of splitting my pants. Once we beat the Hawkeyes, I figured we'd be a sentimental underdog against Notre Dame . . . until Notre Dame lost to Arkansas-Little Rock. So Little Rock was the underdog. And they had a coach who looked like he was right out of Hollywood, named Mike Newell. Hey, Mike, I felt like saying, what's with the *tan?* This is *March*, guy.

As if those weren't enough cards stacked against us, the following week at the Midwest Regional in Kansas City—Big Eight country—we would have to play two Big Eight teams, Iowa State and Kansas. When we finally got the Jayhawks again, I felt pretty good with all the revenge going for us. And I had a confident eye on the Final Four as well, where Louisville, Duke and LSU would wind up. We'd beaten Louisville, we'd lost on a prayer to Duke, and LSU was a team I felt we could compete with.

Eight minutes to go in the Midwest final. North Carolina State ahead by five points. I remember when the young John Madden asked the old Vince Lombardi at a football coaches' clinic what was the difference between a good coach and a great one. "A great coach knows what it looks like when it's right," said Vince. That's a wonderful description, because most of us don't know what we're looking for, much less what it's supposed to look like. And right then, I thought I was one of the greats simply because I realized this looked so right. We were ahead of Kansas at Kansas. We were about to survive and advance. We were going to Dallas to win it all one more time. And then . . .

And then down from the stands, all around us, enveloping Kemper Arena in Kansas City, came the unmistakable sound of the famous Kansas chant from 16,800 Jayhawkers. "ROCK . . . CHALK . . . JAY . . . HAWK . . . ROCK . . . CHALK . . . JAY . . . HAWK . . . ROCK-

CHALK, JAYHAWK!!!" I'm telling you, it was like they were waving the
wheat up there. Anywhere else on this planet, we'd have locked up the
game easily. But then they started chanting and waving the wheat. I think
it was Washburn who came over to the sideline totally bewildered.

"Coach, what's that mean?" he said.

"Chris, that means we are in deep doo doo," I said.

After Kansas came back to beat us 75–67, I was disconsolate. We were
right there on the verge again. I was drained and feeling miserable. I had
had my butt absolutely kicked in. I wanted to go someplace and die, just
to get away from these media hordes. Suddenly I felt a tug in the back of
those pants that I had kept splitting all month. It turned out to be the Old
Perspective, this time in the darling guise of Lee Ann Valvano, age five.

"Daddy, I'm hungry," she said. "Could we get some pizza?"

Kids say the darndest things. They also save the darndest moments.

"Folks, I gotta go," I said. "The lady wants pizza." Tears welled up in
my eyes as I took Lee Ann's hand and walked down the hall.

"Hey, kid," I said, pulling her close. "You want the usual beer with that
pizza?"

Looking back over that season, I still feel a tremendous sense of loss
and disappointment. Not just for what happened, but what could have
happened had we kept that team together. To no avail, I advised
Washburn to stay at State and not turn professional. I told George Karl,
the coach of the Golden State Warriors who drafted Wash with the third
pick (and signed him to a contract calling for 3.2 million dollars over four
years) that at twenty-one, with only one college season of experience
behind him, he wasn't ready. During the short time I had known the
young man, the only problem he *hadn't* had was with drugs. But
Washburn was impressionable, immature, a follower unable at the time
to separate those paths marked good and bad.

If Washburn had been an ornery character battling society every
minute, it would have been one thing. But his ultimate fate was really a
shame: a few substandard years in the NBA, drug addiction, dismissal
from the league. A lot of people have come down on me for not watching
his progress more closely. But the truth is, we did monitor Chris with
tutors, study halls and the like. It may be a valid criticism that N.C. State
took him at all, but it is not valid to say we didn't watch out for him in
Raleigh. Chris Washburn remains the most talented player I ever
coached, but he alone is responsible for his actions.

Ironically, the key guy—or so we thought—the next season, '86–'87,
was not brought in to replace Washburn, but to be our point guard.
Kenny Drummond, 5'10", was another junior-college transfer, this time
from Sacramento City College where he was the MVP of the California
JC championship tournament. Drums was a tough street kid, an in-your-

face defender who backed down from no one and never met a three-point bomb he didn't think he could unload.

Initially, this was beneficial. It was the first year the three-pointer went national, and Drummond's trifecta helped us defeat Navy and David Robinson 86–84 in another Tipoff Classic at Springfield, Massachusetts. (The replay showed Kenny's foot *inside* the line.) Ultimately, it was Drummond's undoing. When he got in a shooting slump later in the season, Kenny kept firing. That—and his unpopularity with his teammates—led to constant booing and catcalls from the N.C. State fans, causing Drummond to leave the program.

The lowlight of this season occurred a couple of days after Christmas when I came down with the flu, was sick as a dog and missed a game for the first time in my coaching career. Our 67–62 defeat at Tampa would become infamous due to some later point-shaving allegations, but I have always doubted that this game could possibly be involved—for no other reason than that Tampa is a Division II school, and this matchup wouldn't even have been on the betting board.

Later in the season, we lost eight of nine games, a streak during which Drummond got into a fight with Shackleford on a road trip to Virginia, stopped trying and then quit the team cold. We momentarily surfaced only when my closest friend in the entire world (at least for that night) showed up, Steve Vacendak, coaching Winthrop, whom we managed to beat 85–58.

A word about Drummond–Shackleford, and you might understand how the perils of a coach encompass more than trying to separate the W's from the L's. Kenny Drummond was very aggressive and hard-nosed. I loved his attitude, but it did cause some friction with his teammates. All of that culminated one day when Drummond asked Shackleford if he could borrow his car. Shack let him, but when Drummond returned and Shack asked for the keys, Drummond said he had already given them back to him. It was one of those "yes I did, no you didn't" kind of arguments that just swelled until we got to Charlottesville, and the two scuffled on the team bus. I had already left the bus, and guys told me about it later. There went my "monitoring the team" reputation again.

Later, I called both of these alleged adults into my hotel room, ordered peace and asked them to apologize. But Drummond would not accept Shackleford's apology. "Even Jesus Christ forgave on the cross," I told Drummond. "You can certainly forgive a teammate." But he wouldn't. That night against Virginia, Drummond played the first seven or eight minutes, but he wouldn't even take a shot. I pulled him. Over the next few weeks we had long talks about his problems, and Drummond stayed around for another half-dozen games, but his heart wasn't in it. He finally packed it in and left. I still feel Kenny was one of the most talented guards I ever coached.

With three games left before the ACC tournament, our record was 14–14. I was understandably concerned that we wouldn't finish with a winning record. In the coaching business you hang onto every little thing, and I was proud of my accomplishment of being the only ACC coach who was currently coaching who had never had a losing season at his school.

Of course, this was my first full season of being both coach and Athletic Director at State. As AD, I had scheduled Chicago State to close the regular season. DePaul in Chicago, Loyola of Chicago, the Chicago Bears, Chicago State. Who knew the difference? Realistically, if we could beat either Maryland or Wake Forest, we'd finish the regular season on the plus side. We wound up beating all three, but the Wake game continued a hellacious series that got more and more bizarre as Bob Staak, one of my best friends in coaching, took over the Deacons in Winston-Salem.

This particular game found us three points behind with four seconds left, when I called our "diamond" play, with all our guys crossing and Vinny Del Negro coming to meet the baseball pass from out of bounds. It worked perfectly. Bob got criticized roundly for not fouling, but Vinny caught the ball, took one dribble, and fired in a trey that tied the score at the gun; we won in overtime.

A sixth-place team in the ACC, only 6–8 in league play during the season, we also won the ACC tournament. Ho hum. You figure it. First, we beat Duke 71–64 in overtime, in the ugliest game ever played on any planet. Then we beat Wake Forest again, 77–73, this time in double overtime, even though Mugsy Bogues scored any time he wanted to. Finally, we played North Carolina, which had beaten us by 18 and by 17 points during the season. Ho hum, again. It was the first time I told the team about my father, that I had told him I wanted to win another championship for him. It was a very emotional pregame, but I believed very strongly that this team could do something extraordinary.

Actually, they did two extraordinary things. Behind by a point with time running down, Del Negro drove the length of the court, went baseline and got fouled. He knocked in the one and one. Then we told our defensive jet, Kelsey Weems, to get in Kenny Smith's face all over the court. Carolina threw the ball in and never even tried to get it to Smith, so oppressive was Weems. The Tar Heels' Ranzino Smith wound up taking a long jumper which missed badly, leaving them on the downside of the ACC championship, which we won 68–67.

If this was the team a future book would term "troubled," you could have fooled those who watched them scream and dance and jump all over each other in one of the most emotional scenes I've ever witnessed. Me, I was the epitome of cool, naturally. My family found me still babbling incoherently three days later.

We weren't that good, of course. In our first-round NCAA game we got blown out by Florida, which had the infant monster, Dwayne Schintzius, at center and the Vernon Maxwell-Andrew Moten M&M backcourt. It didn't help that in the week leading up to the tournament, Shackleford and Chucky Brown hobbled around on bad ankles swathed in air casts. This was another game that has cropped up in the stories about Shackleford and point-shaving. But if a key guy was dumping, wouldn't his injury affect the line the wrong way? I never saw evidence of Shackleford trying any less than his best in any game.

Florida's guards exposed our major weakness, which is why for the '87–'88 season I went out and recruited what I think has been the best college backcourt in the nation for four years: a pure point guard in Chris Corchiani from Hialeah, Florida, and a shooting guard extraordinaire in Rodney Monroe from Hagerstown, Maryland.

Within the '87 Final Four was manifest the vast changes spreading through the game: speed; fast-breaking, all-court defense; three-point shooting. UNLV made it to New Orleans by running and pressing. Providence made it doing the same. Syracuse went to the final game in warp speed. Indiana used outside bombing to win it all. To attract the kind of players needed to keep up this style, I had to change my approach: Press more, run more. Tom Davis at Iowa was one of the innovators of this approach, so over the summer I studied the intricacies of the 1–2–1–1 press and other defenses.

From day one in practice, I had a ball coaching this style. No more tall timbers, stand-around offense. With Shack and Brown and Avie Lester, we could really motor. Again, I remembered Lombardi's line about what it looked like when it was right: This looked right.

Then, in the third game, I turned chicken. We were pressing and running like crazy against Kansas right on our home court. We got a 10-point lead before they recovered and started breaking us down. But instead of plugging the holes like I'd been doing all summer and in the preseason, I copped out. "This sucks," I said to my coaches. "This press sucks. What the hell are we doing this for?" I didn't think I had any control over what was happening. So I went back to our old slow-hand stuff. Confused the players totally. Terrible coaching. They thought we were running the best operation possible, and then we stopped. We lost that game 74–67, Kansas went on to win the national championship, and we went on to lose in the first round of the NCAA tournament to Murray State, which was not a dance studio after all. And *I* was a dunce.

Oh, we had some high notes during the season. We won a Valvano's revenge championship in Hawaii's Rainbow Classic. Remember how I was so upset about losing to Rice several years before? When we got to halftime of the championship game against Arizona State, playing like horses' you-know-what, I chewed some serious butt in the locker room. Not to mention, knocked some down. Unfortunately, as I roared back through the door to give the team another tongue-lashing, I knocked our team physician, Dr. Jim Manly, out cold.

Here's one of those situations where a team wants to laugh out loud at the maniac who's just made an idiot out of himself, but they can't for fear of being murdered by the enraged despot. They knew they'd better not laugh. Meanwhile, I couldn't break the tough-guy mood or we'd be finished. "Goddammit. Somebody take care of that doctor," I snarled. "What the hell is he doing behind the door, anyway?"

We beat Arizona State 83–71 on the way to a 24-victory season in which we'd only lost two games in a row once until the very end, against Duke in the ACC's and against Murray State, which I might add went on to play champion Kansas tougher than anybody in the NCAA's, losing 61–58.

Frankly, we were again first-round flat there in Lincoln, Nebraska. Bob Devaney, the Nebraska AD and former football coaching legend, collared me about my opinion that the NCAA should stage a championship football playoff just as they do in basketball. "Let me tell you this," said Devaney. "Right now we have 36 Bowls so 18 teams go home happy. In your tournament, one team wins and 63 go home unhappy." The next day, I was one of those 63.

Every season, with the increased visibility of our program on television, we always got cards and letters from fans critiquing the players' postgame interviews. I always told the team to try in these exchanges to offer something interesting, different, maybe some key word which would make them sound better. After our final victory, against Clemson in the ACC tournament, Shack was asked how he came to be so effective with either hand.

"Yeah, well, coach told me to work on being more amphibious," Shack said. Which wouldn't have been so bad except that he announced that his *coach* had said it.

"Yeah, well, you should see Shack in the pool," I said.

That year was the birth of what I consider my most effective team ever at N.C. State, the '88–'89 bunch. I had stopped recruiting numbers; I was just going for happy now. Even though Shackleford had gone hardship to the pros, I felt that with Lester, who was a much better defensive player, we'd be better. That summer, whenever I was asked who would play center and I'd mention Avie Lester, the response would be, "Oh." I called it the Avie Count. And I told him about it.

"Nobody thinks you can play, Avie," I said. "I've gone to four Wolfpack Club meetings, and the Avie Count is up to 874 people who think you can't cut it." The whole summer I spent working on Avie's head because I knew he had what it took body-wise; I loved his ability, his rebounding and shot-blocking potential. Moreover, with Corchiani and Monroe, I had the ideal backcourt. Chucky Brown was just coming into his own as a pro-caliber player and Brian Howard, our other forward, was the brightest guy on the court I'd had since Sidney Lowe.

I had great confidence. The longer you coach, the more comfortable you feel about what you're doing. Plus, academically, we were fine; Howard, Corchiani, and Monroe were all on course to graduate. I wasn't worried about the others, either, having been told that Lester had scored the highest on his college boards of any black athlete who was currently in the state university system.

The kinks we had to work out early on were in Corchiani's game and fiery personality. In our first road game at SMU, Chris picked up two technical fouls, which cost us in a two-point defeat. Further, we put all his possessions over our first three games on one videotape and had him look at them. He was on the brink of becoming an outstanding point guard—by the time you read this, he may have set the all-time NCAA record for assists—but he had to become more consistent in his decisions. Chris is the best straight-ahead north-south player I've ever had. He explodes that myth of black-equals-quick, white-equals-slow guards; he's always been able to get by anybody of any color.

We were 12–1 and highly ranked before really getting into the meat of our schedule, but by this time in the growth of our program, in-season rankings didn't mean anything any more unless we were playing number one. The NCAA tournament was everything. On January 7, we played a nationally televised home game against Temple, amid the controversy engendered by newspaper stories which quoted the jacket of an unpublished book cover alleging improprieties at N.C. State, including "changing grades," "hiding drug test results," and the exchanging of "millions of dollars."

In the locker room before the game, I was obviously chagrined and upset—the book jacket suggested that I was the instigator of the improprieties—and I told the team the charges were absurd. Nevertheless, we would play that game and every other game the entire season long in a negative spotlight that was to change every one of our lives. How would we stay focused on basketball? That first game, we held Temple star Mark Macon to six points, the lowest total of his career, and won 71–59.

After splitting back-to-back whip jobs against North Carolina (98–88) and UNLV (80–89), we continued to battle for the top spot in the ACC standings and won the top seed in the league tournament, but only after two of the more fundamentally amazing victories in ACC history.

The first win came at Georgia Tech, 71–69, when, after a severe snow and ice storm in Raleigh, we were unable to leave the Raleigh-Durham airport on schedule. Only a handful of players and myself arrived in Atlanta just 16 minutes before tip-off. Why go to all that trouble to meet a fate that would probably be a losing one? Because, as I found out that morning in the midst of deciding whether or not to brave the trip, Tech's Tommy Hammonds was hurt and would not play. "Get the snowshoes out, men!" I shouted. "We're playing Tech without Hammonds if we have to ski there!"

Two weeks later, we clinched a tie for the regular season title by outlasting Wake Forest in Greensboro through not one, not two, not three, but four overtimes. Remember, two seasons before I had won two personal battles with my buddy, Staak, in one OT and two OT's. Well, this was ridiculous. As Yogi Berra said, it was *déjà vu* all over again.

In regulation time, we again were behind by three points with the ball and with the clock running out. This time, we set up the same "diamond" play we ran before, except Weems got the ball instead of our best shooter, Monroe, who was covered. This time, Staak did foul Weems, refusing to let him shoot for the tying trifecta. Weems, who was a bad free-throw shooter, made the first. Now came a play which a team drills on all season long—drill and drill, sweat and toil—with the understanding that it will never, ever work.

We wanted Kelsey to aim his second foul shot so that it missed off the rim, hard to the right. Meanwhile, our rebounder on that side would go hard to the basket blocking off Wake Forest's inside defender while Monroe spun to the right outside the bodies to try and get the rebound. I was watching closely when, lord knows, the ball punched the rim, smacked the board and caromed directly to Monroe. Falling away, he threw it up over his head toward the basket. Nothing but net. Tie game.

At that moment, I looked over at Staak, who went from his early forties to approximately 186 years old. His face was ashen, his hair had all fallen out. He was one of my best friends. All I could do was form "I'm sorry" with my lips. In the overtimes, Wake kept getting ahead and we kept coming back. By the end of the fourth, Wake was exhausted; we won 110–103 simply because we had more and bigger people.

Did it take something out of us? Why suggest that? Just because in our first-round game in the ACC tournament, playing eighth-place Maryland which we had defeated twice by a total of 40 points and which was playing *without* the team's best player, Jerrod Mustaf, we lost 71–49!!!!! Perish the thought.

Astoundingly, we weren't finished yet. After beating South Carolina in the NCAA tournament, we came out against Iowa, a terrific muscle outfit from the Big Ten which had whipped Carolina in Chapel Hill in a famous midseason contest, and led 25–6, just like that. The Hawkeyes came back, and the game turned into one of the true gems of the decade in the tournament. Down the stretch, I reverted to my fouling philosophy, which meant that it was Rodney Monroe versus the Hawkeye free-throw shooters. At the end of both regulation and the first OT, we fouled, Iowa converted twice, and Rodney had to score from downtown to get us even. I remember on the second one, Roy Marble and Ed Horton admitted to the newspapers that they practically ripped Monroe's arm off. No call. Double OT.

Now, brilliant strategy. I told my team that, no matter what number I call out, give the ball to Monroe. Throw it to him, set a pick, screen, get out of the way, go hide in the corner—do anything, but get the ball to Monroe. Am I a genius or what? Rodney scored 40 points, 11 in the second overtime, and we advanced 102–96.

The team's last NCAA tournament game—I didn't know it at the time, but it was my last, period—was a coaching dream. It was against Georgetown in the Meadowlands. We were in the same sort of situation, psychology-wise, as in 1986 against Kansas: playing a tournament opponent to get to the familiar adversary, Duke.

Georgetown, with Alonzo Mourning and Dikembe Mutombo, did not scare us. In fact, when Tony Kornhiser of *The Washington Post* came to write an article on how a coach prepares for a big game, I outlined exactly what would—and did—happen. Georgetown spurted, we fought back like crazy. We played tough defense in the middle of the second half, holding the Hoyas to 17 points in 18 minutes. We played a variety of gimmick stuff on the Big East player of the year, Charles Smith, who was ill anyway. We were down by only three points, with under two minutes left and Corchiani dribbling the rock.

Chris penetrated through the lane. He let the shot go. And then one of those scenes occurred that will stay ingrained on my mind forever: The ball going in the basket. The referee holding up a fist for the foul. The foul has to be on Mourning, his fifth, he's out of the game. Corchiani, a helluva foul shooter, will make it and we'll be tied. We'll stop Georgetown at the other end, come down, hold the ball and Monroe will sink the game winner. We'll beat Duke, go to Seattle where the Final Four will be the most wide open in years. Michigan. Illinois. *Seton Hall?* Are you kidding? We're going to win the national championship!

And then the athletic director at Bucknell University, who happened to be Rick Hartzell, who happened to be the referee with the upraised fist, somehow happened to come running right toward my face, kicked his one leg up, bounced on his other leg and signaled . . . *travel!*

Believe me, I was beside myself. My eyes bugged out of my head. I couldn't believe it. There was no travel. It wasn't even *close* to a travel. Either the basket was good and no foul, or it was good and a foul. But no travel! Hartzell looked at John Thompson glaring at him, then he looked at me. It was the worst call in history. CBS' Billy Packer, courtside, said it was the worst call in NCAA tournament history. Even a guy named Rick Hartzell later wrote me a letter admitting that it was a horrid call and apologized. But nothing changed it.

As I recall, Georgetown came down and somebody jacked up a 112-footer, a shot from Seventh Avenue or some other ungodly locale. We lost 69–61. Did it hurt? Nah. Devastation, death or a plague of locusts on my face would have been easier to take. I figured a coach was lucky if he got 25 years in Division I, and since I had coached 19 already, I had about six chances left at another NCAA championship. Considering that this ref had just taken one of my remaining six away from me, that he had come as close as he could to ruining my entire existence, I thought I was quite restrained when I mentioned to the press that:

"It certainly could have gone either way. Yessir, this time the ball bounced wrong for us. Maybe next time."

It was the kind of situation that I had often said could be alleviated by the following: When we use three referees, at the end of the game, if both coaches agree, we pick out the worst one and shoot him. There was an incident in Chicago a few years back, when a guy choked a referee nearly to death over a questionable call during a church league game. The newspaper report of the incident said the referee's wife refused to press charges. She probably was waiting to see the replay.

Chapter Fourteen

STILL HARM, STILL "FOULS"

LOOKING BACK, IT WAS ALMOST AS IF THE FIFTEEN MONTHS BETWEEN January 7, 1989 and April 7, 1990 made up a separate tragicomedy of my life; a kind of Theater of the Absurd featuring pain and suffering intermingled with hilarity and constant turmoil that I subcontracted out from all the other years of my existence. I want to say up front that I've never absolved myself from any of the responsibilities of my position as the coach at North Carolina State, the ultimate head guy. I have no feelings, similarly, that "the system" did me in. But responsibility and culpability are two different things entirely. In some respects it was incomprehensible, unbelievable what happened to me. At the same time it was so very real that sometimes I recall that period as one single scene unfolding right before my eyes.

Saturday, January 7, 1989

It was the day of our game against Temple at home. We were appearing for the first time in Nike's new "Unitards," a one-piece spandex outfit, which is probably the uniform of the future. The night before, I had received a phone call from Chip Alexander, a reporter from Raleigh's *The News and Observer,* who told me that his newspaper had received a photocopy of the jacket cover of a forthcoming book about "irregularities" in the North Carolina State basketball program. He read: *"Personal Fouls.* The broken promises and shattered dreams of big-money basketball at Jim Valvano's North Carolina State." Alexander said the book

173

would accuse us of fixing grades, having drug-test results hidden from the proper authorities, and diverting "millions of dollars" from the Wolf-pack Club to the players, as well as paying them off with automobiles.

That morning the headlines read: BOOK TO ACCUSE VALVANO, NCSU OF CORRUPTION. There wasn't much joking about the new uniforms. Chucky Brown's reaction reflected most of the players' attitudes toward the charges levied against the 1986–87 team. "If all this stuff is true, where's my bread?" Brown said in the locker room. "I'm still driving an old beat-up jalopy."

To my mind, there was absolutely no truth to the allegations. I knew that there was no money changing hands between our staff and the players. I knew that we never hid the results of a drug test. What I didn't know was whether a kid had been involved with some booster, fan, or somebody else. There's not a coach in America who can monitor his teams to the degree that he is 100 percent certain every player hasn't done anything wrong.

I decided that the only way to combat the inevitable reaction to the charges was to invite the NCAA in. I was also quite confident about weathering such a probe. When you invite the NCAA in, it's very similar to calling the IRS and baring your financial books: You'd better be clean, because they'll find the spots. But I knew we'd pass muster. What was it Chris Corchiani's father always said when we recruited Chris? "You can't even get a T-shirt from N.C. State."

Personal Fouls did not come as a complete shock. A few months earlier, Sonny Vacarro, Nike's national advisory board director, had told me about a former N.C. State team manager who was trying to sell information about our program. Moreover, a month earlier, Dave Kindred of *The Atlanta Constitution* had written a column about a nameless "academic advisor" who had called him, offering to divulge information in exchange for $25,000 and a job with the paper.

That first column was filled with such bizarre garbage that it gave me a tremendous sense of security. "The coach signed up for a course in music just to show the world he's a well-rounded person," Kindred wrote. "He never attended class. One day his assistant coach was puzzled by his strange request. The boss said, 'Go to the library and get everything on Tchaikovsky. Write a book report on him.' The coach then turned in the report as his own."

I hoped that if this book was composed of patently false drivel such as this, it wouldn't harm anybody.

Focused despite all the diversions, we beat Temple. In the locker room afterward, there was a mob scene of lights, cameras and media action. The foul smell of *Personal Fouls* was everywhere, but nobody seemed concerned about whether the information was true or not. The media's attitude was, it's a great story, get all the soundbites you can. I understood why this was happening; a writer named Peter Golenbock— whom I had never seen, met or spoken with—was out to make a buck. I couldn't do anything about it, but I was seething inside.

Monday, January 9

I met with Chancellor Poulton; we drafted a letter to the NCAA requesting an investigation of the charges. I couldn't say for sure that the players had done nothing wrong, but to my knowledge they hadn't. I also felt confident that no member of our staff had violated any NCAA rule.

Thurl Bailey, the star of our national championship team, and Kenny Drummond, a player who left our team and transferred, were among the former Wolfpack players who denied they received anything illegally.

Dr. Jim Manly, our team doctor, held a press conference to explain that our drug-testing program was a nonpunitive, confidential, voluntary operation. The players did not have to be in it. But if they were, they and their parents had been assured that 1) tests were random, and 2) their names and violations were kept private. Dr. Manly explained that in 1986–87, one N.C. State player tested positive for drugs, but that we couldn't reveal his name or who took the tests.

Our drug program remained in a constant state of evaluation. Some coaches recommended it be mandatory. The student body and administration itself preferred not to have it that way, saying it was infringing on the players' right to privacy. Dr. Manly pointed out that we were hardly "hiding" drug-test results when our own policy prevented us from divulging them.

Hugh Fuller, head of the Academic Skills Program at N.C. State, the man who monitored the progress of all "at risk" student athletes, told *The News and Observer* that the University's basketball players' academic progress was "lacking." It was the first time his name surfaced in the press, and it would not be the last.

Wednesday, January 11

Gordon Griffith, a spokesman for Substance Abuse Consultants, the national firm that handled our drug-testing program, supported our position and defended the program.

Walker Lambiotte, a former N.C. State player presumed to be a major source for the book *Personal Fouls,* said in a release out of Northwestern University: "Due to my lack of knowledge, I don't feel qualified to comment on the allegation . . . but I do want to make it clear that I had no part in the writing or the publication of the book. I was approached by Peter Golenbock to contribute to the book and I declined. Anything that might appear in the book about me is second hand. I have not seen or read the book."

A series of articles emerged naming John Simonds as the major source for Golenbock's book.

Simonds was a kid from Durham, North Carolina who was one of our team's student managers in the 1986–87 school year. I had delegated the responsibility of hiring our managers to our assistant coaches, since they'd be working together closely. In this case, Ed McClain, one of our assistant coaches, who had employed Simonds at our basketball camp the previous summer, had hired him for the season. I never got to know Simonds well.

I was not that concerned about what Simonds was saying. I felt he had the same tainted credibility as some ex-players such as Andy Kennedy and Teviin Binns—young men who did not get sufficient playing time, and who were unhappy at State and had somewhat of an axe to grind. It turned out that some players had even been paid or offered money. Simonds had been a close friend and roommate of Lambiotte, who was never totally satisfied at State due to his lack of playing time.

Lambiotte was not only a good athlete, he was an academic All-American and a wonderful young man. He started the first six games of his freshman year until the vastly improved Vinny Del Negro, a sophomore, beat him out for the position in '85–'86. (Lambiotte did start 22 games as a sophomore.) After we won the ACC tournament in March '87, there were rumors Lambiotte would leave, but he publicly said he was looking forward to his final two seasons playing for us. Toward the end of that season we were trying to get a line on Lambiotte, and my assistants and I talked to Simonds about him quite a bit. We wanted John to help us try to convince Walker to stay.

That summer, Dick Tarrant, the coach at the University of Richmond, told me that Lambiotte had come to his campus not only inquiring about a transfer for himself, but asking if Dick would grant a scholarship to his buddy, Simonds, too. Naïve us. The next fall, Lambiotte did transfer, to Northwestern. But Simonds stayed at N.C. State. When he came to talk to Ray Martin, another one of my assistant coaches, about retaining his manager's job, Ray told John that under the circumstances we didn't think he had supported the program enough and it would be best that he not be manager again.

When Simonds came to see me about the situation, I backed my assistant. He seemed to take the decision well. Soon afterward he dropped out of N.C. State, ultimately enrolling at Florida State.

At the time the *Personal Fouls* story broke, I felt that there was one disgruntled ex-manager and two or three disgruntled ex-players. Every coach had disgruntled exes floating around college campuses. Who would believe their exaggerated tales of woe? Conversely, how was I to suspect Simonds would be so vindictive? In the N.C. State media guide following the 1986–87 season, there is an enchanting picture of our team, taken just after we won the ACC tournament championship, in which my youngest daughter, Lee Ann, whoops it up while sitting on the shoulders of a fresh-faced guy in civilian clothes who has a smile as wide as anybody in the picture. The guy is John Simonds.

Thursday, January 12

Roddy Jones, the chairman of the board of governors of North Carolina's University system—the body that encompassed all the state colleges in the system—announced that there would be no investigation of the N.C. State basketball program.

Dr. Richard Lauffer, former head of the Department of Physical Education, who had been retired for a year, charged that Chris Washburn's grades were changed in the school year 1985–86, and that Chancellor Poulton knew about it.

Huge news. In subsequent weeks, a faculty committee, the NCAA investigators, the butcher, the baker, the candlestick maker and everybody except "A Current Affair" checked into this allegation, and found it to be false. Of course, *that* wasn't reported with banner headlines.

My frustration was mounting. Who recorded a student's grades? Professors, by computers. Since our kids were constantly in academic difficulty, whoever was supposedly changing the grades evidently did a horrible job. First, we were being attacked for lack of academic progress. Now we were being accused of changing kids' grades. Moreover, the Buckley Amendment—a federal law which protects a student's academic records from being discussed in a public forum—was now starting to be routinely violated by professors and by the university itself.

A word on Dr. Lauffer, the former head of Phys. Ed., who was no stranger to me. Traditionally, the athletic department and phys. ed. department at most universities fight constantly. The varsity coaches are well-paid, highly visible entities in the community; the PE people, usually anonymous, hardworking members of the faculty, sometimes resent this. The two sides often clash over facilities. For example, the first time I met Dr. Lauffer, our women's volleyball team was having difficulty getting practice time because of the PE department's aerobics dancing classes.

Dr. Lauffer said he found out about Washburn by calling up his records on the computer. Why would the director of PE look up Washburn's grades? A good question; I don't know. He said he saw that a slew of "No Credit" marks had been changed to "Incomplete" over just a few weeks, the explanation for which was very simple if he knew anything at all about how the system worked. When Chris got into trouble for stealing the stereo and was required to do the 320 hours of community service, he had to drop out of school for a semester. A rule stated that if a student dropped out for medical or counseling reasons, he was permitted to take an Incomplete. So when Dr. Lauffer saw the different grades, he assumed they'd been changed, and went to Poulton. The chancellor told him that there was no academic wrongdoing. Apparently, Lauffer assumed that there had been a coverup of some nature.

Friday, January 13

Editorial writers in the state decried the decision of the board of governors not to investigate the basketball program.

Saturday, January 14

C. D. Spangler, president of the university system, said he wanted a thorough, internal investigation of the N.C. State basketball program.

The NCAA announced an immediate probe into allegations of grade-changing made by Dr. Lauffer.

Pocket Books announced they were delaying the publication date of *Personal Fouls* due to concern over veracity of the manuscript.

Oh yes, N.C. State beat Georgia Tech, 82–68.

Despite the media circus surrounding the team, our guys continued to focus on one game at a time. In the Tech contest, we put 5'10" Corchiani on the Yellow Jackets' 6'7" star, Tom Hammonds, and held him to 9 points. A day didn't go by that we didn't talk about the ongoing controversy. But what we concentrated on was the great opportunity we had to handle pressure and adversity and show our true character. I told the team that this thing could either tear us apart individually, or bring us closer together as a unit. The locker room was like an oasis, the court a comfort zone. A former Wolfpacker, Spud Webb, had a wonderful line: When somebody asked him how, at 5'7", he could go out on the floor with all those giants, he said it was the only place he felt at home. For me, the games had become that.

Wednesday, January 18

The N.C. State Faculty Senate questioned the basketball team's graduation rate.

A couple of months before this, I was asked by the faculty senate, which is composed of professors from different departments, to speak to them about recruiting, academics and college life in general, as it affected the basketball team. In our discussion, I was asked by one professor why we didn't recruit better students. I answered that our goal always was to get the best students we could and I proposed this scenario to them:

Suppose you're the basketball coach, and you go out to recruit a youngster in the state. He's an outstanding student, and his choices are Duke, North Carolina, Wake Forest and N.C. State. In your opinion, if that youngster ranks those schools academically, would he rank State 1 or 2 or 3? Nobody said anything. Let me help you out, I said. Would you assume he'd rank Duke 1, Carolina 2, Wake 3 and . . . "Yes, but not in engineering," interrupted a professor. I pointed out one of the harsh facts of life: that for better or worse, unfortunately, the best basketball players in the state had not recently been leaning toward engineering.

Let me go further, I said. Be objective now. Perception is important here; not reality. If you were a high-school guidance counselor somewhere in America and you were asked to rank the ACC schools academically, would you rate N.C. State number one?

"If it was engineering or textiles," somebody else said.

I had to point out that, normally, in my experience, the number one goal of every blue-chip hoopster in America is not to go into Engineering or Textiles. I'm just trying to be honest here, I said. (Although I detected some hostility.) Let's list the perceived best academic schools in the league: 1. Duke; 2. Virginia; 3. North Carolina; 4. Wake Forest; 5. Georgia Tech. . . . Hey, N.C. State is probably down there in the 6–8 range. I was simply trying to point out the task of a coach who goes into the home of a kid who wants to play in the ACC, a kid who is a great student and athlete and who says he wants the best education he can get. Hey—I love the school; two of my daughters go there. But this was a recruiting reality.

(In fact, *U.S. News and World Report* comes out with their own "best schools" ratings each year, which ranks schools according to both smaller regions and national university categories. For the southern region for colleges and universities, Wake Forest was ranked #1 in the October 15, 1990 issue. In the national category, Duke was ranked #7, Virginia #18, and Chapel Hill was ranked #20 among the best big schools. Even UNC–Charlotte was applauded, but there was no mention of N.C. State in either the 1989 or 1990 surveys.)

I told the faculty senate that I thought I was a very good recruiter, but that I was at a disadvantage trying to get the superior students. We've gotten a few of the Lambiottes and the Gannons. Believe me, we try to get all we can. But it's difficult. As far as rating the basketball programs in the conference, N.C. State had won ten conference championships—the same as the folks over in Chapel Hill. We'd won two national championships—the same as only nine other schools in the history of the sport. We were in the top twenty-five nationally in overall wins and winning percentage. In the ACC, I thought we were second to none, except possibly Carolina. I've lost lots of kids, I said. But I don't think I've ever lost them because of our basketball. I've lost some because of our perceived academic standing.

(Eight months later, a report would come out ranking the fifty states in order of their high-school SAT scores. Lo and behold, my three recruiting strongholds—North Carolina, South Carolina and Washington, D.C.— "boasted" average scores of 836, 838 and 846. They were ranked 1–2–3—the *lowest* 1–2–3 in the nation.)

The faculty senate wanted to know how we recruited. I showed them the pie chart I used when I went into recruits' homes, signifying that of all the players I've signed in Raleigh, 86 percent of them fall into one of three categories: Either they were graduated from N.C. State or another university; they were still enrolled at State or another university; or they had left and were playing pro basketball at some level. I couldn't be more clear than that. Obviously, the other 14 percent did not graduate, were not in school and were not playing pro ball. But I did *not* say that 86 percent were graduated. I was very explicit about the categories.

I dwell on this because in the newspaper article two months later in which the faculty senate questions were reported, the piece intimated that I'd said 86 percent of my players graduated. I didn't come close to saying that.

One more point in my meeting with the faculty. When I asked them if they knew the normal, four-year graduation rate of *all* the students at N.C. State—not merely the basketball players—only one or two had any idea. I was astounded. Well, the rate was *24 percent* over the four years. Yes, it was an incredible statistic. But I didn't elaborate on it. Not then.

Thursday, January 19

The NCAA arrived on campus in the person of Dave Didion, who would be the chief investigator on our case. Didion's initial investigation involved only academics, but soon he turned his attention to other allegations as well, including shoe and ticket sales. Didion was given an office in Holladay Hall, the main administration building just downstairs from Chancellor Poulton's office.

A newspaper story disputed my "86 percent graduation rate" (which I never claimed in the first place) and said the figure was 26 percent.

I never wanted to feel that the media was putting the worst possible twist on events, but it was hard not to. In this case, the supposition was that, of the 42 players I had recruited over my career at State, 11 had graduated. What wasn't mentioned was that 16 of those 42 were still in school. They were undergraduates—freshmen, sophomores, juniors and seniors at N.C. State and various other schools—who couldn't have graduated yet. The actual figure should have been 11 of 25, which is 44 percent; very consistent with university graduation rates.

Friday, January 20

A newspaper story said that after a basketball player had flunked out of school, Chancellor Poulton readmitted him under a special contract.

It was true that a player was readmitted under a special contract. The player was Charles Shackleford. What was not reported was Poulton's motive. The chancellor felt that in the matter of "at-risk" students, neither the school nor the students were living up to their responsibilities. A contract was drawn up for both parties to sign, stating these duties on either side. Poulton felt it might be a prototype for the future that the NCAA could administer between all schools and their athletes. At the time, this was a confidential arrangement known only to the parties involved. Somebody in the Academic Skills program must have informed the papers of its existence.

Saturday, January 21

I came face-to-face with John Simonds.

Well, not really. Through the magic of television, NBC aired taped interviews with Simonds and myself in separate places during halftime of our game at North Carolina (which we lost 84–81). I disputed the statement that I knew Simonds as well as he had indicated, and said I felt confident that the allegations in *Personal Fouls* would prove to be false.

Tuesday, January 24

Bennie Bolton, a prominent four-year player at State during the 1984–87 seasons who is quoted extensively in *Personal Fouls,* said he doubted that allegations in the book were true. He said he had never personally spoken with Peter Golenbock.

Wednesday, January 25

The NCAA investigator, Didion, interviewed Dr. Lauffer regarding his charges of academic wrongdoing.

President Spangler said he was looking into a larger investigation.

The News and Observer ran a lengthy interview with Bolton, in which he lamented the financial plight of the college player. He attacked me personally as being an "uncaring" coach.

Thursday, January 26

We beat Duke 88–73. Two months later, Duke would advance to the national semifinals of the NCAA tournament.

Friday, January 27

The academic deans at N.C. State issued a statement expressing "strong objections to the continuing distortions in the press of information concerning the grades of a former student [Washburn] . . . We have examined the records in question . . . and find the official record does not support the allegations concerning grade changes." It is signed by, among others, Dr. Larry K. Monteith, Dean of the College of Engineering. Monteith's is another name which would appear again in the next fifteen months.

President Spangler appointed a commission headed by Sam Poole to investigate the basketball program.

Poole, a lawyer and administrative assistant to U.S. Senator Terry Sanford, was vice-chairman of the board of governors of the University of North Carolina system. His commission now joined the NCAA and the N.C. State Faculty Senate as bodies holding ongoing investigations. Spangler's feeling seemed to be that, because Poulton was involved closely with the faculty senate in its *internal* investigation, the state university system should take the unprecedented step of investigating a school within its own system, thus duplicating (triplicating, actually, when the NCAA was considered) the process.

A headline at the time said: N.C. STATE WOES TOO IMPORTANT TO BE LEFT TO THE NCAA. I thought this was fairly interesting, since historically, the NCAA was the body that probed college sports programs. What? Was this a job for the FBI? The CIA? Batman? Sam Poole himself called me long distance while I was preparing the team for our game at Maryland, to assure me his investigation was only to verify the academic integrity of the university. He said this was not a "witch hunt."

Funny, but on the way back to the hotel after we beat Maryland, I could have sworn I saw several brooms flapping through the dark clouds on the horizon.

Monday, January 30

A report was published, stating that I had talked with the Los Angeles Clippers of the NBA about a coaching job.

This was not true. The Clippers had called my lawyer/agent in New York, Art Kaminsky, to inquire about my interest, but I told Art I would consider something like that only after the season. I never met with, or talked to, Clipper management, although several articles said that I had. It was just another negative on my side, adding to the public perception that I was planning to bail out amid the turmoil.

Wednesday, February 1

A *News and Observer* editorial referred to Bennie Bolton as a "thoughtful man—straightforward, honest about his strengths and shortcomings and those of others. . . . Mr. Bolton's is a bittersweet story of a poor kid from Washington who scrimped for spending money, struggled in school and gave many hours a day to basketball. He resents—calmly, philosophically—the fact that his school and his coach made a lot of money from Wolfpack basketball and he got $7 for dinner after games."

Tuesday, February 7

The N.C. State Faculty Senate issued a statement saying that, from their investigation, absolutely no grade-changing had been found.

Wednesday, February 8

It was reported that ten of twelve N.C. State basketball players were on academic warning status.

The publicity regarding their study performance came as a horrible blow to both our players and their parents. They couldn't understand why the university itself was revealing this kind of information—in effect taking shots at them. This statistic was part of a lengthy study by the faculty senate which, in addition to commending the athletic department for its stand on Prop 48, also said that the graduation rate of our players was not that different from what would be expected at a university with an overall graduation rate of 24 percent.

In addition, the report compared our school's overall graduation rate with that of other universities, specifically North Carolina (77 percent) and Duke (close to 100 percent), further supporting, I thought, my position that when evaluating a program fairly, a team's graduation rates should be compared to the rates of their fellow students in their own school, not to those in other places.

I was disturbed that these numbers seemed so startling to our university academic personnel. How could they have been surprised? The fact that we didn't admit any Prop 48's in no way insured that the students we did admit wouldn't be on academic warning as soon as they entered the university. They were students within the "at-risk" range— and, as I would soon get a chance to point out, our academic people *should* have known they would be on academic warning from the moment they set foot on campus.

Thursday, February 9

Sam Poole asked the State Bureau of Investigation to help his commission with their probe.

This happened simply because the members of the commission were not prepared for the amount of paperwork as well as man hours and legwork involved in their investigation. But the appearance was that there had been criminal wrongdoing in an academic matter. The parents of the players were furious that the SBI was now involved.

Naturally, under the stress of all that had gone on the past few days, we played spectacular basketball at home and blew out North Carolina, 98–88.

The News and Observer reported a five-year review of Dr. Lauffer's performance as a department head, in which 54 percent of faculty members rated his leadership as "good" and 28 percent rated him "poor or very poor." A memo in the story quoted Dr. Lauffer as writing, "I know the mentality of coaches. They're only interested in players helping them gain glory. They don't have the students' best interests at heart and it's disgusting to call athletes students."

Saturday, February 11

The Associated Press reported that the Poole Commission, "investigating allegations of corruption in N.C. State's basketball program, has compiled 3,000 pages of documents but has found no evidence of wrongdoing."

I would have felt fairly wonderful about this development, except that in the same story, President Spangler admitted that "publicity" had forced him to name the Poole Commission in the first place. He also said that the commission would continue to look into things such as contracts, sneakers and tickets.

Sunday, February 12

The News and Observer reported that a week earlier, the board of trustees at N.C. State passed a resolution stating that the board "unanimously supports the current men's basketball program, the players and Coach Valvano and wishes to acknowledge the significant contribution to the life of the university community made by these students . . ."

Week of February 20

I met with the Poole Commission.

Needless to say, I was eager to talk with these fellows face-to-face, to explain every facet of the basketball program. In addition to Sam Poole, the commission was made up of three other highly respected men in the state community: an ex-chancellor of the University of North Carolina at Charlotte; a banking executive; and an executive in the textile industry. I was excited about our exchange of ideas right up until one of them asked me the very first question: "Why would a player sell his shoes?" I don't have a transcript, but the rest of the conversation went something like this:

"For the money," I said. "Because he was poor and probably needed the funds."

"Don't you give them money?" he said.

Immediately, I knew that we were in serious trouble, being investigated by a group of well-meaning people who knew nothing about the rules of college athletics, save for Sam Poole.

"We only give them room, board, books, tuition and fees," I said.

"What about spending money?" he said.

"You should be on the NCAA committees, because that is something everybody thinks should be done but is not," I said. The man was shocked.

"In other words, they get nothing else. But if they're poor, they need money," he said.

"Which is where the basketball shoes come back into the picture," I said.

For most of the meeting, we discussed the rules and regulations of the NCAA. It was an educational briefing, pure and simple. I was asked why I seemed a bit angry at times. I explained my position: that I felt the investigation by the faculty senate had been a viable one and that the NCAA probe was a proper way to look into the alleged irregularities. But that I felt it was absolutely wrong for the UNC system to have appointed a group such as themselves who weren't versed in the complexities of NCAA regulations—and then to enlist the help of the SBI.

Obviously, there was some testiness on both sides. Sam Poole said he felt our program should be investigated. I asked him if he felt so strongly about our situation—alleged improprieties having come to light from the jacket of a book that hadn't even been published—why hadn't he felt the same way about the University of North Carolina football program, when in a book by Lawrence Taylor called *Living on the Edge,* the New York Giant star admitted he copied from tests, cheated in class and sold tickets to get through Carolina?

I gave them copies of the book with whole paragraphs underlined, where Taylor wrote:

Selling game tickets is one of the standard ways football players have of getting by . . .

If you can't change the system . . . you better learn how to beat it. I did. There were a number of courses ready-made for football players. . . . Large lecture classes . . . you're going to get what the guy sitting next to you gets. The only thing you have to do is remember not to copy the same name on your paper.

My question, of course, should have been directed to President Spangler rather than to the Poole Commission. Why hadn't he appointed them to investigate Taylor's claims?

My meeting with the Poole Commission lasted several hours. I realized that good people had been put in a position to which they were wholly unsuited.

Wednesday, February 22

Pocket Books announced in New York that it would not publish *Personal Fouls*. Adam Rothberg, a spokesman for Pocket, said ". . . the manuscript did not meet the publishing standards established by Pocket Books."

Naturally, with such good news fresh in our minds, the Wolfpack got blown out at Duke, 86–65, in Danny Ferry's last home game in Durham. I was glad the book was gone; I was even happier that Danny was finally going.

Saturday, March 4

N.C. State beat Wake Forest 110–103 in four overtimes, in one of the more memorable games in ACC history.

Things off the court had been relatively calm. Free of distractions, our minds only on basketball, the team wound up the regular season in spectacular fashion. As regular season champions, we were seeded number one in the ACC tournament playing number eight seed Maryland, which we had destroyed twice. No number one had ever lost to a number eight in the tournament.

Friday, March 10

In the first round of the ACC's, Maryland beat N.C. State, 71–49.

Thursday, April 6

The Poole Commission announced it was expanding its investigation, due to the SBI's findings regarding the selling of tickets and sneakers.

Following our loss to Georgetown in the final sixteen of the NCAA tournament, April seemed quite pleasant. The Poole Commission's discovery was hardly a revelation in that the NCAA had been uncovering this stuff for several months. We were working closely with the NCAA in all aspects of their investigation. In effect, they both were going over the same ground, a situation I had been criticizing all along.

It got to be a Keystone Kops arrangement: The NCAA would question our players about certain aspects of the investigation, then the SBI representing the Poole Commission would come in and ask them the same questions. Didion told me that, more than once, he'd be leaving a place and bump into an SBI representative entering the same place. At one point, Didion suggested that the NCAA just leave the campus and wait until the Poole Commission had finished its job. Pure and simple, the two bodies were clashing. Nobody left, of course. But it was a bizarre time.

Tuesday, May 16

Carroll & Graf Publishers in New York announced that they would publish *Personal Fouls.*

Tuesday, June 6

The News and Observer reported that I refused to hand over to the SBI (investigating for the Poole Commission) my personal and private business records.

This report was correct. What's ironic is that I *had* given all these records to the NCAA. I had no problem with that; they were the proper investigative body. But I felt that the Poole Commission was an inappropriate body to investigate college athletics.

Moreover, the chancellor advised me not to give my records to the SBI. His position was that state employees were protected in their private business dealings. And he had written to Thornberg, questioning the use of the SBI in the probe. The chancellor indicated that involving the SBI gave the public the perception that there was criminal intent somewhere, and that this was hurting the university's image on all fronts.

Wednesday, June 7

In one of it's more negative editorials, *The News and Observer* called Poulton the "New Water Boy at NCSU" for athletics because of his stand.

Saturday, June 10

Bennie Bolton (along with his former teammate, Teviin Binns) said he sold complimentary game tickets during the seasons from 1985 to 1987.

I had no reason to doubt the veracity of this; it was the first violation I actually believed *could* have happened. However, I was sure no coach had knowledge of it. Certainly, I did not. In the same *News and Observer* story quoting Bolton as admitting to the ticket sales, his teammate Kelsey Weems said, "I never heard anyone on the team talk about selling tickets. I remember Coach Valvano telling everybody to be careful and do nothing stupid."

It was interesting that Bolton was the same player who, a few months before, said he didn't think any of the allegations in *Personal Fouls* were true; over whose values the Raleigh newspaper rhapsodized.

Bennie Bolton was a quiet young man from outside Washington, D.C. Besides being a fine player, he was an accomplished artist whose paintings we featured at halftime of one of our games. We tried to give his work exposure every chance we got—hardly the efforts of an "uncaring" coach.

Bolton was a big part of the Wolfpack team for four seasons, and I never had any indication he was unhappy at State. But it didn't surprise me he would sell tickets or shoes. Looking back, I remembered Bennie's financial concerns. State was a "Nike school" in that we wore Nike's outfits and shoes, and carried its bags. As his little protest, Bolton would turn up after games in a "Reebok" T-shirt at times. I guess he was saying: "Okay V, I know the deal. You're getting paid with a Nike contract and I'm not." Once we had a serious conversation about a players' union—college players refusing to participate until they got a

189

share of the TV money—the thing Dick DeVenzio, a former Duke player, has been trying to get organized for years. I told Bennie that, though players weren't getting nearly enough financial compensation and everybody knew it, college presidents were not yet ready to share television's financial windfall with the players.

I would never condone violating any NCAA rule, but if anybody thinks the selling of, let's say, ACC tournament tickets, was confined to N.C. State players, well I've got an S&L application waiting for them in a brand new Edsel which will be parked on the Brooklyn Bridge. I also knew that Bolton's "revelations" would open up a whole new can of worms. At the same time, I felt relieved that if it was just tickets and sneakers at issue—and I knew no coaches were involved—that whatever the NCAA found out about that, the transgressions were minor and the penalties would be the same.

Nonetheless, I began to feel that Watergate had been resolved more quickly than the "problems" in the N.C. State basketball program. It was getting ridiculous. I just wished that everything would come out in the open at once, that the officials would announce the findings and that we could get on with a normal existence.

Of course, all this was affecting recruiting. Much of spring and summer we usually spent setting up meetings with high-school juniors in the fall. Basketball recruiting is vicious. Anything negative printed about you or your program is guaranteed to find its way into the homes of the youngsters posthaste. Amazingly, we signed nearly everybody we went after; the problem was, all but two of them turned out to be Prop 48's, and we could not admit any Prop 48's.

Monday, July 17

The Poole Commission gave its report to President Spangler.

Sunday, July 23

The News and Observer called for Chancellor Poulton's resignation. Besides charging that he "shirked his responsibility to . . . N.C. State University . . . failing to see that its basketball program met acceptable academic standards," it also accused him of "failing to cooperate fully with an investigation of the program" ordered by President Spangler.

By the tone of the editorial, it seemed to me that the final straw for the newspaper was the fact that Chancellor Poulton supported me in my right to respond only to the NCAA—and not the Poole Commission—in handing over my private papers, and that he supported the players in their right to answer questions from the NCAA and not from the Poole Commission. (The stand by the players, I might add, was with the encouragement of their parents, who in no uncertain terms had made it known that they did not want their sons talking to the SBI.) We all felt—coaches, players, and administrators—that once we had talked to and given over records to the NCAA, we had done what we were supposed to do. Plus, as I mentioned, the NCAA did not appreciate our talking to any other public agency while its investigation was going on.

This was the first time I realized the extent to which the media would go in targeting individuals, rather than issues. It was clear some were out to get Poulton and, by extension, me. I thought the coverage had crossed the line into the realm of unfairness. It looked like a vendetta now. And I saw no way that Poulton would be able to continue in his job.

Thursday, July 27

A bittersweet summer day.

First, the sweet: it was the 20th birthday of my eldest daughter, Nicole. Now, the bitter: *Personal Fouls* was finally published.

Forget the book's tacky misspellings: the names of ACC Coaches Carl Tacy, Lefty Driesell, Tom Abatemarco, and Mike Krzyzewski; the names of State players Dereck Whittenburg, Vinny Del Negro, and Chucky Brown. Forget the lack of basic knowledge of college basketball—a game is divided into halves, not quarters. Or even the ignorance of personnel —Abe Lemons is the former coach at Oklahoma City, Pan American and Texas, not Oregon State. There were some very basic, hurtful lies in Golenbock's book, which to my way of thinking made the guy a prime candidate for a credibility transplant.

One of the worst came very early in the book and involved Cozell McQueen, who was described as "functionally illiterate," and who was portrayed as stumbling through the meanings of words in a newspaper report of the death of Len Bias, "whom he loved as a friend."

McQueen came to see me after the book came out and couldn't understand why something like that would have been written. Cozell is *not* illiterate, and he wasn't a good friend of Len Bias. Cozell told me that the incident Golenbock wrote about never took place.

From noting that Washburn and Shackleford were on the team that followed our '83 national championship outfit (they weren't), to saying that I assured John Simonds a spot on the team, uniform number 31, and that I would take care of his grades (I didn't)—the book was a compendium of immature, irresponsible mistakes. Surely it was damaging having me portrayed as an uninvolved coach presiding over a rules-breaking, brain-dead, racially torn team. Having said that, I'm convinced that Golenbock's book did not cause me to lose my job at N.C. State. It did serve as a catalyst leading to the NCAA investigation. What caused the worst problems and led to the ultimate downfall of both Chancellor Poulton and myself happened four days later.

Monday, July 31

Under a front-page banner headline in *The News and Observer,* Hugh Fuller, the director of N.C. State's academic tutoring program since 1983, charged that "academic abuses and manipulation of rules to keep athletes eligible were . . . routine."

On the face of it, Dr. Fuller's concerns were important ones. Yet some were more serious than others. For one thing, he charged that tutors in the athletic department—all of whom were high-school teachers—did course work for basketball players who turned it in as their own. Later, this charge would be denied by every tutor who worked in the department. They were so hurt by the allegation, they sent scores of letters both to the chancellor and to President Spangler affirming that this did not happen.

Fuller said that players were withdrawing from classes for medical or psychological reasons in order to remain academically eligible. The truth of this was that yes, in ten years, two of our players took advantage of a university rule already in place that enabled them, if failing, to drop out for a semester and have the grades washed away. In both cases, it happened to be honestly warranted. But, even if it hadn't been, this was a case of the student exploiting the system, not the other way around. If the rule could be exploited, change the rule; don't blame the student. And two in ten years doesn't seem like "routine" to me.

Fuller also said that coaches persuaded instructors to give players who were in academic trouble "incompletes" rather than failing grades. In the ten years I was at N.C. State, I never called a professor, because I was always sensitive to the perception of a coach pressuring a teacher. However, in an attempt to monitor the progress of our athletes, our assistants would call or write the professors, asking for information on our kids' academic progress—or lack thereof. Some professors welcomed our interest and would freely exchange information. Others deeply resented any intrusion by the athletic department into their world.

Regarding Fuller's comments about players going to professors themselves— Whoa, stop the presses. I've worked in six universities, and I haven't known many flunking kids who have gone to their professors and said, "Lemme have it, Prof. I need that F. I want it. I deserve it. Don't give me a break. Lay it on me. F, F, F." No. A common occurrence for any college student who is struggling with a grade is to go to the instructor and try to get the incomplete, to work out another option.

Finally, Fuller said that coaches steered players to the easiest courses. Again, through word of mouth over the years, our assistants came to know which professors were more receptive to ballplayers, and which weren't. It stands to reason that we wouldn't send our players to a professor who was vocal in his dislike of athletics. In the same way, fraternities and sororities keep historical lists of the preferred easiest teachers.

Fuller also said that basketball players would seek out the easiest courses or the easiest instructors in those courses. Whoa, again! Dog Bites Man! Does an English major try to get the absolutely toughest professor he can find for that *chemistry* course he has to take? Give me a break!

In the midst of his charges, Fuller insulted Dr. William Beezley, a professor of Latin American history and of sports history. Fuller said there seemed to be a preponderance of players who had a strange affinity for that part of the world addressed in Dr. Beezley's course. Dr. Beezley didn't think he taught an easy subject. Anyway, if the university offered the course, wasn't that course viable? Were players to be slandered for taking *any* course the university offered?

My most favorite cynical statements by Fuller were when he said that 1) Because of the medical/psychological withdrawal rule, N.C. State had several students "whose parents and grandparents died several times while in college." Now, who was being glib and ridiculous? And 2) Because he was an Air Force captain in Vietnam, it was Fuller's reading of the history of the Vietnam War that convinced him to make his assertions public. "In Vietnam and at NCSU there have been abuses of power," Fuller said.

Pardon me!

For the past six years, I had worked with Hugh Fuller on many occasions. He was a quiet, unforceful man. We had always disagreed about how to motivate "at-risk" students, but it wasn't until now that I realized how deep-seated his feelings had been. We had been together in meetings constantly; he had written me maybe one memo in all that time.

Why had Fuller waited for at least five years to make such a public statement—for which, incredibly, *The News and Observer* later called him N.C. State's "Most Valuable Player"? Fuller said himself that it was because *Personal Fouls* had finally been published. Apparently, he felt safe now. We were being attacked on so many fronts, he could also come forward.

Let's be honest about what "at-risk students" means. When we start saying "minority" and "at-risk," we're talking about black male student-athletes. To this day, I feel strongly that Fuller was never fully prepared to deal with black student athletes. In Fuller's position as head of the Academic Skills Program, it was his responsibility to provide the best opportunity for them to do well.

Fuller always spoke of the athletes in "suspended maturation." Okay, I'd say, you've got that one right too. Now, what can we do to give these guys the chance to make it?

Fuller claimed he had written memo after memo to administrators blowing the whistle on academic abuses—but, hey! He was telling them things they already knew. That's why they weren't alarmed. Athletes struggle in class? Seek out easier courses? *Really?* Fuller would have everyone believe he was the lone wolf calling for academic integrity; that through his years at N.C. State, two chancellors, two directors of admissions, several deans of schools and one basketball coach had been corrupted by the system.

The everlasting shame of this fifteen-month period was that many people swallowed Fuller's story.

Tuesday, August 1

The News and Observer editorial cartoon portrayed the "NCSU Chain of Command Flow Chart": a pyramid with a basketball at the top, and "Academe" at the bottom.

The "Most Valuable Player" editorial stated, ". . . it is understandable why State's faculty would be reluctant (to speak). Dr. Poulton has made it clear that he stands with his winning coach, stands with him even in the hip-deep embarrassment of academic scandal. Dr. Fuller, for example, says he repeatedly complained to administration officials with no luck. His frustration and his belief in academic integrity finally forced him to speak out. . . . Those like Dr. Fuller who help sort out the truth are not being disloyal. They are the most faithful of all to N.C. State's historic devotion to academic excellence. When they come forward, the university moves closer to the truth and to a day when that luster is restored."

And, boy, did they come forward! This type of press had everyone jumping on or off the bandwagon, depending on the perspective. It became apparent to me that the newspaper had its own agenda in its choice of coverage.

Wednesday, August 2

Albert B. Lanier, Jr., vice chancellor for university relations, who five days earlier had called *Personal Fouls* a "work of fiction," said that the university's official position had changed in the wake of statements by Fuller.

Thursday, August 3

William Friday, former president of the University of North Carolina, said that athletics at N.C. State were out of control.

Friday, August 4

Ed Weisiger, former chairman of the N.C. State Board of Trustees, threw his support behind me and the athletic department.

For the first time, the UNC Board of Governors acknowledged talking about firing me.

Saturday, August 5

Terms of my contract were published in *The News and Observer,* with a discussion by board members about the buyout clause of $500,000.

This had been public information ever since I signed the contract. Only now did it become a source of "news."

Sunday, August 6

A hurtful article appeared in *The News and Observer,* saying that N.C. State's '83 national championship team may have been successful on the court, but team members hadn't been since.

(There were 14 players on that team. Of the fourteen, eight graduated; seven from N.C. State and one from the University of Alabama. Of the six who didn't graduate, four played professional basketball; three in the NBA, and one in Italy. Those who aren't in pro basketball range from TV basketball analysts to a stockbroker to a president of his own production company. Does this sound like an unsuccessful group of people?)

Monday, August 7

The faculty senate announced that, while their committee had found no academic abuses, if abuses had occurred the faculty would not be to blame. They absolved themselves of any responsibility, inasmuch as athletics were so enormous and the faculty was under such constant pressure to make sure the kids didn't foul up.

Neat trick, guys—the faculty has nothing to do with academics!

Wednesday, August 9

Barbara Bain, an English professor, said she was pressured to help a freshman basketball player who was flunking her course.

Well, he went ahead and flunked anyway. Must have been terrific pressure.

Friday, August 11

The News and Observer editorialized: "Members of the (Poole) Commission who were appointed by Mr. Spangler have their own stake in the accuracy of their findings. Mr. Poole, industrialist William Klopman, C. C. Cameron, the state budget director and Dean Colvard, former chancellor of UNC–Charlotte, lent their names and credibility to investigating a sensitive issue. If it looks as if the work was incomplete and sloppy, their reputations will suffer. So will that of Dr. Spangler."

It became pretty obvious to me the intent of the newspaper and in what direction it was heading. The groundwork was being laid for Chancellor Poulton's resignation and for my dismissal.

Tuesday, August 15

I met with the Poole Commission, the chairman of the UNC Board of Governors, Roddy Jones, and the president of the University, C. D. Spangler.

Again, I was chomping at the bit for this confrontation. I had refrained long enough from speaking out because I didn't want to get into Ping-Pong journalism with charges flying back and forth. The atmosphere was tense. Remember, the Poole commission members were the people to whom I had refused to give over my business papers. I got that out of the way quickly. I told them that even though the university had advised me not to change my position, I would be more than happy to provide any records they wished. These were the same records I had given to the NCAA. I had decided to show them I wasn't hiding anything from anybody.

One of the men on the commission, William Klopman, the former CEO of Burlington Industries, was about as nasty to me as anyone had ever been in my life. In fact, it took all of my self-restraint not to walk around the table and pop Mr. Klopman upside his nasty head.

The problem was, he continuously badgered me with a line of questioning that hardly let me get a word in edgewise. To the best of my recollection, the ensuing conversation went as follows. Klopman would say: "You had kids take easy courses? Why did you do that?"

"No, Mr. Klopman, I didn't have anyone . . ."

"It says here that the kids took these courses . . . Why did you let them do that? . . . That's wrong . . . You shouldn't do that."

"I'm trying to expla . . ."

"I understand the kids were selling sneakers? What kind of a program are you running? What about this: I see the kids aren't graduating."

On and on he went. I tried to explain graduation in relation to the graduation rate of the rest of the students.

"I don't care about the rest of the student body," he said. "I just care about your basketball players. You brought them here. What about them?"

I said I didn't admit any students.

"You admitted them. You admitted them," he said.

The guy was just impossible for me to deal with. However, aside from the experience with Klopman, it was a very constructive meeting.

When I got past Klopman, I was able to address the points of which I thought the commission should be aware. On the incredible beating we had been taking for the lack of academic progress of our basketball players, I trotted out some statistics that I thought were revealing, the first of which was the average SAT scores of the entire university.

Did anyone on the commission know what they were? Of course not. They were 1055. That was the average college board scores, men and women, white and black.

Next, I wondered if the commission knew what the graduation rate of the student body as a whole was. They didn't. In the standard four years, the graduation rate at N.C. State was approximately 24 percent. For students remaining for five years, it rose to 46 percent; in six years, 56 percent; and in seven years or forever, 58 percent. These were all approximate figures, and they compared quite unfavorably with other schools such as North Carolina and Virginia, where for example the "forever" figure was in the 80th percentile, and Duke, which graduated nearly 100 percent of its students.

I then told the commission about a confidential report—and I stress *confidential*—done annually by the Admissions Department at State and sent to the varsity coaches. This report showed what the expected GPA (grade point average) of a student would be who entered N.C. State at a certain GPA/SAT level. For example, the student who began at N.C. State with a 2.0 high school GPA and 700 on the SAT's (the minimum score; under 700, a kid becomes a Prop 48) predicted out at a 1.4 GPA as a freshman. Remember that a student needs a 2.0 over four years to graduate. So, when N.C. State admitted a kid with a 2.0 and 700 on the boards, the Admissions Department, the administration, the Academic Skills people, the coaches, the athletic director, me, *everybody* knew that that kid would probably go on academic warning immediately, and that the kid's chances to graduate were lousy—*to begin with.*

That understood, the numbers got worse. An entering student with a 2.5 GPA/1000 SAT was predicted to earn only a 1.85 his freshman year, still not a high enough average (over four years) to graduate. The minimum GPA/SAT numbers a student needed to be predicted to a 2.0 freshman average were 2.5 GPA and 1200 SAT. Now when you figured that most of the entering basketball players were between 700 and 900 on the boards (nowhere near 1200), it was fairly easy to discern that the entire team could possibly be on academic warning from the moment they entered the university to whenever they (hopefully) graduated.

My point again was simply that since these numbers were compiled by the Admissions Department and available to people in the academic administration, the situation hardly should have been as shocking as everyone seemed to act like it was.

As far as I knew, very few of the top high-school basketball players anywhere in America scored 1200 on the boards. Very few black basketball players, likewise. In addition, my guy, Avie Lester, was the highest-rated black student athlete in the entire University of North Carolina system.

I challenged the commission on this point. Since the university knew these athletes were on academic warning from the get-go, it seemed to me blatantly unfair to now attack them for their academic performance. And, yes, I deemed this an attack. When neither the university nor the Poole Commission stood up and stated the situation for what it was, they were permitting a constant attack from the faculty, the public and, especially, the media.

It wasn't just my players who were being attacked, of course. The obvious prime target was me. I was under fire, first for bringing ill-prepared students to the university and, second, for their not making it academically. In reality, how responsible should a coach be for his athletes' academic performance? I didn't have the article then, but let me quote the much-respected John Thompson of Georgetown, who informed *Washingtonian* magazine in March, 1990:

"The biggest con in education is kids saying they were exploited. *I'm not responsible for them getting an education.* [Italics mine] And as long as I let them think I am, they won't get it. It sounds cruel, but it doesn't work with sympathy. If they understand that they are responsible, they'll get it. I'm the coach; I'm not their mother and father. If the kid doesn't get an education, it's his fault. He gets the credit, too. I mean, I never met a coach who told a player to not go to class . . ."

In a later article in *GQ*, Thompson is quoted by Thomas Boswell: "The biggest problem I see in college athletes is that the kid is never made responsible for his own actions. And he knows that. And he plays it like a piano. . . .He knows that regardless of what happens with him, there is always somebody else that he can blame and the public will accept it."

(We've never been close friends, but John took the time to call me and my family on several occasions during this period to offer his support.)

Let me explain—as I did to the Poole Commission—the chain of command of education at N.C. State.

Number one, there was an admissions committee, the only body that admits students to the university. I never met with this group to discuss any athlete. On occasion, I would call the director to plug for a player because I thought he would be a good addition to the team and the university. In just the same way, a music professor might plug for a charmed violinist. But neither the music teacher nor I did the admitting.

Number two, there was a faculty committee from the faculty senate which set the standards for academic progress. They worked along with the provost, the head of academics at the university. They set the levels of progress—the GPA a student had to retain based on the number of credits he was taking. The important number here was 2.0; anything below that was considered Academic Warning.

Number three was the faculty itself. The faculty taught. The graduation rate, it must be noted here, seemed to me a direct result of both the faculty's teaching ability and the students' desire to learn. If N.C. State had a graduation rate of 24 percent over four years, and 58 percent forever, where did the fault lie? Whose responsibility were those numbers? The average board scores at N.C. State were 1050, the average GPA of entering students was 3.3. And yet only 24 percent graduated in four years?

In this regard, I felt that it was also instructive to consider N.C. State's record for overall graduation rate of black male students. Are you ready for this? In the past thirteen years, there had been a continual decline in the graduation rate of black students in a four-year period. Starting in 1977, the rate was 18.2 percent over a four-year period; by 1988, the rate was 7.5 percent. In 1989, it went even lower. And in 1990, figures showed that of the 214 black male students that entered in 1986, only eight had graduated, or *3.7 percent.* (This information comes from the N-CHED A-7 report, filed by North Carolina universities with the state university system.)

Is it any wonder that I felt I was being dealt with unfairly?

Another figure I told the commission about was the "GGPA" or "graduated" grade point average, of which a student needed a certain level to stay in the university. Everyone talks about Eligibility this, Eligibility that. We had no Eligibility at N.C. State. If you were in school, you were eligible. You were either in school or you were out. If you were in, you could participate in any university activity. To stay in, though, you needed to retain certain academic standards. From zero to 27 credits taken, no GPA was required. After the 28th credit hour, a kid needed a 1.25 GGPA. Not exactly genius material, right? Thirty credit hours meant you had passed your freshman year, and you were now a sophomore. You needed a 1.3; that's all. This was *not* an athletic department rule, but a university rule.

Were these people with this GGPA on academic warning? Of course they were. How could this be a shock to anyone in the university? And yet, here were my players being absolutely grinded for something common throughout the campus. I suggested to the commission that if they found this system wanting, maybe the system should be changed rather than dumping on the basketball team and its coach.

Getting back to the chain of command, number four would include the Academic Skills Program, created for all "at-risk" students university-wide. Shouldn't the administrators, professors and tutors involved in this program be somewhat alarmed at the graduation rate?

With all these statistics available to everyone, and with this chain of command in place, I said it was totally absurd that a basketball coach was being blamed for the academic deficiencies of the entire campus. Get a life here, folks. N.C. State was the sixth college I'd worked for—always within the framework of the admissions policy. At Bucknell, Johns Hopkins, and Iona, over a nine-year period, to the best of my knowledge, only two players did not receive their degrees. Those universities have very high overall graduation rates. I hadn't changed my approach at all since coming to N.C. State.

After all this, I told them that in ten years at State, no one had at any time said I hadn't worked within the framework of the university. I'd been given a raise every year, won the national championship, been offered the athletic directorship, worked in that job for free, had funded a scholarship for both an athlete and a student, and was honored at a luncheon for outstanding service to the university. Was I supposed to feel anything other than that I was doing my job in an appropriate manner? I told them I took full and complete responsibility for any wrongdoing that any athletes had done. But if there were problems that I hadn't known about, I wanted to help in the solutions.

Klopman kept insisting that all the players should graduate.

Poole was tough but fair. "Why did you bring in Washburn? You shouldn't have recruited him," he said. I told the Commission that, in hindsight, Poole was 100 percent right. But were they aware that a kid such as Ernie Myers, who came from a much tougher background than Chris Washburn, stayed five years and graduated. On Shackleford, they questioned Poulton's going out on a limb with the contract. But I pointed out that when Charles came back the following semester, he had the best academic semester of his career at State.

"I'm not embarrassed to give kids a chance," I said. I also reiterated that I would be sending them all my financial records, which is when President Spangler spoke up for the first time.

"Sam," he said to Poole, "I think we should applaud the coach for that. I don't think any of us would feel behoven to giving up our private business dealings to the damned newspaper."

Spangler acknowledged that it had been a long, drawn-out controversy and a difficult time for everyone. He said he thought Dr. Fuller had some valid arguments, but that he had chosen the wrong forum in which to air them. He said he was sorry the situation had become so hurtful and divisive. He said he felt the system had been abused, but didn't believe I was guilty of doing that. "The one thing we shouldn't have done, Coach Valvano," he said, "was place you in the position of being the coach and the athletic director. That's going to change." He also said he thought I was a fine basketball coach and he looked forward to our winning another national championship and to his being there to see it.

I left the meeting happy that finally my position was understood. Though I would be leaving as AD, I didn't think that would be the only change. That wasn't going to appease enough of the media, to "feed the dog." Though nothing was said about Dr. Poulton in the meeting, I felt that Spangler had made up his mind that heads would roll; I'd be gone as AD, and Poulton's job was also in jeopardy.

When I met with Poulton later that afternoon, I didn't mention those thoughts; only that my meeting with the commission had gone well and that I was staying on as coach. Poulton said that he sensed I hadn't read between the lines; that he felt I might be fired from both jobs. He indicated that he thought my only chance might be if he remained as chancellor. In retrospect, I think he was actually looking for support from me. But at that point I was very confused.

I was so concerned that later I called Spangler back to ask if there was any hidden agenda concerning the coaching position. But he reassured me that I would remain as coach. "Dr. Poulton has served the university well; he's under a great deal of strain and pressure right now," Spangler said.

If that wasn't a bell of doom tolling, I had never heard one.

Monday, August 21

Dr. Bruce Poulton resigned as chancellor at North Carolina State.

Dr. Poulton hadn't hired me, but he was there when we won the national championship and he had supported me throughout this latest ordeal. I felt terribly depressed when he was forced to step down. I felt especially bad because he lost his job over a basketball issue, and didn't deserve to. It only surprised me because he was such a fighter. Obviously, Dr. Poulton felt a resignation would help heal the wounds.

In retrospect, I believe that one reason for his forced leave-taking was that they wanted a fresh guy in there, someone to sit on me. Remember, Dr. Poulton had been probably my strongest ally. He also had come out firmly in support of a new Centennial Center all-purpose basketball and entertainment arena, a $50 million project that had become a political football in the area.

202

Thursday, August 24

"A Clean Sweep At State" headlined the lead editorial in *The News and Observer*. ". . . Now Chancellor Poulton has resigned," the editorial ended. "It is an example Mr. Valvano should follow and thus relieve Mr. Spangler and the Board of Governors of the necessity to see that the coach does so."

Don't tell me the media doesn't try to dictate policy!

Friday, August 25

The *Charlotte Observer* ran a piece saying that Shack and Weems had lived in apartments owned by me. The story implied that this could be a violation of NCAA rules. Charles Chandler from the *Observer* called me the night before the piece ran, in order to get my comments. The next morning, I called the NCAA to let them know this would be appearing, and to explain the situation, since I knew it was not a violation. For seven years, I had owned several apartments in the Raleigh area, which were run by a management agency, and were rented to students and other people in the area. Shack and Kelsey had rented apartments through the rental agent. Unfortunately, the agent had to ask them to leave after only two months, because they were loud, and had broken a window. They paid their rent and the damages, and left.

I explained all this to the NCAA. They looked into it, realized there was no violation, and dropped the matter.

It is worthwhile to note that it's not uncommon for athletes to rent apartments from university personnel on campuses all over the country. In fact, Ralph Sampson actually lived in Terry Holland's home, in his renovated basement, for a year.

In a report to the UNC Board of Governors, President Spangler announced in a press conference televised live throughout North Carolina the results of the Poole Commission's report to him. The most serious of his findings were that academic standards were "misused" and that players sold basketball shoes and tickets. Among his recommendations were that I step down as AD, that no athletes be admitted to the UNC system without the potential to graduate, that athletes in academic difficulty should not be allowed to play, and that freshmen be barred from the varsity teams in football and basketball.

True to his word, Spangler did not suggest that I be removed as head coach. What he said was that that was a trustees' decision. (The trustees had spoken, at least for the time being, back on February 17.) What he said he did *not* find was any illegal changing of grades or of drug tests. Or that academic regulations and standards were broken to benefit basketball players. It was "the spirit of the law" that was broken, he said.

A few of his suggestions, I felt, were direct results of my own meeting with the Poole Commission. Moreover, I took confidence in the fact that the president wanted me to stay on as athletic director until December 31, another four months, to help in the transition period.

An August 4 memo from me to N.C. State counsel Becky French was released, detailing the team's new set of self-written rules regarding grades, drug use, attendance, a dress code and overall conduct. This was an important gesture by the players themselves to get their own house in order. The most serious recommendation they made was that anyone on Academic Warning 2 would be ineligible to play. The players had not yet stated when this rule would go into effect. On August 9, a second memo went to Larry Clark, chairman of the Athletics Council and our faculty rep to the NCAA. In this memo, we explained that all of the players' recommendations needed to be discussed at an Athletics Council meeting as to when the new rules would begin to be in effect. This second memo was sent to clarify the team's position regarding Avie Lester, as he was the only player currently on Academic Warning 2. Obviously, no player would have voted himself ineligible for his senior year. The other team members were willing to accept this new guideline for the upcoming year, so that if they did fall to Academic Warning 2, they would be ineligible.

Saturday, August 26

My favorite story appeared in the *Charlotte Observer,* headlined: UNC PROBE EXONERATES VALVANO. It began: "A university investigation . . . criticized the basketball program but cleared Coach Jim Valvano of wrongdoing, and policy makers moved to tighten academic standards for athletes."

Monday, August 28

I met with several members of the board of trustees and asked to be relieved of my duties as athletic director as soon as possible.

After working at the job for no compensation for three years, I had spent the last three months being attacked and humiliated in the position by the press and from certain elements in the university. I really wasn't enthralled with staying on any longer.

Wednesday, September 6

The NCAA ended its investigation. Dave Didion presented N.C. State with an official inquiry, listing eight violations.

Didion had been in Raleigh off and on since January 19 investigating our program. In fact, he'd been around so long I nearly started calling him "Diddo," which was his nickname in the NCAA offices back in Shawnee Mission, Kansas.

We both had preconceived notions of each other, of course. He figured me to be some slick-talking sleazoid from New York who had ransacked the whole of higher education; I guessed he was a CIA trench-coat guy working in secret codes, out to nail another coaching scalp to his belt. Bottom line: We weren't supposed to like each other at all.

The truth was, Dave was in his mid-thirties, a former basketball player at Ohio State whose wife is the dean of the University of Tennessee law school. At first I didn't really know how to act around him. If I asked him out for a beer and pizza, I wondered if the first thing he wrote in his notebook might be: "Aha. Trying to get close. To influence investigation. Scumbag tendency." So I didn't know what to do. It was like a first date. So, most of the time I got to treating him like the plague.

The more we talked, however, the more I understood he wasn't trying to nail us; he was just trying to do his job. And he understood I wasn't trying to hide anything. Didion turned out to be eminently up front, fair, honorable and a pleasure to be around. Beyond the investigation stage, we did a lot of talking about college athletics, what was wrong with it, what needed to be done. I asked him if there were schools where it was really tough to do his job and he talked about getting thrown out of homes and coaches' offices, being verbally attacked and abused, being called anti-American. We became friends.

That wasn't the only thing that surprised me about the NCAA

investigation. Dave never used a tape recorder; he only took notes in longhand. It's one of the few arguments I had with their procedure, and yet the results of his interviews with me turned up no errors of fact or substance. We never went out to lunch or dinner—I guess social meetings with an investigatee were *verboten*—but as time went on, I think Dave realized I wasn't trying to withhold information or hide anything. Nor were any of the other dozens of people he interviewed in Raleigh.

To show how paranoid I got, however, the first time Dave wanted to work out and play a little hoops, he asked if I could get him a pair of shoes and some sweats. I didn't know if that was a trick or what. I told him no. He was stunned. Then he realized why I was apprehensive. "You don't have to worry," he said. "I'm only borrowing."

We both laughed. "Okay," I said. "You get the full equipment load. But I'm making you sign it out. You keep nothing."

Didion was competent, thorough, very professional. He was by himself the whole time, no double-teaming anybody. A player can have the coach or a school's attorney sit with them in the initial interview with the NCAA representative, or they can go it alone. The NCAA investigators can probably judge when someone is being influenced by somebody else in the room, anyway. I sat in on some of the interviews, but most of our kids met with Dave alone. One of the impressive aspects that stuck in my mind was the way Dave told everybody right off that he had been around a long time, he was an expert at this stuff, he would find out everything. He *guaranteed* them that. So it behooved them to tell the truth at all times. He told them the Infractions Committee decided things, but that he as the chief investigator would have input. "If you tell us the truth," he said, "if you help us throughout and cooperate, things will be better for you and the University. If you lie, you're going to hurt yourself and everybody else. At that point, we won't help you because we can't help you."

The questions were quite direct at times. "Did you sell tickets?" "What did you do with your basketball shoes?" Initially, Didion came to look into academics only. That's the area in which he spent most of the early days. While he was in Raleigh, he received multiple phone calls from anonymous sources advising him to look into other things. People came out of the woodwork, and he sifted through thousands upon thousands of transcripts, letters, paper trails.

Didion mentioned to me that he felt our case was similar to a number of cases he had worked on, where no coaches were involved or had knowledge of wrongdoing. While the media was trumpeting the unbelievability of the abuses at N.C. State, Didion was telling me our transgressions were nothing compared to what was going on elsewhere out there. No coaches were involved in money changing hands. There was no organized pattern of abuse here. Most importantly, he said that there were no recruiting violations, which is where most schools are found guilty of breaking the rules. Didion told me that from his reports, the Infractions Committee would decide whether this was a major or secondary case, but that the reams of publicity generated probably guaranteed we would be in the major category. And that meant we would have to appear before the Infractions Committee itself.

Ultimately, our official inquiry was nine pages long and mentioned eight violations. To give you an example of the kind of answer we were supposed to provide, take just one of the violations. In the matter of selling tickets, the NCAA found that our players sold $1,500 worth over three years. In our reply, we were to provide the names of every person who received a complimentary ticket over the previous three-year period. At four tickets per every one of the fifteen players times thirty games a year over three years, that amounted to our trying to find and identify 5,400 names. Try that sometime. Within thirty days.

Sunday, October 1

Dr. Larry K. Monteith, dean of the College of Engineering, was appointed interim chancellor at N.C. State.

I remembered Dr. Monteith as one of the deans who sat in on some of the chancellor's monthly meetings with the department heads of the university. I also knew he had signed that Deans' Report back on January 27, stating they had found no illegal grade-changing. Soon after he was appointed, he came to my office and said that though he had no preconceived idea about what had taken place, he was going to make a study of his own on the academics of the athletic department and the basketball program.

He also said—and I should have felt some degree of foreboding here—that he felt there should be no correlation between the graduation rate of the student body and that of the athletes. He said he would accept nothing less than 100-percent graduation rate, or at least 75 percent moving toward 100 percent. I pointed out to Dr. Monteith that the university as a whole graduated only 24 percent. Once again, he said he didn't care about the rest of the university, but he wanted the basketball team at 75 percent.

Dr. Monteith appointed Hal Hopfenberg, an associate dean in the College of Engineering, as interim athletic director.

Monteith told me I would love Hal because he was just like me: fast-talking, from New York, spoke Italian and was another engineer. Right, just like me.

When I met Hal, he reminded me that we had already met. "Don't you recognize me?" he said. Then I remembered. I had run into him once at the Raleigh-Durham airport as he was on his way to Italy. He had given me his card, and told me he'd been to Italy so often, he spoke fluent Italian. This time he told me he felt I hadn't been speaking out to the press enough, that my biggest strength was talking to everybody. He said his job as the new AD was to be an advocate for me. I wish I had heard it from him in Italian.

Sunday, October 15

Afterthought. Preseason practice for the 1989–90 basketball season began.

Thursday, October 26

The NCAA investigation complete, Dave Didion wrote me a letter from Shawnee Mission, Kansas. He said that before he met me, he suspected he "might encounter some smart-ass egomaniac who would try to bullshit me. Those impressions vanished after I met you and spent some time around you. . . ." The nicest thing he said was that if he had a son, he would feel comfortable with me as his coach. Obviously, I was heartened by such a letter.

Monday, October 30

A press conference was held—"Coming to you *live* from the Holiday Inn," said an excited radio announcer—featuring Peter Golenbock, John Simonds, Dr. Richard Lauffer and Bennie Bolton. Lauffer demanded an "apology" from N.C. State "for the derogatory statements they released about my creditability (sic)." Golenbock said he hoped I'd coach at N.C. State "forever" as a living example of influence gone wild. Simonds said, "The fox is still in the hen house, so to speak." Bolton said he never met

Golenbock until two weeks earlier. Nobody looked up the definition of
Dog and Pony Show.

Friday, November 3

I appeared before the NCAA Committee on Infractions at the El
Conquistadore Hotel outside Tucson, Arizona.
The eight allegations resulting from the investigation were:

1. Players sold complimentary tickets.
2. Players sold or traded basketball shoes for cash or sports
   equipment.
3. Players received free jewelry.
4. Players received meals at the home of a booster.
5. Players received meals purchased in town by a booster.
6. An assistant coach took a recruit to a TV station to meet a
   former player.
7. A player slept in the home of an alumnus.
8. We had not properly administered an eligibility progress form.

Following the hearing, a month later when the NCAA Committee on
Infractions announced its sanctions, the report dismissed all the allegations except in three areas which were violations: the sale of tickets, the
sale of shoes and the ever-popular "lack of institutional control," under
which came illegal lodging, meals and an illegal recruiting visit.
Everyone who reads these reports assumes the worst: Oh no, the
players are getting cars and clothes and taking dining halls full of friends
and relatives for free meals at Lutece. But here were the meal and lodging
violations: Chris Corchiani had mono his freshman year, and the doctor
told him not to stay in his dorm. After he remained in the hospital for a
week, the school's insurance ran out and he needed someone to take care
of him. Chris called an adult friend (an N.C. State booster) named Larry
Hall and stayed there one night. Then another booster, Nick Sirrocco,
had four of our players sleep overnight at his house on Christmas Eve and
eat Christmas dinner the next day. And here was the recruiting error: An
assistant coach took a recruit who was interested in broadcasting as a
career to the WRAL-TV studios near our campus and introduced him to
a former Wolfpack player named Alvin Battle.
The two more serious violations were the sale of tickets and shoes. To
explain about complimentary tickets, it is only necessary to understand
that every player gets four comped tickets for each game, three to be given

to family members and one a "wild card" for anyone. The problem is, suppose that "Joe Blow" is listed to get the wild card and he shows up with "Joe Blow" ID. How are we to know whether Joe paid a ballplayer for it or got it comped? It's impossible, that's how. Yet we are held responsible for knowing. Or how about the case where a player's mom and dad and two neighbors drive up for the game. Now, the player can get mom and dad and *one* of the neighbors in as a wild card. But the other neighbor? He has to say he's the player's "uncle." Again, how are we supposed to know if he's not?

As I said before, you and I know, the NCAA knows, and the Shadow surely knows that this ticket situation is prevalent all over America. Most people in what we in North Carolina call "the Triangle Area" realize that ACC tournament tickets—from the player allotment at the local universities—can readily be had at a good price on the street. In our case, the NCAA found a total of $1,500 in comp tickets that were sold over three years. And they found this because we ourselves had done the research into all the lists of names.

In the matter of the basketball shoes, most coaches are under contract with a shoe manufacturer who provides all of their players with five or six pairs of shoes a season: practice pairs, loaf-arounds, game shoes, one for each walk of life. Some players weren't using all of these sneaks; they were trading some of them in to stores or selling them themselves (obviously, mostly to big-footed fellows). And we weren't keeping track. We solved that problem by making each player take only one pair of shoes at a time; when they wore it out, they had to turn the old pair back in before receiving the new one.

Yes, we were guilty of some NCAA violations; players should not sell shoes and tickets. We corrected those problems; we cleaned our own house. In this case, the rules were pretty clear-cut. However, I'd like to point out that some of the NCAA rules are very difficult to understand. Oh, yeah, and the rules get changed just about every other hour as well. For example, four or five years ago, if I was recruiting a youngster who came on our campus and said he was interested in the banking profession, I could take him down to the big bank in town and introduce him to the bank president, who could tell him about the business of banking. That was one year. The next year, the rule changed; now I could still drive the youngster to see the big bank, but he couldn't talk to the banker. Then the third year, the banker could come on campus and talk to the youngster. You could still drive the youngster to see the big bank, and then on your campus he could talk to the big banker. But alas, they changed that, and now I could drive the youngster to see the bank, but he couldn't talk to the banker anywhere—on campus, his house, your house, didn't matter. No problem. You know what we did? We had the big banker write the youngster a letter about the banking industry and give the youngster a call. But guess what? Now I could still drive him by the bank to look at it, but now the banker couldn't talk to the youngster on your campus or his campus, at his house, your house, in the bathroom, anywhere, nor could he send a letter from the bank about banking nor give the banking-interested youngster a bank phone call about how nice it was to bank at his bank.

And everybody thinks coaching's easy.

Of course, then there were the family recruiting visits, wonderfully cheery experiences unless that NCAA pariah—the spare sibling—came along.

"Hi, Mr. and Mrs. Jones. Just calling to verify your Johnny's visit. I understand you're going to drive? Great. Do you realize we can give you twenty-six cents a mile on that trip? So, please keep a good odometer reading for us. What time are you getting in? Oh, good, you'll be here for dinner? We'll check you into the hotel and have a nice meal. See you then? Oh, what's that? You're bringing Johnny's little brother, Jimmy? Uh-huh.

"Well, inasmuch as we've already spent eighty thousand million dollars recruiting your older son, I'm sorry to say the rules prevent us from housing Jimmy with Johnny. The two brothers cannot room together. Unless of course little Jimmy stays up and doesn't go to sleep. Then he's just visiting. What's that? No, sorry. You can't get a separate room for him either, not on us at least. If he wants to stay up the entire time he's here, now that's fine. But if he wants to sleep, you're going to have to pay for that. We can give Johnny a room and you a room. But not Jimmy a room. How about if Jimmy sleeps in with you? Aha. Uh, sorry again. No, he can't do that either. He's not permitted to sleep on this particular visit.

"Now when we go out to dinner, we can wine and dine you and get the finest meal money can buy for Johnny. Now Jimmy, unfortunately, will have to pay for his own meal, no matter where he goes. And remember, on Saturday night you're all coming over to my house, meet the family, munch on some pizza and chicken. By the way, we're going to have to count how many wings that little rascal Jimmy chows down. Not to mention the size and quantity of the pizza slices the little bugger puts away because he's paying for every penny of the food he touches. The solution, Mr. and Mrs. Jones? Next year we're recruiting only single children."

If the point needs reaffirming, I present the 1990 Metro Conference Survey of NCAA Recruiting Rules, a test of no less than 119 questions on proper procedures in recruiting.

Question 5: Subsequent to a prospect's signing of the National Letter of Intent, a member institution may not make contact at the prospect's educational institution unless the contact occurs during a permissible contact period and does not exceed the one-visit-per-week limitation. True or false?

Question 17: If coaches in different sports are recruiting two different prospects at the same high school, it would be permissible for one coach to visit the high school on Monday and the other coach to visit the high school on Wednesday during the same week, provided only one of the two prospects is contacted on each occasion. True or false?

Question 57: For purposes of the contact rule, a "day" is defined as:

A. 24 hours from the exact time of the first contact (e.g., 3 P.M. on day one to 2:59 P.M. on day two).
B. 12:01 A.M. to midnight.
C. 8 A.M. on day one to 8 A.M. on day two.
D. None of the above.

If you answered True, True and B, pass Go and head straight for the NCAA tournament without passing through the NCAA Committee on Infractions.

I was not so fortunate. The official inquiry having been presented and our replies having been organized, our new chancellor Dr. Monteith, new AD Hal Hopfenberg, counsel Becky French and I met with the Committee on Infractions in Arizona. Through this entire process, it was obvious that everyone had been affected by the amount of publicity our case had generated. Didion once told me that the NCAA is overly sensitive about how it's portrayed in the media regarding these investigations. We already knew that, minus the extreme press coverage, our violations might not even have reached the "major" category. That said, I must separate the investigative branch of the process from the hearing. Everyone talks of the NCAA investigators as trampling all over rights with no regard for people, but I never felt this to be the case. We all found the investigators, from Didion to Chuck Smrt to David Berst, the head guy, to be fair. They conducted the investigation in the spirit of getting at the facts, with no hint of a lynch-mob mentality. Nobody was out to bury anybody. This may not be everyone's experience, but it certainly was mine.

In fact, if I had it to do over again, I would hire a company with these methods to come in and investigate my program with an eye toward preventive maintenance. We could have solved a lot of these problems a lot earlier.

Unfortunately, the hearing before the NCAA Committee on Infractions was not such a rewarding experience. First of all, the committee is made up of college administrators, who have little to do with the NCAA main office. For our hearing, the chairman of the committee, Alan Williams, a professor of law at the University of Virginia, had removed himself due to his ACC affiliation. The committee hearing our case was composed of Roy Kramer, presently the commissioner of the Southeastern Conference; Beverly Ledbetter, a faculty member at Brown University; Milton Schroeder, a law professor at Arizona State; John Nowak, a law professor at Illinois; and Tom Niland, who was the athletic director at Le Moyne College in Syracuse.

It would have been an intimidating environment even without the physical setup: tables arranged in a horseshoe configuration with the committee at the top, our people on the left and the investigative staff across from us. In the open end of the horseshoe was all the electronic apparatus, essentially microphones which were so sensitive we were told not to whisper to each other lest our conversations be picked up.

Standard opinion holds that the investigative staff has a lot of influence with the committee in deciding penalties; I don't believe it. In fact, the relationship between these two groups seemed totally different than what I had imagined. The findings and tone of the investigative report were the basis for the decisions; if the investigators thought the parties involved were truthful and cooperated, they made that known to the committee. But that seemed to be as far as it went. Rather, it seemed to me that a confrontational relationship developed during our hearings. The investigators appeared to be on trial at the same time that we were.

Nowak, for instance, kept asking Didion why he didn't pursue certain lines of questioning. He would ask us if we were asked something and then fire away at Didion: Why didn't you ask that? Why didn't you follow up? Of course, Didion got off easy when compared to me. Nowak obviously was the Hit Man of the operation. To me, his questions were suppositional, demeaning. I think he wanted to send all of us straight to the electric chair.

It was similar to my confrontation with the Poole Commission. Nowak was nicer than my old buddy, Klopman, had been. But he still tried to make me feel like an idiot. A transcript isn't available, but here's how I recall it:

"I see here where you had 685 violations of the ticket policy. Who was in charge of tickets?" Nowak said, not bothering to wait for the answer. "I see here an Ed McLean from your staff had a great deal to do with the tickets."

"Yes," I said. "Ed is a part-time assistant coach."

"A part-timer? You gave such an important aspect of your program over to a part-timer? I find that incredible!" Nowak said.

213

"One second. Ed McLean is not a kid. He was the athletic director for many years at Broughton High School in Raleigh. He is a man of integrity and value," I said.

"Yes. But still a part-timer. You did not see fit to have a full-time member of your staff handle this?" Nowak said.

"One second again. Ed McLean is bright, intelligent, extremely competent," I said. "He's fifty-three years old, an ex-Marine, organized. When the rest of us are out on the road scouting or recruiting, Ed is the guy in the office. He's *the guy.* He's our anchor."

"You were the athletic director, you had a part-timer doing tickets and there was nobody checking up on you, either?" Nowak said.

This Nowak was concerned about a system of checks and balances while he questioned my integrity in holding the jobs of coach and athletic director. Of the three hours we spent before the committee, the exchange with Nowak was only a small part. The rest of the time was less rigorous, but this particular incident left a bad taste in my mouth. On the other hand, I don't know which was worse: being cross-examined by Nowak, or sitting there with my future being debated while two members of the committee . . . well, I don't want to say they were asleep, but if they weren't, they must have been calling up some long-lost relatives in a personal séance.

Tuesday, December 12

The NCAA Committee on Infractions announced the results of the investigation of the N.C. State basketball program. The Wolfpack was put on probation for two years for violations of NCAA legislation and declared ineligible to play in the 1990 NCAA tournament. The university was instructed to develop and implement "a system for administrative control and monitoring to ensure compliance with NCAA legislation."

Chuck Smrt of the NCAA investigative staff appeared in Raleigh at a press conference to outline the details of the infractions and the punishment. On the positive side, Smrt said: "The committee said it did not find that any clear and direct competitive advantage accrued to the N.C. State program as a result of the violations in this case." By actual definition, ours were not "major" violations in that the NCAA's definition of "major" is that the school received a clear and direct competitive advantage.

However, Smrt went on, "The committee determined that the case was major in nature because the University failed to control its intercollegiate athletic program in compliance with the rules and regulations of the NCAA in two primary areas."

Those were tickets and shoes. After all was said and done, it came down to tickets and shoes. For that, they banned the team from the NCAA tournament for the coming season. They also accepted our own self-imposed punishments which we had detailed a month before in our hearing with the Committee on Infractions. These included no off-campus recruiting or official paid visits by recruits during the 1989–90 academic year; a limitation on scholarship grants-in-aid to twelve for the combined seasons of 1990 through '92; and a reduction of one man from the coaching staff.

"The NCAA membership has given the Committee on Infractions the authority to impose lesser penalties if it determines that the case is unique," Smrt read from the report. "The committee cited the University's commendable approach and concluded that the case was unique for the following reasons: when public allegations of possible violations in the men's basketball program were made, the University contacted the NCAA immediately and cooperated with the enforcement department; the University acknowledged the existence of the violations of NCAA rules; and the University is taking significant actions to reorganize its athletics administration and to self-impose penalties. As a result of these mitigating circumstances, the committee adopted the University's self-imposed penalties and did not add sanctions that would have prevented N.C. State's basketball team from appearing on live television."

From the menu of punishments available, what the NCAA actually did was penalize N.C. State *less* than the required minimum of punishments.

As if I didn't feel relieved enough, imagine my feelings after the following exchange in the press conference.

Reporter: "One of the minimum violations is possible termination of all staff members who condoned this violation. Could someone respond? What I read is that Coach Valvano and his staff could have been subject to firing. Could someone respond to whether that action will take place?"

Smrt: "I'll be happy to respond. There was no athletic department staff member found in violation. In the past the committee has imposed actions against a staff member if they were involved so there was no staff member involved for the committee to do that."

Reporter: "Are you saying Coach Valvano's job was not at risk?"

Smrt: "What I'm saying is that there was no staff member including Coach Valvano to be found in violation. Coach Valvano was not involved in any violation in this case."

Reporter: "I'd like to ask Becky French [N.C. State University legal counsel] regarding Coach Valvano and his contract. Would the sanction voted by the NCAA break that contract?"

French: "Under the contract, the contract would be terminated if he was found in violation of a major NCAA coaching violation. That was not the case here so it does not involve any major NCAA violation under his contract."

Reporter: "OK, Becky, so you are saying that nothing has happened in these violations that would negate or break Jim Valvano's contract with N.C. State?"

French: "These violations have not named any individual as being guilty of a major violation as listed in Mr. Valvano's contract."

At this point, my attitude was: Case Closed. I felt almost total vindication in that we'd weathered these incredible allegations from a book; investigations from the faculty senate, the SBI, the Poole Commission and now the NCAA itself; and attack after constant editorial attack from the local newspaper. Now it was finally over. Under the most intense national scrutiny imaginable, there were no recruiting violations —the major business a coach involves himself in. No unfair competitive advantage. Zero. No academic irregularities. Zero. And unlike a lot of things in life, the punishment certainly fit the crime. Yes, we were barred from the tournament, but we hadn't been taken off television and the season had started anyway. We could focus on other things; we were only banned for one year; our underclassmen had a future after all. That was the best part.

During a meeting at Becky French's house to go over the ramifications of the NCAA announcement, I couldn't have been more upbeat. Wow, I could get back to the court, get on with coaching my team, return to basketball. Finally, all the other stuff was behind us. At one point Dr. Monteith asked me if we could talk privately and we went into another room and closed the doors.

Imagine my surprise when he informed me that he was about to go ahead with his own private investigation of the basketball team's academic situation. "I don't feel I can fully support you until I look into this myself," he said.

Since he had mentioned that he would look into academics back when we met in October, I thought he had been doing this all along. At that very moment, I didn't think about "hidden agendas" or "frameworks of the University" or "axes to grind," or anything else. I was too shocked, disappointed and numb. All I could think was: Here We Go Again.

Chapter Fifteen

FORGET THE OLD ITALIAN PROVERB; IT'S OVER BEFORE IT'S OVER

FORGET MY PARTY-POOPING MEETING WITH MONTEITH. THE OVERALL SENSE still was one of relief. I felt vindicated; the NCAA had found no indiscretions by our coaching staff. The team was relieved that finally the investigation and its aftermath were over. Yes, we were disappointed we would not be able to play in the NCAA tournament, but we committed ourselves to winning every other tournament we were scheduled to play in that year. Let's go back a few weeks. Back to basketball. For the better part of a month since we went before the Committee on Infractions in Arizona, I prepared the team for the worst. N.C. State was a "major" case; we had admitted guilt. We told them what the required punishments were for situations such as ours. "We can expect no tournament and no television," I told them. In fact, that's not what happened.

Since the postseason penalty was only for a year, and since we would remain on TV, there wouldn't be a devastating impact on recruiting, or on this particular team—remember, we were already well into the season. And what a team we expected to have!

Coming off the disappointing ending to the previous season when we were one game away, and (to me, at least) one worst-call-in-the-history-of-the-world from playing Duke and Danny Ferry to get into the Final Four—and this despite incredible turmoil—I knew we had tough, resilient, terrific kids. It was my 10th year at N.C. State and, following that stretch of star-struck seasons, we had hit upon a proper recruiting balance between marquee names and role players. The team was happy. We had lost Chucky Brown, but the dynamite backcourt of Rodney Monroe and Chris Corchiani would be juniors. Two thirds of our

forecourt, Avie Lester and Brian Howard, were seniors; and in 6'9"
sophomore forward Tom Gugliotta, I felt we had our next Del Negro: an
unknown sleeper who was ready to step forward and be The Man.

We had a great early season, despite the turmoil. I'll retrace my steps
for a moment to describe them.

The basketball season started the same day our tryst with the NCAA
ended; if that hadn't been marathon enough, I flew back from Arizona to
be with the team for our opening exhibition game against the team
from—ready?—Marathon Oil. Then, on November 8, we were to play a
second exhibition game, this one against the national team from Venezuela. However, a mind-boggling situation had developed concerning
Avie Lester's eligibility.

According to our players' self-adopted rules which they had voted on
back in the summer, the stiffest penalty was that if a guy went on
Academic Warning 2—the most serious state of academic problems—in
the upcoming season, he would be ineligible to play until he had gotten
off. Obviously, this was not to be retroactive. At the time the players
voted on this, only Avie was on Academic Warning 2, and as I said
before, the team's intention was that Avie be exempt from this new rule
so that he could play his senior year.

Back in August, I had sent the memo to Becky French, with a copy to
Larry Clark of the Athletics Council, explaining the team's newly
adopted rules. These players were eligible by NCAA standards, eligible
by ACC standards, eligible by N.C. State standards. But they wanted to
make the *team* standards more strict. A few days later, I sent a second
memo directly to Clark, to clarify the fact that these rules were not
retroactive, nor were they meant to punish any players *currently* on
Academic Warning 2 (and Avie Lester was the only one). The new rules
went into effect as the team went into the new season.

Following this, I was called in by the interim athletic director, Hal
Hopfenberg, and told that, according to the new rules, Avie Lester could
not play. I told Hal that there must be some mistake; that he had my
second memo stating that this was not meant to punish any current team
member, and that the time frame needed to be discussed. Hopfenberg
then told me that the second memo had not been read by Chancellor
Monteith or President Spangler, and that the first memo indicated that
Lester would be ineligible. "It was ambiguous," Hopfenberg said.

"It's only logic," I said. "Nobody is going to vote himself off a team for
his last season. The second memo clarified the first. This kid can't be
penalized because somebody didn't receive a memo!"

Hopfenberg said the perception—I guess he meant the perception of the administration, the press and the public—was that Avie, who was currently on Academic Warning 2, was now ineligible according to the team's own rules, and that if they went back on that now, it would be seen as another educational sham.

I walked out of that meeting, my head spinning. Could anyone possibly envision a player voting himself ineligible for his senior year? Our differences on this matter simmered between August and November. But since Hal had said he'd look into it, I was waiting to hear back from him.

Hopfenberg came to me right before the game against Venezuela and reiterated that, to the faculty's way of thinking, Avie Lester was ineligible. If he played, there would be serious problems, not the least of which would probably be a no-confidence vote sent down by the faculty senate. Hopfenberg said there would be a movement on the campus that I should be removed from my job, that I had violated academic principles. He suggested we "redshirt" Lester.

I told Hopfenberg that this was a good idea, but unfortunately, we couldn't redshirt Avie, because he had already played against Marathon Oil. He said that he thought that didn't count because it was only an exhibition game. I told him that, yes, it did count. Because of Hopfenberg's lack of experience with NCAA rules, he thought he could wait, that he could head off the crisis, that we didn't have to make a decision on Avie's eligibility until our game against Richmond, the first "official" game. But according to the NCAA, one exhibition game is equivalent to an entire season of eligibility.

"Let's play him against Venezuela, then don't play him the rest of the year, then appeal to the NCAA," Hopfenberg said.

"No. Let's not play him in the Venezuela game. Let's tell the NCAA that a mistake has been made," I said.

My position was that we should show the NCAA our mistake. Show them we made it, we realized we made it, and that we stopped then and there and held Avie out. Which is what we did. But now we had to explain to the media why he didn't play against Venezuela. Since the Buckley Amendment protected Avie's grade situation, we couldn't say he was on Academic Warning 2. So we announced that, according to the team's new rules, the administration viewed Lester as currently ineligible and he couldn't play. And that we were asking the NCAA to give Avie his last year back next season.

The firestorm that followed included:

1. The press insisted (correctly) that if Lester was eligible, we should go ahead and play him. The NCAA would never give him back a year.

2. A member of the university's Athletic Council writing me a letter saying he would judge *my* character on whether Avie played or not.

While Hopfenberg prepared an appeal to the NCAA, I really hoped the University would understand that Lester's chances of winning the case were virtually nil, and that N.C. State should let him play his final season. I even called Dave Didion to ask his opinion. He said the rules stipulated that one game (Marathon Oil) constituted a season. We had no chance with an appeal. The NCAA has no mechanism to overturn that eligibility rule. I asked Dave for some advice. He said we should play Avie, or else he was going to lose his last year. He said that since the school had misinterpreted its own rule, it should go ahead and let him play. I told Dave the school had already determined he should not play this year.

After we beat Venezuela without Lester, I met with Avie and his parents (who had come up from Roxboro for the game) to explain the situation. It was a terrible time. Here was a kid who had worked his butt off and was on the brink of what I thought would be a terrific year, a year in which he could prove he belonged in the NBA. And now he was being told he couldn't play. It wasn't just frustrating and sad—it was tragic. Oh, the administrative fathers did come up with a small bone. They said Lester could get off Academic Warning 2 if he attained a grade point average close to 3.0 after the first semester; a higher average than he had ever reached in his career. Avie thought he was capable of getting there, but it seemed difficult and unfair.

That night, I met with Avie and his parents in my office. I explained what had happened and the consequences, and Avie's parents couldn't believe it. Avie stormed out of the Case Athletic Center, actually tearing a huge metal door from its hinges. As bitter as he was about N.C. State and basketball in general, Lester continued to practice with us, knocking the heck out of our frontcourt in preparation for the ACC wars, never saying a negative word. Of course, for the next six weeks, we hoped against hope that our center would reach the required GPA and be able to join us.

We opened in the preseason National Invitation Tournament on November 15, and, even without Avie, we beat Richmond 57–48. The only way to beat a Dick Tarrant–coached team is to be smart, don't make mistakes and score when you get the chance. Beginning a string of games in which he proved to be an amazing offensive weapon, Monroe scored 20 points and also had six rebounds. In addition, in Avie's place, 6'10" senior Brian D'Amico started, and contributed a good effort with seven points and eight boards.

For our second-round NIT game on November 18, we traveled to Chicago to meet DePaul. Every time we played DePaul in Chicago, three things happened: 1) It snowed. 2) I went to eat at Mike Ditka's. 3) We got beat. It was 70–63 this time, but afterward I didn't feel so bad. I thought we were going to be all right without Avie. There were some things we couldn't do—like run fast. But in general, we were all right.

On December 1 and 2, we played in the Tournament of Champions in Charlotte. I really wanted to do well. This was the second year of the tournament, which was to be hosted by us and North Carolina in alternate years. In the inauguaral event, the Tar Heels had easily defeated Arizona; now it was our turn to show what we could do. It reminded me of the old days and the North-South doubleheaders: Carolina blowing people's brains out, N.C. State struggling for its life.

On the eve of the tournament, the hosts treated the teams to a dinner where the coaches competed in one of those "Pop-A-Shot" games. Randy Ayers, the young coach at Ohio State, tied with me, so we went into overtime. The teams cheered, the fans went wild, and I wound up winning, which seemed a precursor of things to come when we beat Ohio State the next night. In the game, Tommy Gugliotta had 10 points and 11 rebounds, and generally played great. He ran the floor well, and was blossoming right before everyone's eyes.

I say "ran," but as the score (68–54) indicated, we didn't do that much running. It was obvious this team would be playing to its opponents' style. We were counterpunchers, which is why the next night in the championship game against run-and-gun Pittsburgh, I decided to go up and down the floor with the Panthers. I was worried that, without Lester, we wouldn't be able to keep up the pace. But we did that and more. We beat Pitt 100–87, with Monroe scoring 30 points and—get this!—Gugliotta adding 21, with 10 more rebounds.

Following the game, Gugliotta was named the most valuable player of the tournament. My God, what a moment! You've got to understand that "Gugs" was a youngster whom hardly anybody in the big time wanted. He had played at Walt Whitman High School in Huntington, Long Island, where his father, Frank, who was a longtime friend of my own dad, had coached. Frank Gugliotta had worked for my dad at his summer camp and, when my dad retired, Frank took over as camp director.

The first Gugliotta son, Frank Jr., came of recruiting age when I was the coach at Johns Hopkins. The second, Charlie, was looking for a basketball scholarship when I coached at Bucknell. I missed on both those Gugliottas. "I've got one son left," Frank Sr. had told me a few years before. "He's going to be the best, and you'd better not miss out on him."

When I went to scout Tommy, he was a skinny, 6'6" bag of bones who had sprouted from 6'1" after his freshman year of high school. He just wasn't big enough or good enough. He was thinking about either Fairfield

VALVANO

or Iona, and I thought that that was just about his level. I told Frank Gugliotta I didn't think I could use Tommy.

"Jimmy, my son is going to be a player," Frank said.

On Gugs' visit to Raleigh, we had a long talk. Meanwhile, his father had taken ill. Maybe that was a factor. Maybe the relationship between our fathers was another factor. Whatever the case, I knew I had to offer Tommy Gugliotta a scholarship to N.C. State. "I'm not sure you can play here," I told Gugs, "but I sat here and told Vinny Del Negro the same thing."

Tommy's father passed away in his freshman year. After the fifth game of his sophomore year, he became the MVP of the Tournament of Champions. As he ran off the court beaming and hugging his trophy, I pulled Gugs aside. I did a lousy job of holding back the tears. "You know something, Tommy?" I said. "Somewhere tonight there are two very proud fathers looking down on two very proud sons."

While not one of the best physical teams I had at N.C. State, this was surely one of the more enjoyable to be around. Everyone got along, the relationships were tight. Sure, we missed Avie's quick athleticism, but D'Amico was giving us some solid stuff in the middle. We were slow there, however. And we couldn't substitute speed either. I always felt that when you make a substitution, if you became a faster team, you don't necessarily hurt yourself. But when you come off the bench slower, it affects your efficiency. Since our subs were mostly slow and inexperienced, we had to find a way to get quicker, which had to be through Mickey Hinnant.

Ironically, when we beat St. John's in the first annual ACC-Big East Challenge in Greensboro on December 5, we didn't need much from Hinnant. Monroe and Corchiani split 44 points, and we won 67–58.

Unlike most of the coaches, I thought these inter-league matchups were great; good for the schools AND the conferences. And I didn't pooh-pooh the rivalry between the leagues. I reveled in it, used it, motivated with it. I told our guys we were playing for a lot of things, including conference pride. I didn't want to spend the summer Nike trips listening to Jim Boeheim of Syracuse and P. J. Carlesimo of Seton Hall crowing about their league being better. Wake Forest had been beaten in overtime by Seton Hall in the first game of our doubleheader, so the ACC was behind the Big East by one in the games that week. I told our players we had to win to get back even.

It was a close game all the way, but it turned when St. John's Boo Harvey slammed the ball down in anger and was charged with a technical foul. We made the free throws, took the lead and never looked back.

* * *

222

On December 7, Monroe and Corchiani played bombs-away again as we beat Duquesne 126–77. We had now scored 68, 100, 67, and 126, victories all, showing versatility everywhere. N.C. State's '83 championship backcourt of Lowe and Whittenburg certainly had earned their spurs; they'd played together for so long in high school and college that they'd become one word: LowWhit. But I wasn't so sure Monroe and Corchiani weren't now challenging them in the State record books. They were the two biggest-name recruits I'd ever signed together who made it together. Rodney will probably wind up the leading scorer in N.C. State annals; Chris will probably finish as the leading assist man in NCAA history.

Cheered by all this and a 6–1 record too, we prepared for a long, 12-day layoff and the semester exams.

The NCAA announcement of sanctions on December 12 caused no chair-throwing or cursing, but there was palpable depression. One thing that kept the players' spirits high during the break was knowing that Avie Lester was studying hard. Surely, if he did well, common sense would prevail, and the administration would let him play the next semester. If he did make his grades, Avie would take the floor for our next game, just one week away.

However, on December 19, I had to tell the team in the locker room before the game against East Tennessee State that Lester had not made the required GPA—and remember, this unrealistic 3.0 goal for Avie came about solely from a misreading of the team's new rules—and that he would not be joining us for the rest of the season. Avie *was* eligible, but he wouldn't be allowed to play.

It was "the coach's decision" to keep Lester off, of course. It was always "Valvano's decision." The administration would tell me to announce these things, and to say that it was *my* decision. My decision would have been to have played him the *first* semester. Again, I was told to do this because the school did not want the perception that we were going against any of our own rules or regulations. Again, the faculty senate made it known that they considered my first memo of August 4 to be binding, that the second memo did not count. Again, I was told that if I attempted to play Avie Lester, they would start proceedings to have me censured or fired.

I'm still embarrassed to this day that I didn't take a stand for Avie at that point. Avie Lester was a casualty of the university's concern with public perception at the time.

But what could I tell the team? They were disappointed, hurt, furious. They said it was not fair; that it was ridiculous. They were right. To say the Wolfpack didn't want to play the game against East Tennessee would be an understatement. The team was totally dead and gone; I wasn't even sure they wanted to continue the season. To demonstrate how flat we were, we fell behind by 20 points in the first eight minutes, and we lost 92–82. The ironic thing about the whole evening was that the East Tennessee coach, an N.C. State grad named Les Robinson, would later succeed me. Think his team's whipping us that night created a favorable impression of State for Les, or what?

Meanwhile, Avie Lester couldn't have acted with more class. It was a bitter disappointment, an absolute travesty of justice for the young man. Not having played his entire senior year, he went unwanted in the NBA draft. Last fall he tried out for the Denver Nuggets, but after being cut there, he wound up playing in Portugal. Given the right opportunity, which he didn't get at N.C. State, Avie Lester may still play in the NBA someday.

The Holiday Festival in New York got the juices flowing again. This was my third Christmas tournament in the Big Apple. The two other times we had split titles with St. John's, but this year we played teams coached by two of my best friends, Florida State with Pat Kennedy and Seton Hall with P. J. Carlesimo. When I was at Iona with Pat as assistant coach, P.J. was the coach at Wagner. This was like the ECAC, revisited. We played Pat's club in the first round, and won easily. Monroe had 35 points and Corchiani had 16 assists.

Two nights later, Tommy Gugliotta had 18 points and 11 rebounds as we defeated Seton Hall for the championship, 65–62. Though neither Pat nor P.J. had teams anything like the year before—when Seton Hall came within a basket of being national champions, and Florida State was ranked in the top ten before being upset in the NCAA's—I was ecstatic over our showing in New York, especially coming as it did so soon after our double setbacks earlier in the month.

Bring on the ACC schedule.

On January 3, 1990, we opened the conference season at home against Clemson, a team that wound up winning the ACC regular season, advancing to the Final Sixteen in the NCAA tournament. The last play was designed to get Monroe the free shot, but when Rodney was doubled, he threw it to Gugliotta, who drained a jumper with two seconds left, giving us a 79–77 win. Was this turning into a dream season for Gugs or what?

Of all the years I'd been coaching, in terms of terrific teams, the two best were the very last two.

* * *

In our game against Temple in Atlantic City on January 6, Monroe made 33 points and we won 74–71. However, standing proud with a record of 11–2, over the next 11 days we lost more games than we had lost up to that point. Inasmuch as we played Georgia Tech, Wake Forest, North Carolina and Duke—among them one team which would go to the Final Sixteen of the NCAA tournament and *two* to the Final Four—and that three of the four games were on the road, I'd say we didn't have much to apologize for.

Tech's Lethal Weapon Three—Kenny Anderson, Dennis Scott and Brian Oliver—beat us 92–85 in a game which just proved my old philosophy that a team can stop one star player and maybe two star players, but that it's awfully difficult to stop three. The funny thing about Georgia Tech is that two other Techsters, Johnny McNeil and Malcolm Mackey, are kids we tried hard to recruit.

Our series of games against Wake Forest continued to be close even though my friend, Bob Staak, had been replaced by the former Virginia assistant coach, Dave Odom. We won 61–57, mostly because Dave was still trying to impart Virginia's cautious, deliberate, halfcourt offense to a crew of dazzling runners and jumpers. It was going to take a while before the coach and the players adapted to each other. I'm kind of glad Dave didn't let them push the ball down the floor faster until later in the season.

Carolina beat us 91–81; beat us every which way. It was the only game all season I could safely but sadly say we weren't in. Duke, however, was a different story. It's strange how certain teams give other teams fits; we'd always been very fortunate that way against Duke. We had them again this time: With only seconds to play, N.C. State led by two points. Duke freshman Billy McCaffery was on the foul line, and he threw up a horrid brick.

In a bizarre sequence of events, Gugliotta jumped up for the rebound, grabbed the ball, lost control of it and—Boom!—the thing went through the hoop to score for Duke! Now, the game was tied, and we went into overtime. I'd lost games a lot of ways, but this was unbelievable. Now, according to Coach Mike K., "So and so came across and blocked out and somebody tipped and . . ." Sorry. Hey, we've played the tape back a thousand times. Gugliotta fumbled the ball up high, it slipped off and went in the basket and we lost in overtime, 85–82.

Off the court, the debate about the team's academics continued.

Monday, January 29, 1990

Interim Athletic Director Hal Hopfenberg spoke to the weekly luncheon meeting of the Raleigh Sports Club, emphasizing his support for
me to continue as coach. "And if it turns out that there was no academic
scandal and that he is found to be nonculpable in his actions, then yes, I
very much would like to see him remain as basketball coach," Hopfenberg told the club.

Wednesday, January 31

Interim Chancellor Larry Monteith called me to his office; it was the
first time we had spoken since the day the NCAA sanctions were
announced and he told me of his ongoing personal investigation.

Monteith asked me if there was anything I would like to discuss with
him about academics: changes, reforms, graduation rates, what have you.
He said that it appeared that we had a better level of student on the
basketball team in my first three years. Then following that, I seemed to
have had a very bad three years in terms of students. Again, he brought
up the forty-three players I had recruited. Again, he asked me if I felt
there had been severe academic abuses. I said no. It seemed a total rehash
of everything all the investigative bodies had gone over. But I did feel he
was being more and more negative toward me regarding the academic
situation.

We beat Virginia, a team we usually have difficulty even showing up
for, by the stunning score of 84–58. In a battle of two fine junior point
guards, Corchiani outscored John Crotty—are you ready for this?—
20–0.

Friday, February 2

An editorial appeared in *The News and Observer,* which heretofore had
had nothing but praise for Hopfenberg, entitled "Hopfenberg Out of
Bounds." In it, the newspaper replied to the AD's comments at the
Raleigh Sports Club meeting.

"In praising Mr. Valvano's come-lately support of reforms, Dr. Hopfenberg ignores the painful facts of the past year," it read. ". . . There are
no 'ifs' about the academic scandal or Mr. Valvano's culpability. . . .
Perhaps Dr. Hopfenberg has been temporarily seduced by the glitz of the
games or the glibness of Jim Valvano."

That night, we were in Las Vegas for our game against UNLV the next
afternoon. Having been invited by Vegas Coach Jerry Tarkanian to a

dinner in honor of the N.C. State traveling party, I of course invited Hal Hopfenberg and his wife to join us. Chancellor Monteith was not there, and my assistant coaches had other things to do. At first, Hopfenberg said he'd love to come along. Later, he showed me a fax of *The News and Observer* editorial, which somebody had sent to our hotel.

Hopfenberg said he didn't think he should go to the dinner with me that night, and asked if I agreed.

I don't know if I was more shocked or disgusted. "Sure, Hal," I said. "If that's the way you feel . . ."

My God! Here was a grown man and a distinguished educator allowing himself to be told how to run his business (not to mention his personal social life) by a newspaper editorial! It was just another indication to me of the total paranoia in Raleigh regarding how the media reacted to anything—specifically, anything to do with me. Surely, Monteith was blazing down the warpath set by *The News and Observer,* and now Hopfenberg seemed to be the advance scout. Still, I didn't feel my job was in jeopardy. I thought I'd only have to survive one more shot from Monteith, one more set of strict academic guidelines, and I'd be able to continue.

Up to now, while Monteith had been virtually silent, I had been getting positive feedback from Hopfenberg. But now, the writing was on the wall. This being Vegas, the message was in neon, and I couldn't even see it.

Saturday, February 3

I've talked about the difference between systems coaches and seat-of-the-pants coaches. The decision I made in the Vegas game was to play an offense we hadn't used all season. Remember, we were up against a team so strong, deep and talented that, two months later, they would break just about every record for a national championship game known to man. I knew we couldn't play Vegas head-up, honest injun. We had to come up with something special.

So we stacked our entire offense above the foul line. We passed and cut to the basket all day long. We stayed in front the entire first half, but Vegas made a run at the end of the half, leading 43–42. We regained the lead and held on into the second half. As unbelievable as it seemed, the fearsome, defensively pressuring 'Vegans were forced to lay back in a zone, so tough were we on our angled cuts. I was ecstatic that we had forced one of the truly great defensive crews out of its game plan. Tark's sharks were in a zone, right where we wanted them, against which we were most effective.

Then suddenly that hydra-headed defensive formation Tarkanian called the "Amoeba" glommed all over us. We turned the ball over twice in a row, and I'm not talking about harmless entry passes, either. We were just calmly throwing the ball around the perimeter when the Amoeba got us, stole the ball twice, and went the length of the court for morale-busting dunks. We lost 88–82; still, it was an excellent effort.

Wednesday, February 7

In the last meeting I'd had with Interim Chancellor Monteith, he had asked me to think some more about anything that might be unusual in our approach to academics. I went to see him on February 7 to discuss a university policy which I felt needed to be changed. I said that the university needed to look at the policy whereby a student—and not only a student athlete—could drop a semester full of bad grades in order to reenter and be eligible. That's that one loophole that a couple of basketball players had taken advantage of in my ten years here. I told Monteith that if he felt that policy was a mistake, it should be changed. "If you want to get together again, please call me," I said.

Monteith didn't call. This meeting was the last time he talked to me. Then. Now. Or ever.

That night, we played UNC in Chapel Hill, where no team I'd coached had ever won. Where we'd lost in all kinds of nefarious ways. Where we'd lost from the first time, when Kenny Matthews took that charge that wasn't called . . . to the last time, the year before, when the Tar Heels' Scott Williams threw the ball directly into the arms of Chucky Brown so that Chucky could fire up an unmolested three-pointer to tie the game—except that Brown missed.

This time proved to be different. The game was close all the way. With 12:55 to play, the score was tied. Then something marvelous happened: We had a great run and actually led by as many as 17 points before we settled into an 88–77 win. And we did it without a few key guys whom I had disciplined prior to the game. Remember those stringent team rules we had voted in? One of them concerned class attendance. That afternoon, I had received a report that Brian D'Amico and a couple of important freshman subs, Bryant Feggins and Kevin Thompson, had missed classes. So D'Amico didn't start, and the other two barely got into the game until the second half. Instead, we went with a smaller, quicker lineup: Mickey Hinnant became the third guard with Monroe and Corchiani, and we just ran. We didn't press much; we just ran.

We won going away, even without these players. As we walked off the court at the Dean Dome, I remember thinking we'd finally done it. We'd overcome everything. The kids had played hard. They'd stayed focused and together. We imposed the strict standards. They didn't get away with missing class. We enforced the rules. We beat Carolina at Carolina. What else could a school possibly want from its coach?

Thursday, February 8

The next day, I went to my meeting with Hopfenberg. Before I could get a word in edgewise about academics, Hal gave me a big grin. "Pretty shrewd, Jim," Hopfenberg said. "A small lineup against the big Heels. Sting 'em. Scatter 'em. Run 'em to death. Great move."

"Hal," I said. "It had nothing to do with coaching. I made those other guys sit because of academics."

"Come on, Coach," he said.

Saturday, February 10

In a rematch with DePaul, we extracted some vengeance in an 80–71 victory. No Chicago. No snow. No Ditkas. But a win's a win. At that point we were 17–6, looking at a strong finish. I even let myself think about the following year, when our lineup of Monroe and Corchiani at guards and Gugs, Feggins and Thompson up front would be as strong as any team's in the conference.

Monday, February 12

Clemson. Away. 6'11" Elden Campbell, an about-to-be NBA first-round draft choice. 6'11" Dale Davis, a junior, better than Campbell. "We're going to play Paul Westhead basketball," I told our troops. I knew we couldn't stand around with Clemson or we'd get our brains bashed in. "We're going to run and keep running and unless I miss my guess, we're going to shock 'em. We'll put one big man in the game and four quick ones. They'll be able to play either Campbell or Davis, but not both of 'em at the same time." After the first thirteen minutes or so, we led by fifteen points.

Now for the bad news. We weren't deep enough or in condition enough to play Paul Westhead basketball. I've never seen such a tired bunch as the N.C. State Wolfpack after Clemson came from behind and beat us 89–81. Even though we lost, it was such a fun game! I vowed right then that if I could choose one style, this would be it: I'd get ten medium-sized guys who could really motor and jump, and then I'd run and press and alternate them until the cows came home. That was obviously the wave of the future.

229

Saturday, February 17

Georgia Tech beat us for the second time, playing confidently and comfortably. We were ahead by seven points with seven to play, when Dennis Scott hit two three-point shots in the next two minutes. After we missed again, Scott hit another bomb. Just like that, Tech up by two. We had a chance to win the thing both at the end of regulation and at the end of the first overtime, but Brian Oliver latched onto Monroe like Velcro Man and Rodney couldn't get in good position for his pet shot.

In Tech's 95–92 double overtime win, the difference was that Scott could get his shot in the clutch and Monroe couldn't. Rodney was a great player, but needed some more work off the dribble to make an impact; Oliver's defense went a long way toward proving that to him. As a result, I firmly believe this was the game that made up Rodney's mind to stay in school and work on his game before turning pro.

Wednesday, February 21

We won another Duke game, 76–71. Five weeks later, of course, the Blue Devils would advance all the way to the national championship game. But as the ACC season wore down and we realized we'd be staying home while a lot of our peers advanced into the tournament, I can honestly say we didn't seem affected. I felt terrible for Avie Lester and our seniors, D'Amico and Brian Howard. But the feeling was that we would have the bulk of the squad back together next year.

With away games at Virginia and weak Maryland, and a home contest against struggling Wake Forest, I figured we'd win at least two of our last three games and go into the ACC tournament with a 20–9 record.

We were 18–8 after our win against Duke.

I had absolutely no hint that it was the last winning game I would ever coach at N.C. State.

Monday, February 26

Becky French, the N.C. State University legal counsel, told *The Charlotte Observer* that Charles Shackleford's agent, Salvatore DiFazio, admitted to her that Shackleford had accepted nearly $65,000 from two men before and during the 1987–88 basketball season while he was still playing for the Wolfpack. In *The Observer*'s story, the State Bureau of Investigation's William Dowdy said the agency was making its own inquiries of criminal allegations "which may be unrelated."

Meanwhile, Shackleford himself told *The News and Observer* he took the money from a sports agent. " 'You don't think it will come back to hurt you,' he said. 'But in the long run, it does. What I did was wrong, but I don't think it was major. I was a kid in college and I had no money, so I took money.' "

Wednesday, February 28

In the locker room at College Park, Maryland, the N.C. State sports information director, Mark Bockelman, hit me with a bombshell. That very afternoon, I had met with my agent, Art Kaminsky, in the hotel about a possible book offer. The bus ride to Cole Field House was uneventful. I had given the team the pregame chalk talk, they had gone out for the warm-ups and I was feeling fairly good about life, when Bockelman informed me that "ABC News" was about to go on the air with a former North Carolina State player's claims of a point-shaving scandal at State.

I don't remember every detail of what happened then, just that I felt as if I'd been kicked in the gut. I walked out of the locker room, past the training room and over to the other side of Cole, near the home team's dressing room. Somebody had a television on. My team, live, was just about finishing their warm-ups when somebody from one of my former teams appeared on the "ABC News," his face shadowed for anonymity, and said something about point-shaving. From his silhouette and the inflection of his voice, it looked and sounded like Kelsey Weems, a guard who played for N.C. State in the '86 through '89 seasons before leaving because of personal problems. I was in such an emotional state, it was all I could do to walk back over to our locker room.

Not that this development came as a total surprise. Eight days earlier, I had been warned by Armen Keteyian, a reporter for ABC, that something like this was looming on the horizon. On February 20, Keteyian had appeared in my outer office and handed my secretary, Beverly Sparks, a note which said: "Coach, I believe it is very important that you at least listen to my questions about Shackleford and a suspected point-shaving conspiracy at State in early '88. You're not implicated, but obviously I need a comment. Armen."

Keteyian was accompanied by another ABC reporter from Atlanta, and we talked for about half an hour in my office. What Keteyian told me was that he had some information regarding point-shaving. He asked me if I had ever suspected such a thing from any of my players. I said of course not; that if I had, I would have done something about it. We're talking about a coach's worst nightmare here—beyond defeats, ineligibilities, recruiting violations, the works. I asked Keteyian all sorts of questions about where he had received his information, who was involved, when, what games, etc.

Personal Fouls had intimated that an N.C. State player had thrown the game we played against Florida in the 1987 NCAA tournament (we lost 82–70) to avoid taking a drug test. However, as far as I knew, that was only speculation and rumor. It had never been implied that there was point-shaving involving gambling. Keteyian would not elaborate on his information, except to mention that our game at the end of the 1987–88 season against Wake Forest (which we won 86–82) was supposedly under suspicion. He also asked if I knew a man named "Robert Kramer," whom he said was involved with Shackleford in the point-shaving conspiracy. Again, I told him I knew of no such individual.

As I told Keteyian, these charges had emerged before. During the Poole Commission investigation, in fact, the SBI had looked into point-shaving, but had come up with nothing. So I wasn't as alarmed as I might have been if this information had sprung out of nowhere. We had FBI representatives come in every year to talk to the team about gamblers; and our games were all so competitive! At no time did Armen mention anything about having a former N.C. State player ready to go on national television and claim he personally knew of point-shaving.

Subsequently, much was made of the fact that Ralph Kitley, the Wake Forest center, scored 22 points against us for a career high. The implication was that Shackleford permitted him to score in order to shave points. Whether this was true or not, there is no way any coach would be alarmed at an opposing player's having a good game. Kitley had played very well that year against Georgia Tech, as well. Although not a prolific scorer, Kitley had good games against other teams. In twenty-three years of coaching, there are many occasions when an opposing player will perform above his normal statistics.

After the reporters left my office that day, I immediately called Hal Hopfenberg and Becky French, the university attorney, to tell them about the meeting. I gave Becky a copy of the note Keteyian had given me. I'm sure they alerted Interim Chancellor Monteith. Other than that, there wasn't much else I could do.

But now, here came a TV report with a nameless man sitting in shadows. Did I believe him? I certainly hoped it wasn't true, but I had no way of knowing.

Obviously, coaching the Maryland game became extremely unimportant. I did not want to coach the game. At that point, I didn't know if I *ever* wanted to coach again. Anticipating the process after just a mere allegation—and I had been through Allegation Hell for almost thirteen months now—I realized that whether anybody was innocent or guilty wouldn't come to light for months and months. It would be so difficult, so draining, so damning.

As distraught as I was, I had to tell the team about the television report; they would have seen something was wrong just by looking at me. I told them that I hoped this was not true, and that I couldn't believe any of our former players engaged in such an activity. "But fellas," I said, "get ready for another onslaught of questions. The media will be all over us about this. We're all going to have to suffer again."

That pregame locker room meeting at Maryland effectively ended our season. Oh, we didn't quit playing or trying or even mentally getting ourselves prepared. But our hearts just weren't in it. That night, I barely was able to go through the motions. We lost 96–95, and the feeling was like . . . some sort of scrimmage. Shirts and skins. Winners out. Have to win by two. Only we didn't.

After the game, my agent, Art Kaminsky, and I met with Hopfenberg in my hotel suite to discuss the ramifications of everything that had happened in the last few days. Immediately, some miscommunications and misconceptions occurred. I think that Hal didn't really understand what I was going through.

It was after midnight. I'd just come face-to-face with charges of a point-shaving scandal. My team had lost another game on the road by one point. I'd done a terrible job coaching. We'd been through so much turmoil. The acting chancellor, my boss, was in the process of a review or an investigation or an inquisition to determine my future. Former players had not only let me down, but possibly had been involved in dumping games. Jesus God! What else? I was incredibly depressed.

"Hal," I said, "I don't know if this actually happened. I hope to God it didn't. But I also know the position this puts Monteith in. Everything is going to start all over again. How much can the university handle here?"

"Just relax," Hopfenberg said. "Let's let Larry make his decision. Maybe he'll conclude everything's okay."

But I knew everything wasn't okay.

"Hal, let's get serious," I said.

I told Hopfenberg that we should both do what was best for the university. If that meant parting company, so be it. I knew that, even if there had not been point-shaving, the taint would always be there. If there had, though in the past a coach was not held blameworthy—for instance, Tom Davis moved from the point-shaving scandal at Boston College to prominent jobs at first Stanford, then Iowa. I told Hopfenberg that maybe we should get our lawyers together to talk in an amicable fashion about how I could step down in the easiest way possible. I thought he understood what I was talking about: that I believed Monteith's decision had now been made for him; that he would have to fire me. I assumed that, like any athletic director should, Hopfenberg would know I was talking about concluding our business under the terms of my existing contract.

I assumed wrong.

It was a few days later that Hal said he thought from this conversation that I meant to say I was quitting.

But no coach is going to quit in a situation where, by doing so, he gives up $500,000. The clause in my contract read that if either party broke the deal, they would receive a half million dollars from the other. (I also had a separate deal with the Wolfpack Club, wherein if I was fired by the university, the Club would pay me an additional $375,000.)

We did agree that night to get our respective lawyers together as soon as possible back in Raleigh.

Thursday, March 1

In New York, I met with Art Kaminsky, who agreed with me that Monteith and the university had no choice but to let me go. Unless we got a more positive signal that I was still wanted, Art planned to come to Raleigh over the weekend to meet with N.C. State officials about my separation from the university.

Friday, March 2

I flew back to Raleigh and met with Hopfenberg. I wanted to know exactly how he felt, how Monteith felt, just what N.C. State wanted me to do. I won't deny that I was still looking for any sign at all that somebody wanted me to remain as coach.

Hopfenberg said Kaminsky should come to Raleigh.

Saturday, March 3

Kaminsky met with Hal Hopfenberg, Becky French, and George Worsley, N.C. State's vice president for financial affairs. I had never been involved in anything like the settlement of a contract before. Art and I had discussed what was fair. By the terms of the contract, if I was dismissed, I was to get a total of $875,000 (from the university and the Wolfpack Club, combined). But N.C. State had been very good to me. I'd had a terrific ten-year run. I loved the people, the state and the school. My home was in Raleigh, I had one daughter in the university and another about to enroll the next year. A settlement figure in the area of $600,000 seemed fair to me. We assumed the meeting would be a short, friendly session in which everyone would abide by the tenets of the contract, shake hands and arrange for a press conference to announce my leaving.

I had finished our last regular-season practice with the team and was sitting in my office early in the evening, when Art called.

"Brace yourself," he said. "You're not going to believe this."

I didn't know what he could mean.

"They don't want to pay you anything," he said.

"What?" I said.

"They say since you wanted to quit, they're taking you at your word. You're quitting. They don't have to pay you a thing," Kaminsky said.

Forget the potential money loss. The unconscionable hardballing. The sandbagging of a legitimate contract. I can't explain the hurt and the pain I felt, that the university, to which I'd given my working life for ten years, would now treat me like that.

"Guess what, Art," I said. "I don't want to quit. I want to coach. Are you telling me they want me to keep coaching?"

"No. They don't want you to coach, either," he said. "They don't want you here, period."

"Whoa," I said. "They don't want me here, but they don't want to honor the contract either?"

"That's what I'm telling you," Kaminsky said.

"Well, now they have to fire me," I said. "I'm not quitting."

Kaminsky called back a little while later. "They'll give you one year's salary," he said.

By this time I was too angry to think straight. "End of discussion, Art. You might as well leave right now. Tell them I'm either going to coach the basketball team at N.C. State or they're going to fire me and live up to the full terms of the contract."

Kaminsky met me back at my office. He was bewildered at what had taken place. He's a pretty high-powered New York agent/lawyer, a guy who's been around and dealt with all kinds of contracts, not to mention people. He said he had never seen a client treated as poorly as this. To think that a university which had always approved of what I'd done—had re-signed me, promoted me and extolled me beyond my wildest expectations—would now turn around and do this, was incomprehensible.

Sunday, March 4

Our final game at home against Wake Forest was one of the more emotional times I'd ever known. Our problems had been spread all over the papers, of course. In addition, it was public knowledge that Monteith was nearing the end of his internal investigation, that my contract negotiations were under way, that my job was hanging by a thread. As I walked out onto the court at Reynolds Coliseum, the place exploded. Yellow ribbons in the shape of a "V" were everywhere. There were V posters and V placards and V signs. People shouted and applauded and carried on something wonderful. To hear such support was incredible. It was a humbling experience, and a teary one.

I can't explain what such an outpouring of affection meant to me and to my family. These were the real people supporting me. I might be getting my butt kicked in the electoral college, but the popular vote was all mine. That afternoon convinced me to follow my course. I was committed to staying at N.C. State now. I wanted everybody to know I didn't want to leave.

We lost to Wake Forest, 93–91.

Thursday, March 8

To negotiate my case—read: fire me—N.C. State hired an independent lawyer named Howard Manning, aged seventy-five. In a meeting with the board of trustees, Manning said he'd take care of the situation "in a couple of days."

Friday, March 9

Before N.C. State's opening game in the ACC tournament in Charlotte against Georgia Tech, I found myself in the men's room with none other than Bobby Cremins, coach of the Yellow Jackets. "Mark it down, Bobby. Whoever wins this game will win the tournament. If we get by you today, nobody will stop us. If you win it, you're going to the Final Four." (Which naturally they did, and they did.)

Nevertheless, I was again amazed at the amount of support I was receiving from N.C. State alumni, friends, and fans in general. One group calling itself The Friends of N.C. State University passed out thousands of four-page flyers, listing my accomplishments. Even I had forgotten one of my proudest: recruiting and coaching the only two-time basketball academic All-American in ACC history, Terry Gannon. I used to joke that if I was to be blamed for all the future nongraduates I coached at N.C. State, I should be given credit for all the future doctors and lawyers I coached at Johns Hopkins.

We led Georgia Tech by 10 points at halftime, but couldn't hang on down the stretch against the Lethal Weapons. We lost 76–67, after which several players, when asked about my future, said that if I was going, they were gone. Corchiani, especially, vowed to transfer from N.C. State unless I was retained as the coach. (Later, I would help Chris and his parents decide whether or not he would stay and finish out his senior season.)

There was a lot of crying in that locker room following my last game. I told the team that I was clearly fighting to keep my coaching job. I said I wanted to remain at State, that I'd never quit, that if I was not here the next year it would be because the university had fired me. It was a tough time and place for me. But it will remain the most special of all those locker room times and places.

Saturday, March 10

Happy 44th Birthday, Dad. For the first time in my life, I sat up in the stands with my family and watched the ACC tournament. Took pictures with the fans. Signed autographs. Shook a lot of hands.

A card from my middle daughter, Jamie, seventeen (who shares my particular brand of humor), said:

> For Dad on his birthday . . . You have devoted your entire life and spent every cent of your money trying to find ways to make me happy . . . I like that in a guy . . . Dad, I don't think you ever had a normal birthday. This year is not an exception. This has been a tough year for all of us. I think we should use today as a new starting point . . . It's time you started being a little selfish and make yourself happy. This whole ordeal has taught me one special thing. The Valvano family can make it through anything because of our love for each other. The only thing we may not be able to live through is a severe loss of income. Ha! I love you.
>
> Jamie Jill.

In fact, throughout this period, one of my greatest supports was my family. In the morning, I was often greeted by "refrigerator notes" from my youngest, Lee Ann. How many ways can a nine-year-old tell her dad she loves him? Well, Lee Ann found many. She made bookmarks and paperweights, and wrote notes, the gist of all of which was, "Dad, I love you."

My oldest daughter, Nicole, who was attending State, also left many votes of confidence, like the one I found in my office one day: "Hey, Dad, just came by to give you a big hug and kiss, but I missed you. I'll see you at home. I love you, Nicole."

Of course, it goes without saying that Pam was my mainstay throughout all of this.

Week of March 12

Hal Hopfenberg invited me to go to lunch (I guess Jerry Tarkanian and Las Vegas were sufficiently far away). "Lunch" consisted of a walk around the new Centennial Campus at N.C. State. As we walked, he told me about the time he once owned a restaurant with a business partner. As I recall, the conversation went as follows. After a few years, Hal said he left the partnership, but didn't ask for any part of the restaurant.

"Uh-huh," I said.

As we walked past a new building, Hopfenberg pointed out where his office would be if he was still in that school as associate dean of engineering. That is, if he hadn't taken the position of interim athletic director.

"Uh-huh," I said. "As soon as the interim is over, you'll go back there, right?" I said.

"No, I don't think I can get my old job back," Hopfenberg said. "In fact, I'm not sure Larry Monteith can go back as dean of engineering, either."

"Wait a second, Hal," I said. "You're telling me that the university asked both you people to take these interim positions, and when they're over, you have no jobs back where you came from? I may not be that smart, but something doesn't sound right there."

"I'm just telling you the way it is," Hopfenberg said. "Everyone has to sacrifice in some way."

"Uh-huh," I said.

Did I hear this straight? I should just walk away from my job?

"Hal," I said, "I see my situation a bit differently. You've been in the Athletic Department less than a year; I've been here ten years. I'm a guy who, after three seasons, was given a ten-year contract and then won the national championship; who, after five seasons, was made the athletic director; who, after seven seasons, was given a new contract to keep me forever. Just this past fall, you folks gave me the highest award a nongraduate can get. At no time has anybody ever found anything wrong with what I did. I do love this university, but what you and your friends are trying to do now is wrong. It's not the way to treat people. And I'm not walking away from anything.

"Oh, and Hal," I said as we concluded our walk. "You shouldn't have walked away from that restaurant, either."

While the hardball lawyer activity was progressing, I received an

238

amazing amount of emotional uplifting, not only from family, but also from friends, coaches and fans. My favorite note came from an anonymous donor. It was a paraphrase from a speech by Albert Schweitzer: "In everyone's life, at some time, our inner fire goes out. It is then burst into flame by an encounter with another human being. We should all be thankful for those people who rekindle the inner spirit."

My spirits were rekindled by many people. One day, a phone call came from a man who said he was "Ollie North."

"Yeah, right. Who is this? Eddie Janka?" I answered. Janka was a former coach and a dear friend of mine who now travels the country for Nike. "Eddie, I don't need this right now."

"Jim, this really is Oliver North," said the caller. And it was. What Colonel North told me was that I knew the truth, and that was what mattered the most.

Another night, I got a phone call that made me laugh. The phone rang, and the caller jokingly said he wanted to thank me for making him a ton of money in the last few weeks. "Jim, I earned about forty grand picking up all the speeches from the organizations that canceled you. It's not hard times for everybody," he said. "Hey, Terry!" I said. I knew it was Terry Bradshaw. He went on to tell me to hang in there, and that I'd get through all this fine.

Then there was Notre Dame football coach Lou Holtz. I had gotten to know Lou over the past few years through the Washington Speakers Bureau. It's ironic that he also once coached at N.C. State.

"I'm getting very sentimental, being at home so much," I told Holtz. "I've never felt so close to my wife."

"Which reminds me of an old farmer friend of mine," said Lou. "He died a few years ago at the ripe old age of eighty-seven. Lying on his deathbed, every once in a while he glanced over and saw his wife, Edith, sitting vigil. 'You know something, Edith?' he said to his wife. 'Remember when we first got married and we had that farm that failed? Edith, the whole time you were right there by my side. Then remember when we went into that business venture that lasted three years before it got plowed under? Again, you were right there by my side. Then the three kids we had, my jobs kept running out, they couldn't go to college and they always blamed me? Edith, there you were, always by my side. Here I am on my deathbed and, Edith, you're still by my side. Edith, you know what? You're a goddamn piece of bad luck!' "

When I hung up with Holtz, I was laughing so hard my wife, Pam, asked me what Lou had said.

"Oh nothing, hon," I said. "Lou just said you were a goddamn piece of bad luck."

Another phone call wasn't so humorous. It was from Bob Knight, the basketball coach at Indiana, and it concerned a column in *The National* sports newspaper in which he was quoted. What Knight had said had really crushed me. "It would have been much better for Jim Valvano and for college basketball if he had lost that national championship in 1983," Knight said. "Because Valvano's biggest moment, in my opinion, turned out to be the beginning of his downfall . . . Let me ask you a question," Knight said to the columnist, Mike Lupica. "Do you really think he (Valvano) had any other priority other than winning basketball games? . . . No. End of discussion. Now he sends in his agent. Education isn't done through an agent. It's you and me. Coach and school. As soon as a coach sends an agent in, he removes himself from being an educator."

With most criticism, I considered the source. But in my profession, Knight was considered by everyone to be a man of integrity. I never knew him well, but I had heard him speak many times at summer camps, and I respected him. What I was sure of was that he didn't know me well enough to take that kind of a shot. I felt that it was not worthy of him, and I was terribly disappointed.

Knight called me soon after the article appeared and, true to character, did not back off from what he had said. He only apologized that his thoughts and words had gotten into the newspaper. He insisted that his conversation with Lupica was just between the two of them, and that he never intended it to be public.

"Nobody should have to read that in the paper," Knight said. "With what you're going through, you especially didn't need it."

I thanked Knight for that at least, and then I shared a few things with him.

"Since you apparently care how I feel," I said, "I want to tell you how much it hurts me that you would say those things to anybody, because I have great respect for you and your accomplishments. What you don't know about me is that I love this game. I grew up with the game. My father grew up in it and taught me in it. Winning the national championship was *not* the worst thing that happened to me. It was by far the greatest thing, and I cherish it above everything else I've done in the game.

"Bob, I think I love basketball no less than you do," I said. "I respect it no less. I have given to it no less. I have never done anything to undermine that respect or love. I want you to know that. I care deeply about the game and the coaches and the players, and I want you also to know that my father coached for thirty years and our entire family loved basketball."

We had a nice conversation which lasted the better part of an hour. I felt much better for it. Just after Indiana lost in the NCAA tournament a few days later, Knight called again. He said he had thought about our conversation all weekend. He agreed he had not known me or my feelings. He said he called up Mike Krzyzewski at Duke—his close friend who had played for Knight and coached under him—to see if I was pulling his leg. I'd known Mike since we played against each other in college. Mike must have given me the thumbs up, because Knight said he had misjudged my motives and that if I needed any help to feel free to call him. I really felt that here was someone who listened, accepted me for what I'd said and reached out, again someone who rekindled my spirit. I'll always be grateful to Bob Knight for that.

During this time of the contract talks, I continued to be buoyed by some incredible support. Petitions to keep me as coach had circulated, and some 30,000 signatures were sent to the chancellor, the same guy who had not talked to me since February 7. I had faculty members coming to my door to offer help. One told me there was a silent majority on campus who didn't want to say anything on my behalf lest they be branded as anti-academics.

All the while, the local newspapers had me out, a *fait accompli*. The national critics zeroed in on the money-grubbing Valvano, the guy who was only out for the almighty buck, a charge that was especially galling considering what loyal N.C. State had done to me the last time my contract came up.

There had always been lucrative offers for me to leave the Wolfpack. In 1986, ABC wanted me to quit and become their lead college basketball color guy. Following the 1987 season, I interviewed with the New York Knicks. This was after the Knicks made a run at Rick Pitino, then at Providence, who initially turned them down. I wasn't the first choice, but I was willing to listen. Funny. During that time, a huge banner headline appeared in the *New York Daily News* over my picture. The headline said: HIRE HIM. Funny. The article urging the Knicks on was written by Mike Lupica. Yep; the same guy who criticized me three years later. In fact, one of the hard things for me to deal with was when writers like Mike, whom I considered to be my friends, attacked me daily. Don't believe any public figure who says he doesn't read the papers, and that the words of others don't hurt him. At the time, I wasn't ready to move back to New York, but when Pitino changed his mind and made himself available, the point was moot.

In 1988, however, the magical name of UCLA came up. When I kept getting phone calls marked "Urgent" from Greg Robinson, an assistant football coach for the Bruins, I finally called back. Robinson had worked at N.C. State for a while, and I assumed he was calling me in my position as athletic director to inquire about a job. Greg *was* curious about a job:

the head basketball job in Westwood. He said he had been authorized by Peter Dalis, the UCLA athletic director, to contact me and see if I would be interested if the coaching job there became open.

We were playing Murray State in the first round of the NCAA tournament in Lincoln, Nebraska the next day. After we were smashed to smithereens, I returned to Raleigh and called Dalis. He told me that they were not renewing Walt Hazzard's contract at UCLA, and in meetings to discuss a new coach, John Wooden had recommended Mike Krzyzewski and myself.

"Coach Wooden is an idol of mine," I told Dalis. "Of course I would be interested in talking."

The week before the Final Four, I flew to San Diego, where I was to give a speech. Dalis called me there and asked me to come up to Los Angeles to meet with UCLA Chancellor Charles Young. I remembered my theory that the bigger the job, the fewer people with whom you have to deal. At the end of a five-hour meeting at the Marriott Hotel by the Los Angeles airport—during which everything from poetry to business to economics to the cinema was discussed—Chancellor Young got up and said to Dalis: "This is our man. You two work out the details. But I think Jim is the guy to get the job done at UCLA."

A few years ago I would have jumped up, shook hands, looked for those cute Bruin mascots to hug, and said, "Take me to the gym." Now, though, I told Dalis that before I did anything, I had to talk the whole move over with my family back home.

"Do you have any contractual problems?" Dalis asked me.

"I don't foresee any," I said.

The reasons I didn't mention the buyout clause in my contract were simple. First of all, I felt it was premature to discuss my contract until I spoke to the N.C. State officials. Second, I knew that there were several scenarios: N.C. State might waive the buyout clause; since the clause stipulated that *I* could buy my contract out, I had that option; and, if my family didn't want to move, I could call UCLA's athletic director and say I'd decided to remain at N.C. State, and the contract need never be discussed.

In any case, I felt my contractual situation with State wasn't UCLA's problem.

Back in Raleigh, I told Chancellor Poulton of the UCLA offer, and I said that if the university wanted to invoke the clause, I would understand. I certainly wouldn't ask UCLA to pay half a million dollars for my buyout, if I did decide to go to UCLA, so I'd have to decide if I wanted to foot the bill myself.

Poulton really surprised me. He said he knew what a dreamer I was, and that if I wanted to leave, he wasn't going to hold any employee there if he felt he had a better opportunity somewhere else. He told me to forget the clause, and that if the UCLA job was what I wanted, nobody had to pay anyone anything.

If Poulton surprised me, my daughters surprised me even more. Nicole, firmly entrenched at N.C. State, said, "Good luck. I'll watch your games on TV." Jamie, in typical teenage understatement, said that if we went, it would ruin her life. Lee Ann, sensing my disappointment, said that she would be more than happy to move to L.A. with me.

Although realizing the difficulty of uprooting the family at this stage, Pam said, "Let's go take a look." However, she did remind me about what I've always said about "don't mess with happy." "This is messing," she said.

When we arrived in L.A., UCLA had arranged for us to look at homes with a real estate agent. Needless to say, L.A. is a very expensive proposition. I commented to Pam that I did believe we could find our dream house on the West Coast, although I thought it would have to be in Seattle.

When Dalis came to the hotel to pick us up for dinner, I could see he wasn't happy.

"Jim, our attorney has received a call from the N.C. State attorney saying that if we progress with you as coach, it's going to cost us $500,000. You said there wasn't any contractual problem."

I was just about speechless, if you can believe that. I told Dalis I hadn't mentioned the clause because I didn't foresee any problems, and in fact, Chancellor Poulton had exempted me from the clause. I told him Poulton had given me permission. I told him I had no idea what had happened.

Dalis was angry I had not told him up front. He said Chancellor Young also was very upset. I explained my options, and reiterated that Poulton had told me there'd be no problem. At dinner it became obvious that the relationship had been irretrievably sabotaged. "I think it would be best if I withdraw my name from consideration," I said to Dalis.

"That's probably the best idea," Dalis said.

Upon arrival at the Final Four in Kansas City, I called Becky French back in Raleigh. I was absolutely livid. "How could you people have embarrassed me like this?" I said. "Poulton gave me permission. You people made it look like I was pulling a fast one here."

French said that she'd only done what she had been told. When Poulton called up the members of the board of trustees, they refused to let him give the basketball coach away free. They demanded that he adhere to the buyout clause.

In other words—back to the future, March, 1990—upstanding, loyal, compassionate N.C. State University was now trying to get out of the very same clause that the school had used in 1988 to keep me from pursuing the UCLA job. Me, the money-hungry opportunist; N.C. State, the bastion of integrity.

That's the reason I was so adamant about my contract. I was sick of this stupid posturing by representatives of the university. I'd taken all this academic bashing when I knew how poor the statistics and gradua- tion rates of the whole university were. Now I was taking more bashing about being a capitalist pig when the university itself was the party that had negotiated the contract, invoked it on me before, and now didn't want to live up to it. Could there be any more questions about why I wanted to fight?

Tuesday, March 20

According to later press reports, this was the day that Monteith, unbeknownst to me and a whole lot of other people, called a special, private meeting of the Board of Trustees. He again went over the academic records of the basketball players I had recruited, and painted a sordid picture of kids not making it. More than one month later, on April 21, *The News and Observer* reported details of the meeting, saying Monteith wrote: " 'We cannot let this series of events that have occurred over the past 14 months occur again in our lifetime.' " . . . It added that "After hearing the presentation, the board voted 9–3 to fire Jim Valvano as basketball coach."

Wouldn't you think that if a man was going to have fired another man who had spent ten years at a school, he might tell him about it? I'm still waiting to talk to Monteith.

Thursday, March 22

Because Hal Hopfenberg himself had told me that people in North Carolina probably would not be as receptive to a lawyer from New York, I called Art Kaminsky and we talked about the benefits of hiring a lawyer from in-state, who might be viewed as less confrontational, to work with him. He readily agreed. Rufus Edmisten, the North Carolina secretary of state who became a friend during the days when we got some anti-player- agent legislation passed, recommended Woodward (Woody) Webb, a former candidate for Congress who was much respected throughout North Carolina.

After his first meeting with State's lawyer, Howard Manning, Webb reported back to me that Manning was adamant that N.C. State pay me nothing. Initially, the school's argument was that I said I was quitting. Now, they were changing theories. Manning went to the newspapers with the claim that I had violated the academic clause in my contract. But my contract was very clear in the termination department. If I violated an NCAA rule or if I committed a felony, yes, I was gone, with no compensation. But the NCAA had already absolved me from any wrongdoing, and I wasn't on any police blotter. My contract lawyer looked at the wording and said N.C. State would not have a leg to stand on if this thing ever went to court.

Thursday, March 29

In a letter to Howard Manning, Woody Webb *renewed* my request to appear before the N.C. State University Board of Trustees to give my side of the story. I also had been asking to speak to the board of governors. To quote from Webb's letter: "What possible harm can it do for Jim to appear before either or both of these bodies to discuss, face to face, the past, present and future situation respecting the North Carolina State University basketball program and his prospective relationship with the program?"

Repeated efforts to speak to these boards were all in vain. I never was given the chance to reply to Monteith about his charges. Webb even sent letters to each member of the board of trustees, but they responded that only the chancellor could call a meeting of the full board. At the same time, the N.C. State football coach, Dick Sheridan, one of the most honored and respected men in the profession and a favorite of Monteith's, was trying to see him to speak on my behalf. Monteith declined to see Sheridan. Ultimately, even N.C. State Senator Wendell Murphy, one of N.C. State's most loyal supporters tried to reach Monteith to speak to him about me. I was at Senator Murphy's home when he made the call.

An aide to Monteith told Murphy the chancellor would not talk to him.

Saturday, March 31–Monday, April 2

The Final Four played out in Denver and, yes, I missed it. I watched every second of every game on TV. The tournament is the second love of my life, it's why I coach, my *raison d'être*. It was like a knife in my heart watching Vegas, Duke and Georgia Tech—three teams we had battled gamely with during the season—play during the Final Four. In addition,

245

in the aftermath of all the controversy, a speech I was to have given at a Final Four banquet sponsored by the University of Colorado on the campus at Boulder got canceled. Worse yet, the invitations with my name on them had already gone out to over 200 CEOs from around the country. *The Denver Post* headline read: VALVANO BENCHED AS FINAL 4 SPEAKER. Ugh.

Monday, April 2

In a memo, a member of the university board of governors related a phone call he received from Bill Burns, a member of the N.C. State Board of Trustees.

"Mr. Burns said that he voted with the majority position on the board of trustees, which was to dismiss Mr. Valvano. He added that the university must take an honorable position. He said that if we do not succeed in negotiating an agreement, we must honor the Valvano contract.

"Bill Burns does not think that we can point a finger toward Coach Valvano relative to the issue that athletes were admitted with low academic grades, and went on to play four years of basketball and dropped out of college. He stated that by and large the grade issue was an administrative decision and he would not support an effort to hang this on the basketball coach.

"The opinion expressed by Mr. Burns is closely allied to a number of calls I've received over the past two weeks. We must face the facts. There is strong support for Jim Valvano the man and Jim Valvano the basketball coach."

Wednesday, April 4

Seeking to show that my commitment to N.C. State was not merely tied to finances, I agreed to an interview on Tom Brokaw's "NBC Nightly News" broadcast for April 6, 1990. In this interview, I said that I would coach basketball at North Carolina State for free. To make it legal, I said I'd coach for a dollar. This wasn't an issue of finances; it was an issue of fairness. In my heart, I knew I did nothing wrong. That knowledge was at the core of my battle to remain at N.C. State. To be the scapegoat for a university that had serious academic problems didn't seem right to me. I wasn't going to buckle under that easily. When I said that if I was part of the problem, I wanted to be part of the solution, I meant it.

246

Thursday, April 5

We received a letter from Andy Vanore, the chief deputy attorney general for North Carolina, which said: "In response to your letter of April 3, I am instructed by the Chairman of the Board of Trustees of N.C. State University to advise you that Mr. Valvano's request to appear before the board is denied."

Friday, April 6

Woody Webb called me to say that tomorrow, N.C. State would announce that I had been terminated from my job as basketball coach. Did I want to go to court? Webb felt positive there was no way in the world I would lose. Did I want to settle for their offer? Instead of paying me under the terms of the contract, $500,000 over the next five years, the university would give me a total of $238,000 all at once. The school had nothing to do with my separate contract with the Wolfpack Club. Charlie Bryant, the director of the Club, promised to honor every penny of the $375,000 contract with the Club. The Wolfpack Club had always been fair and honest in their dealings with me. So I would leave with $613,000—just about what I would have asked for if the original negotiations between Art and the university had started on a civil level. However, no price can be placed upon the pain, the anguish, and the damage to my reputation that the university inflicted on me.

I met with the Valvano family at the house. They said they would support me in whatever I chose to do. But we had had enough. I wasn't about to put them through a nasty court case.

Saturday, April 7

Interim Chancellor Larry Monteith made the announcement; he took no questions from the media. A representative from the university brought papers to my office for me to sign, promising that I would not sue N.C. State. The representative was not Monteith. It was not Hal Hopfenberg. It was not Becky French. It was French's administrative assistant.

I held a press conference. I took questions from the media. Somebody asked what happened. "You figure it out," I said. "They gave me a lifetime contract. Then they declared me dead."

247

April 1990

In "NCSU Today," an N.C. State University April Fool's spoof on the newspaper *USA Today*, the quick-read items in the left-hand column on the front page included:

Weather: According to sources at Raleigh's *News and Observer*, recent snow and rain in Rockies, Northeast; thunderstorms in Midwest, South Central; all to be blamed on Jim Valvano.

Wall Street Down: Dow drops 15.99 points . . . Investors pumped money into stock mutual funds in February despite shaky market. N&O claims Valvano to blame.

Ozone Hole: Sources at Raleigh's N&O cite hearsay linking Valvano to 1000 mile hole . . .

U.S.A.'s Homeless: America homeless tops 28 million . . . Point fingers at Coach V, resignation only solution.

Challenger Disaster: NASA, unaware of N&O's Valvano bashing, deny N.C. State coach designed faulty o-ring.

On the "Saturday Night Live" weekend update, Dennis Miller reported: " 'Saturday Night Live' News has learned that the Stock Market Crash of '87, the Greenhouse Effect, and the Vietnam War were all caused by this man, Jim Valvano."

On a nationally broadcast radio show, Robin Williams was asked why he lost the Oscar for his performance in *Dead Poets' Society*. "I blame it on Jim Valvano," he said.

Friday, May 11

Larry K. Monteith was elected Chancellor of N.C. State University by the University of North Carolina Board of Governors.

Saturday, September 15

N.C. State University Chancellor Larry K. Monteith announced to the N.C. State Board of Trustees organizational changes which included realignment of the structure of top-level administration. Effective November 15, Dr. Harold Hopfenberg would move from the position of special assistant to the chancellor and associate dean of engineering to executive assistant to the chancellor.

Chapter Sixteen

PROBLEMS AND PRESCRIPTIONS

As PAINFUL AS IT IS FOR ME TO ADDRESS THE SUBJECT OF THE BOOK *Personal Fouls,* I would be negligent not to acknowledge the impact it had on my personal as well as professional life. The fact that the critics tore apart the book's multiple inaccuracies—in such things as spellings, dates, scores and general knowledge of the game of college basketball, as well as quoting "sources" such as Bennie Bolton, who didn't meet the author until after the book was published—did little to assuage the hurt it caused my family and myself.

The book had nothing to do with my dismissal from N.C. State. I have always believed that *Personal Fouls* was only the catalyst for the NCAA investigation, which we then welcomed and which inevitably found violations only in the matter of kids selling shoes and tickets. Following the initial furor from the publication of the book came Dr. Hugh Fuller's charges and the in-house investigation of academic abuses, and that set the scene for the ongoing controversy and the never-ending criticism from the local press.

That said, *Personal Fouls* did raise some valid points about the operation of a Division I basketball program. Certainly there were areas in which I could have done better. It is possible that the success I had in monitoring academics at my prior coaching addresses gave me a false sense of security. To the best of my knowledge, in the years I was at Johns Hopkins, Bucknell and Iona, only two players that I recruited did not graduate from those schools. I never had a problem with graduation rates or academics. At N.C. State, knowing the poor percentages in the graduations of black males and of students overall, I should have realized we were going to have difficulties with graduation, and acted accordingly.

I could have had tougher rules regarding class attendance. It's not enough just to say you want the kids to graduate. It's not even enough to monitor their progress through tutors. We had tutors travel with us on all our road trips. Obviously, this just wasn't good enough.

When Peter Ueberroth was running the Los Angeles Summer Olympic Games in 1984, he said he felt that the head of any organization has an important obligation to anticipate problems and to solve them before they happen. I should have realized that a youngster who had low college board scores and a low class rank would have difficulty in competing with those of his peers who had scored in the 1000's on the SAT's. This was my mistake, something I should have focused on a lot more than I did. In addition, I should not have vigorously recruited players who had so little interest in college. Some kids we recruited were obviously below normal admissions standards, but they had a deep interest in university life, and they wound up graduating. I speak not only of Ernie Myers, but of Harold Thompson, Dereck Whittenburg and Alvin Battle. These were kids who would have liked to have played professional basketball, but they came to N.C. State to get a degree. Was Chris Washburn interested in graduating from college? Was Charles Shackleford? Obviously, higher education meant something different to these fellows, namely a vehicle to get to the NBA. Of course, it's difficult to predict in recruiting. Still, I could have given more thought to particular recruits' interest in school.

Hindsight always being 20–20, I do have some ideas about the unremitting problem of athletes with poor grades. The easiest solution, naturally, would be to form an alternative minor league supported by both the NCAA and the NBA. This would be for those future professional players who had no interest in college.

Failing that, universities must get together with athletic departments to raise their admissions standards. Prop 48 standardized the qualifications to a 700 score on the SAT and a 2.0 grade point average. But think about that: at N.C. State alone, we're talking about a player trying to compete with other students who have entered school equipped with over 1000 on the boards and a 3.2 GPA. If the standards were raised, these kids would have a better chance of graduating, as well. Whether the numbers are raised or not, however, I believe that no entering students who were admitted below the normal standard of admissions for that particular school—be they high-school graduates or junior-college transfers—should be allowed participation in the first year until they have earned at least a 2.0. Then and only then should they be permitted to play; and this rule would establish an added incentive for the player to keep up a passing GPA.

Concerning the shoes and tickets, once again, in retrospect, I should have put a system into place to monitor the situation. As I mentioned, the shoe problems at N.C. State occurred when a youngster either sold or exchanged a new pair of his team shoes for money or other clothing. Bennie Bolton said he sold his because he didn't have enough money to live on. This is a sad situation, obviously, but Bennie's solution was to break an NCAA rule. We trusted our players not to sell their shoes. But after the shoes issue hit the fan, we instituted a new policy whereby we issued only one pair of shoes to each player. When that pair was worn out, the player would bring the shoes back to us in exchange for another pair. A simple solution—each player only had one pair at a time.

The ticket situation was more complex. Under the former policy, four complimentary tickets were given to each player per game (three had to go to relatives, and the fourth could be a "wild card" for a friend). There was never any guarantee that the wild card holder hadn't in fact paid for the ticket. Say the wild card was issued in Joe Shmoe's name. If a guy who came to pick up the ticket bore the identification of Joe Shmoe, there was no way to tell if Shmoe paid for that ticket. Again, if I could have foreseen such a serious problem, I could have taken measures to prevent it.

One measure would have been to eliminate the wild cards and say that the comps could only go to family members. That's the most severe solution. Another, much more logical, was precisely what I did in my last year before the season began. First, every player made a list of his friends and relatives, and anyone else who would be getting tickets. Next, we wrote to all these people informing them of the list and requesting their address, phone number and relationship to the athlete. We then had an assistant athletic director follow up with phone calls to insure that the people were who they said they were. If you spoke to a guy who had no conceivable relationship with the player, you'd have a pretty good idea he might have bought the ticket.

Paying the players a salary is a solution that has been bandied about for years. A kid's scholarship consists of room, board, books, tuition and fees. Many people still don't realize that the players are not permitted to work if they're on scholarship. They can only work during the summer. Players from less than wealthy families, then, have a tough time getting through school financially.

I used to be strongly against paying players; I always figured that if their scholarships didn't provide enough support, they could apply to the federal government and receive a Pell Grant of $1,400 for the school year. But this may not be a justifiable position, after all. I can see why players are bitter about coaches making a ton of money when they themselves can't get a flight home for Christmas. Once I was sitting at our training table before a game with Mike Giomi, discussing coaches' salaries. "You know, we should be getting a piece of that TV money," Mike said at one point. At the time, I made the statement that the reason

251

coaches earned money on these things was because coaching was our profession. It was the same situation as when the engineering professor made more money than the engineering student; yet the engineering student was the one paying the tuition, I told Mike. Someday, of course, the student would go out and build the better mousetrap and get his own windfall.

But let's face it. Every player knows how much money is coming into a university and how much the coaches are making; it's not hard to see why some players would resent it. And so I've come to believe that there should be some type of stipend for a player. The problem with this is that if you do it for men's basketball, you need to do it for all the other teams as well: women's basketball, the track team, tennis. This is a real problem, but my position would be that a school must bite the bullet and pay the stipend to all the scholarship athletes. What's fair is fair.

The university should devise a formula based on need for all the athletes. This might include reimbursement for transportation to and from school at the beginning and end of the year; one trip home for the holidays; and perhaps a monthly salary. The financing could come from the millions of dollars the schools get from college basketball.

On drug-testing, I have also shifted gears. The fact that our testing program at N.C. State was voluntary, nonpunitive and confidential rendered the book's charges that we hid the test results ridiculous. We told the kids from the beginning that they did not have to take part in the program, that there would be no punishment and no information about the testing released to the public. In the five years that we had drug-testing at N.C. State, there were a handful of positive tests, but these athletes were not permitted to play unless they had entered a counseling program, had been retested and found clean. The rule was that the NCAA tested only the winning teams after their tournament games; never did we have a positive result.

If I had it to do over, however, I would lobby to change our program to a mandatory one—punitive and nonconfidential, besides. If a youngster tested positive, immediate dismissal. No questions asked. There is much to be said for "compassion" on the drug question, but ultimately the attempts to help these players in any other fashion but punishment hasn't worked. On the contrary, too often the good samaritan has turned into the naïve chump; the result being harm to the youngster, the athletic department, the coach and the university. Moreover, the NCAA should drug-test both the winners and losers in the NCAA tournament, to avoid even the hint of anybody playing *not* to win, to avoid such a test.

This brings up the allegations about an N.C. State player throwing a game to avoid a drug test. Let me categorically state again that at no time did any member of my staff or myself suspect any of our players of doing anything but playing to win. I've always been passionate about winning, and demanded it of everyone around me. If I had ever sensed anything amiss, I would have contacted the proper authorities immediately—as I did when the rumor of alleged point-shaving was brought to my attention by ABC.

And yet, in college basketball, there has been a point-shaving scandal in every decade since the fifties. Even with a stipend, there are probably some players who would still break the law. It's the old story: You can hardly legislate morality for all players.

At the time of this book's completion, none of the point-shaving charges have been proven. An ongoing investigation by the New Jersey Crime Commission may lead to indictments and a trial, but I certainly hope and pray that no player at N.C. State was involved. I would be shocked, disappointed and personally crushed if they had.

Many people blame college athletics' ills on the alumni and rabid fans and booster clubs that have proliferated around the country. While it's true that my strongest support group was the Wolfpack Club, let me point out that these fine folks were with us in both victory and defeat. Their backing wasn't based on the W's and L's. All boosters aren't wild-eyed fanatics who only care about winning; we had some really wonderful people behind us at N.C. State. The problem comes when well-intentioned individuals don't understand the rules and regulations, and overstep the boundaries of the recruiting process. To avoid this, schools have to do what we started at N.C. State; namely, an educational system of mailings and seminars, instructing the Club members in the proper procedures as set up by the NCAA. Schools also must make sure that any booster who violates a rule should be denied participation in the program. If there's education and if there's punishment, I've got to believe booster clubs and individuals would toe the line.

Another point I'd like to make concerns coaches' contracts with their universities. While I'm not in favor of tenure for coaches, I am wholeheartedly for honesty between coaches and their employers. Let's get serious: Anybody who thinks coaches can retain their jobs if they don't win would sign up Milli Vanilli for the Metropolitan Opera. Just take a look at the newspapers following each football and basketball season. Coaches are constantly being fired by institutions; the reasons are spelled "D-E-F-E-A-T-S."

Early this season, Denny Crum, who has won two national championships and done a marvelous job for twenty seasons at Louisville, came under attack by the local media for his players' academic deficiencies. The university followed suit. Where had everybody been for the last twenty years? The simple truth is that we need more honesty from our institutions of higher learning. If schools admit youngsters below the normal standard of admission, they should say so: "We're doing this because we want to compete on the highest level of intercollegiate athletics." But too often, schools have concealed their academic standards in the same way they've concealed their campus crime statistics. The latter, for fear of dwindling enrollment. The former, for fear of dwindling victories. Our universities must be honest about graduation rates and progress toward graduation, both to the public and to the coaches. Because if a coach doesn't win, he's going to get fired. Because if a booster cheats, the coach is going to get fired. And because, now, if his players aren't making progress toward graduation, he's going to get fired.

Meanwhile, the universities seem to take no responsibility, absolving themselves of blame.

Solution: The coach's contract should spell out just what is expected of the coach regarding academics and graduation rates. If the university's overall graduation rate is 50 percent, but the administration wants the basketball team to graduate at 85 percent, fine; put it in the contract. And then let the public know that this is what the coach is to be judged on. (But don't be surprised at the lack of applicants.) There's a crazy rule now in effect which states that if *anyone* violates an NCAA rule, the *coach* gets fired—well, that's absolutely absurd. It's impossible for the coach to monitor everybody connected with his basketball program.

Now, if the coach knows about violations, obviously, he's out. But when such violations are beyond his control, it's patently unfair to heap the blame on the coach. The way the contracts are written today, coaches are left responsible for aspects of university life that are entirely out of their domain.

I don't want to let the young athletes off the hook here, either. Nothing will elicit a bigger laugh from coaches than the concept that his players are "exploited." I've said this before and I'll say it again: Student-athletes exploit schools far more than the other way around. The kids we deal with at the Division I level are hardly naïve or unsophisticated. From the moment they have been designated as "blue-chippers," they have been courted, wined and dined. Half of them already have agents, whether they are schoolyard acquaintances, parents, teachers or the high-school coach himself. These kids know the score, the stakes and their own value.

To maintain some sense of balance on campus, to insure a quality of college life for a young athlete, I have come to believe that the NCAA should abolish athletic dormitories. N.C. State didn't provide housing for the athletes, so it was difficult to recruit a youngster—offering room, board, books, tuition and fees—and then say, whoops, sorry, there's no room for you. Universities need to permit all entering athletes to live on campus in guaranteed housing just like any other freshman. In short, treat them no differently from their peers. Living and associating with the other kids on campus has to be a better experience than being isolated.

Which brings me to another sore point I had about *Personal Fouls:* the charge that I was not a players' coach, that I didn't care about the kids. Again, that was absolutely ridiculous.

Obviously, a coach becomes closer to some players than others, but much of the time that determination is made by the player; not every kid is dying to hang out with his coach. In the case of three specific players mentioned in the book, I have my own side to tell.

At one point, there was mention of my "taking a music course" at N.C. State. Wrong. But what I did do was try to help Charles Shackleford with a problem he had in his music course. One day Shack came by my office after class. He showed me some of his books and I picked up his music book and began to read. In it, I came across the interesting concept that music had predated speech itself. Shack and I talked about that for a while and then I noticed that in the back of the book the very first question in a review of that chapter was to discuss why the birth of music was an enigma.

I'll never forget what happened next. When I asked Shack that question, he couldn't answer it. It wasn't that he had trouble with the concept; it was the word "enigma" that stumped him. He had no idea what it meant. Now, I would venture to say that if you went out into the street right now and asked ten people the definition of "enigma," you might get five correct meanings. Anyway, in discussing this with Shack, I asked him why the birth of music would be "puzzling," and he immediately knew the answer, which we had just covered: It was puzzling because music came before speech. I realized then that many of our players' academic problems might derive from vocabulary, rather than from grasping concepts. Later, I talked to Chancellor Poulton about the fact that we needed to do a better job in tutoring the players on the simple meaning of words, which might help them improve in a lot of other areas. How this got twisted into the *Personal Fouls* version is beyond me.

Let's take another player, Kelsey Weems; ironically, the guy whom I've always suspected was the veiled figure on that "ABC News" report who charged that there had been point-shaving at N.C. State. Weems had had problems in Raleigh, which led to his leaving the school. When that happened, his mother, father and minister came to N.C. State and asked us if we would please stay in touch with Kelsey, that he needed to hold out hope. My staff and I called Kelsey on a weekly basis to check on his progress at his home in Atlanta. We always guaranteed him that if he could take care of himself and clean up his personal problems, the school and the team would gladly take him back. When Kelsey did return, I'll never forget him standing up in the locker room and speaking to the team about how he had changed his life; how the support of everybody at N.C. State had meant so much to him; how it was a special day for him to come back to school and rejoin the team.

In the cases of Shackleford and Weems, could I have cared about them or communicated with them any more than I did? I sincerely don't think so. The fact is, my relationships with my players, from stars such as Sidney Lowe, Thurl Bailey and Dereck Whittenburg, to role-players such as Alvin Battle, Mike Warren and George McClain, have always been solid, valuable and rewarding to me. In fact, McClain, who did not finish in our program, holds a job working with underprivileged children in the area, and each year we provide them with game tickets. Vinny Del Negro called me all the way from Italy to wish me good luck on my debut with ESPN; last summer my wife and I took a cruise with the Thurl Baileys. Recently, Spud Webb called and invited me to speak at a roast for him. And when Chris Corchiani was contemplating leaving N.C. State last year in the wake of my firing, I flew to Florida, had dinner with his family, and pointed out that I would support Chris whether he decided to stay at State and finish his career there, or not.

Over the years, many wonderful letters I've received from the families of my players have done far more than offset the scurrilous charges made in a book based on inaccuracies.

I stand by my record. I'm secure in the feeling that, whatever my mistakes in coaching, I never did anything to cheat, hurt my players, or abuse the system.

Epilogue

LYNN SWANN: "HEY, JIM, LOOK AT THAT PINK CADILLAC!"
Jim Valvano: "It might be. It could be. It is! Miss Piggy!"

In six months, I've gone from the pits to the pigs. My new job with
ABC Sports finds me a long way from the April Massacre at North
Carolina State. I'm at Disney World in Orlando, Florida, to be specific,
working on a special with the Harlem Globetrotters to be shown on
"Wide World of Sports."

But there are crises in all walks of life. At my first production meeting,
there we were with our clipboards going over the game plan when Geoff
Mason, the executive producer, told us the sequence of plays. "Jim and
Lynn, you'll have as your guests Mickey Mouse, Minnie Mouse and Miss
Piggy."

For my very first notes as a big-time TV star, I wrote: "Mickey,
Minnie," and "Mademoiselle Pig." I was perfectly content with all of this
so far when, whoops, to the left of me came the concerned voice of one of
the Disney executives.

"Wait just one minute," he said. "We aren't promising any Miss Piggy.
The Mice, fine. Mickey and Minnie will be there. But Miss Piggy? We're
not sure she can make it."

Uh-oh.

"Hold it. I thought we were getting the pig," said Mason. "I thought it
was all set."

I knew Miss Piggy was one of the Jim Henson entourage, more Muppet
menagerie than Disney World. And a very big star, as she has made it

257

known many times. But there was something amiss concerning her schedule. And our show would have to go on without her. Maybe.

"Tell you what," said the Disney people. "If we can't get Miss Piggy, we're sure we can get you Pluto or Chip and Dale and maybe we can throw in Goofy."

Although I was a rookie, this sounded like a heck of a deal to me.

However, I knew Geoff was still adamant that we get Miss Piggy. I kept my mouth shut—honest—until somebody asked my opinion. "I think we should hold out for the entire pig package," I said. (I stole this line from Katherine Love, the assistant producer.)

Finally, the Disney people made some phone calls and came back to say they could get the porcine damsel herself, if only for a couple of hours.

"Only a couple of hours?" I asked.

"Yeah," somebody said. "The pig is Teamster's Union."

If that wasn't enlightening enough, when I began my big interview with Miss Piggy right there out on the court—all I could think of was that Jimmy Hoffa was hiding under that cute little visage—I mentioned that she must really love basketball to be spending her precious time here, watching the Globies. How about it, Miss Piggy? How much *do* you love basketball?

Then . . .

Nothing.

Why of course, folks. Miss Piggy, the live character actress, doesn't talk. Embarrassed, humiliated, on the brink of television disaster before I'd even started my new career, I did what any red-blooded American TV reporter was brought up to do. "Over to you, Lynn . . .." I said.

Well, yeah, there *is* another world out there after basketball. In the months since I left the game, I've discovered my wife and daughters, friends, golf and contentment. Have I missed hoops? Never more so than the beginning of the season when practice started, that time when a coach becomes a teacher. With my new jobs at ABC and ESPN, though, I intend to take full advantage of two of my most favorite things in life: talking and watching college basketball.

In the meantime, I've done rock collections with my youngest daughter and gone to parents' day at my other two daughters' sorority house. I've learned all the golf lingo: Bite! . . . Work, baby, work! . . . It's leaking . . . and, most of all . . . What Club Did He Use, Rossi? Some friends and I have even started our own tournament, the Rossi Open, named after Bob Rosburg, now a colleague of mine on ABC. We may even invite Rossi next year. Of course, if he doesn't come, he'll never be invited again. That's the first rule of the Rossi Open.

I've gone to museums. To Broadway shows. On a cruise. I've met a whole bunch of folks who don't know the difference between a pick and a roll. I've gained ten pounds, but I'm healthy again. With my new-found time to watch late-night TV, I've become hooked on the Home Shopping Network. I've ordered every gadget imaginable, including my new Snack-Master, at which I've become very handy. My family got worried when I started to order the vacuum cleaner attachment that also cuts hair. Jamie said, "We'd better get him out of the house soon."

I've learned to treasure my family more, to value my friends and co-workers, and I've figured out that it's not wise to try to predict the future. Once, I thought I'd coach forever at North Carolina State. Now, I'm just trying to perfect my banana pancake recipe and learn the ropes of broadcasting.

Got to go now. There are snacks to create, golf courses to annihilate, and at least one beauteous pig to appreciate. This time, I'm not messing with happy.